DATE DUE

JAN 1 1 2005	
MAY 1 4 2006	

Mind and World

MIND AND WORLD

· · ·

With a New Introduction

· · ·

John
McDowell

HARVARD UNIVERSITY PRESS

Cambridge, Massachusetts

London, England

First Harvard University Press paperback edition, 1996

Library of Congress Cataloging-in-Publication Data

McDowell, John Henry.
Mind and world : with a new introduction / John McDowell.
p.   cm.
Includes bibliographical references and index.
ISBN 0–674–57610–1
1. Philosophy of mind. 2. Knowledge, Theory of. 3. Concepts.
I. Title.
[BD418.3.M37   1996]
121'.4—dc20   96–22268

Contents

Preface

The main text of this book is a sort of record of the John Locke Lectures that I delivered in Oxford in Trinity Term, 1991. I have done some recasting of the lectures from the form in which I gave them. I have tried to make improvements in clarity and explicitness. I have also eliminated phrases like "next week" and "last week", which it seemed absurd to leave standing in a version meant to be taken in through the eye, perhaps—at least for the texts of the lectures—at a single sitting. But apart from correcting one inessential falsehood at the end of the last lecture, the texts I offer here, headed "Lecture I" and so on through "Lecture VI", aim to say just what I said in Oxford.

They aim, moreover, to say it with a mode of organization and in a tone of voice that reproduce those of the lectures as I gave them. There are at least three points here.

First, even where I have made revisions at the level of phrases and sentences, I have preserved the order of the lectures, as I delivered them, at the level of paragraphs and sections. In particular, I have not tried to eliminate, or even lessen, repetitiveness. I hoped that frequent and sometimes lengthy recapitulations would be helpful to hearers, and I hope they will be helpful to readers too.

Second, in a brief set of lectures, it seemed sensible to try to pursue a reasonably linear train of thought, and I have not tried to make the revised texts any less two-dimensional. The footnotes, in so far as they go beyond merely bibliographical information, and the Afterword are meant to give some indication of what a more rounded treatment of these issues might look like. But they are no more than an adjunct to the record of the lectures, more or less as I gave them.

Third, I have tried not to erase an unguardedness that seemed proper for the lecture format.

I have many substantial debts to acknowledge.

Someone who read these lectures superficially might suppose Donald Davidson figures in them, after the first page or so, as an enemy. I hope it is clear to less superficial readers, even from the texts of the lectures themselves, that I single out Davidson's work for criticism as a mark of respect. I define my stance against his by way of a contrast that it would be easy to relegate to the edges of the picture, with massive agreement in the centre. For my purposes in the lectures, I play up the contrast. In the Afterword I try to make some amends. The fact is that Davidson's writing has been an inspiration to me ever since, at David Wiggins's urging, I first read "Truth and Meaning" or perhaps "On Saying That" (I am not sure which came first for me).[1]

I have been more strongly influenced than footnotes can indicate by P. F. Strawson, especially by his peerless book on Kant's First Critique.[2] I am not sure that Strawson's Kant is really Kant, but I am convinced that Strawson's Kant comes close to achieving what Kant wanted to achieve. In these lectures I follow Strawson directly when I exploit Kant in the context of considering the first person (Lecture V); and my use of Kant in saying how we should conceive experience—the main thing I try to do here—is Strawsonian in spirit and often in detail.

Strawson's influence operates on me both directly and at one remove, through Gareth Evans. Evans did not live to write a preface to his seminal book, *The Varieties of Reference;*[3] if he had, he would surely have tried to convey the extent to which his teacher had shaped his thinking at its most central points. Evans's direct importance for me is incalculable. For a decade or so what mattered most in my intellectual life was my collegial life with him. Anyone who knew him will know what this amounted to: a non-stop barrage of intellectual stimulation. I have no idea how I could so much as begin to separate out the difference he made to me; I cannot imagine what sort of philoso-

---

1. Both now reprinted in *Inquiries into Truth and Interpretation* (Clarendon Press, Oxford, 1984).

2. *The Bounds of Sense* (Methuen, London, 1966). I should also mention *Individuals: An Essay in Descriptive Metaphysics* (Methuen, London, 1959).

3. Clarendon Press, Oxford, 1982.

pher (if any) I would have been now if it had not been for him. He is one of the two people now gone with whom I most wish I could discuss this work.

The other is Wilfrid Sellars. His classic essay "Empiricism and the Philosophy of Mind"[4] began to be central for me long before I ever thought of coming to the University of Pittsburgh, and it is an abiding regret for me that I became a colleague of his too late in his life to profit from talking to him as I have profited from reading him.

Robert Brandom's writings, and conversations with him, have been very important in shaping my thinking, usually by forcing me to get clear about the differences, small in themselves, that transform for me the look of our wide measure of agreement. The way I put things here bears substantial marks of Brandom's influence. Among much else, I single out his eye-opening seminar on Hegel's *Phenomenology of Spirit,* which I attended in 1990. Thoughts Brandom elicited from me then show up explicitly at a couple of places in these lectures, but the effect is pervasive; so much so that one way that I would like to conceive this work is as a prolegomenon to a reading of the *Phenomenology,* much as Brandom's forthcoming *Making It Explicit: Reasoning, Representing, and Discursive Commitment*[5] is, among many other things, a prolegomenon to his reading of that difficult text. I am also deeply indebted to Brandom for detailed help and support while I was preparing the lectures.

Many other people have helped me with this work. I try to mention specific debts in the footnotes, but I am sure there are many places where I have forgotten who first taught me to say things as I do, and I am sorry about that. Here I want to thank James Conant, John Haugeland, and Danielle Macbeth for special help and encouragement.

I made my first sketches of the kind of formulation I have arrived at here during the winter of 1985–86, in an attempt to get under control my usual excited reaction to a reading—my third or fourth—of Richard Rorty's *Philosophy and the Mirror of Nature.*[6] I think it was an earlier reading of Rorty that put me on to Sellars; and it will be obvi-

---

4. In Herbert Feigl and Michael Scriven, eds., *Minnesota Studies in the Philosophy of Science,* vol. 1 (University of Minnesota Press, Minneapolis, 1956), pp. 253–329.

5. Harvard University Press, Cambridge, Mass., 1994.

6. Princeton University Press, Princeton, 1979.

ous that Rorty's work is in any case central for the way I define my stance here.

I used those first formulations in lectures in Oxford in that academic year, my last there, and in my Whitehead Lectures at Harvard in the spring of 1986. That initial work was done while I was a Radcliffe Philosophy Fellow, and even though this fruit of my Fellowship is rather belated, I want to record gratefully that this book owes a great deal to the generosity of the Radcliffe Trust. I also thank the Master and Fellows of University College, Oxford, for giving me permission to accept the Fellowship.

I am very grateful to the Sub-Faculty of Philosophy in the University of Oxford for doing me the great honour of inviting me to give the John Locke Lectures, and to many friends in England for their kindness during my stay.

Introduction

1. This book first appeared without an Introduction. Since then, however, I have been made to realize that it is harder to understand than I thought. I hope an overview, omitting some details in order to focus on the central theme, will help at least some readers.

My aim is to propose an account, in a diagnostic spirit, of some characteristic anxieties of modern philosophy—anxieties that centre, as my title indicates, on the relation between mind and world. Continuing with the medical metaphor, we might say that a satisfactory diagnosis ought to point towards a cure. I aim at explaining how it comes about that we seem to be confronted with philosophical obligations of a familiar sort, and I want the explanation to enable us to unmask that appearance as illusion.

It matters that the illusion is capable of gripping us. I want to be able to acknowledge the power of the illusion's sources, so that we find ourselves able to respect the conviction that the obligations are genuine, even while we see how we can, for our own part, reject the appearance that we face a pressing intellectual task.

2. A good way into the picture I offer is to consider the plausibility of a minimal empiricism.

To make sense of the idea of a mental state's or episode's being directed towards the world, in the way in which, say, a belief or judgement is, we need to put the state or episode in a normative context. A belief or judgement to the effect that things are thus and so—a belief or judgement whose content (as we say) is that things are thus and so—must be a posture or stance that is *correctly or incorrectly* adopted according to whether or not things are indeed thus and so. (If we can make sense of judgement or belief as directed towards the world in that way, other kinds of content-bearing postures or stances should easily fall into place.) This relation between mind and world is normative, then, in this sense: thinking that aims at judgement, or at the fixation of belief, is answerable to the world—to how things are—for whether or not it is correctly executed.

Now how should we elaborate the idea that our thinking is thus answerable to the world? In addressing this question, we might restrict our attention, at least tacitly, to thinking that is answerable to the *empirical* world; that is, answerable to how things are in so far as how things are is empirically accessible. Even if we take it that answerability to how things are includes more than answerability to the empirical world, it nevertheless seems right to say this: since our cognitive predicament is that we confront the world by way of sensible intuition (to put it in Kantian terms), our reflection on the very idea of thought's directedness at how things are must begin with answerability to the empirical world. And now, how can we understand the idea that our thinking is answerable to the empirical world, if not by way of the idea that our thinking is answerable to experience? How could a verdict from the empirical world—to which empirical thinking must be answerable if it is to be thinking at all—be delivered, if not by way of a verdict from (as W. V. Quine puts it) "the tribunal of experience"?[1]

That is what I mean by "a minimal empiricism": the idea that experience must constitute a tribunal, mediating the way our thinking is answerable to how things are, as it must be if we are to make sense of it as thinking at all. And this is one side of a combination of plausibilities that promises to account for the philosophical anxieties I alluded to. The other side is a frame of mind, which I shall come to (§4 below), that makes it hard to see how experience *could* function as a tribunal, delivering verdicts on our thinking.

Fully developed, of course, such a combination would amount to an antinomy: experience both must (minimal empiricism) and cannot (the line of thought I have yet to broach) stand in judgement over our

---

1. "Two Dogmas of Empiricism", in W. V. Quine, *From a Logical Point of View* (Harvard University Press, Cambridge, Mass., 1961; 1st ed. 1953), pp. 20–46, at p. 41.

attempts to make up our minds about how things are. But consider a stage at which reflection is subject to such a pair of pressures, but not self-consciously enough for it to be clear that what they generate is an antinomy. With an inexplicit awareness of the tension between such a pair of tendencies in one's thinking, one could easily fall into an anxiety of a familiar philosophical sort, about that directedness of mind to world that it seemed we would have to be able to gloss in terms of answerability to how things are. In such a position, one would find oneself asking: "How is it possible for there to be thinking directed at how things are?" This would be a "How possible?" question of a familiar philosophical kind; it acquires its characteristic philosophical bite by being asked against the background of materials for a line of thought that, if made explicit, would purport to reveal that the question's topic is actually not possible at all.

3. It may seem surprising that I am associating empiricism with a philosophical anxiety about the possibility of *thought*. Surely, it may be objected, empiricism is an epistemological position, and the relevant question should rather be this: "How is it possible for there to be empirical *knowledge*?" What that comes to, in terms of Quine's juridical image, is something on these lines: "How can experience, standing in judgement over, say, a belief, return a verdict sufficiently favourable for the belief to count as a case of knowledge?"

But suppose we are prone to have our thinking shaped by the second element in my combination of plausibilities (which I have so far brought into view only in terms of its effect). That is just to suppose that we find it hard to see how experience can function as a tribunal, standing in judgement over our beliefs. This would be a difficulty about how experience can return any verdicts on our thinking at all, and that is surely more fundamental than a difficulty about how experience can return a particular kind of verdict, one that reaches some high level of favourableness.

It is true that modern philosophy is pervaded by apparent problems about knowledge in particular. But I think it is helpful to see those apparent problems as more or less inept expressions of a deeper anxiety—an inchoately felt threat that a way of thinking we find ourselves falling into leaves minds simply out of touch with the rest of reality, not just questionably capable of getting to know about it. A problem about crediting ourselves with knowledge is just one shape, and not the most fundamental, in which that anxiety can make itself felt.

4.   What is the pressure on our thinking that makes it hard to see how experience could function as a tribunal? I can bring it to light by rehearsing a central element in Wilfrid Sellars's attack on "the Myth of the Given".

Sellars insists that the concept of knowledge belongs in a normative context. He writes: "In characterizing an episode or a state as that of *knowing,* we are not giving an empirical description of that episode or state; we are placing it in the logical space of reasons, of justifying and being able to justify what one says."[2] It is a way of repeating what I have just been urging (§3 above) to say this: though Sellars here speaks of knowledge in particular, that is just to stress one application of the thought that a normative context is necessary for the idea of being in touch with the world at all, whether knowledgeably or not.

One way of putting what Sellars is driving at is to say that epistemology is liable to fall into a naturalistic fallacy.[3] In the more general version I have insisted on, the thought is that the risk of a naturalistic fallacy besets reflection about world-directedness as such, whether knowledgeable or not. If we put Sellars's point this way, we are identifying the natural—as indeed Sellars sometimes does—with the subject matter of "empirical description"; that is, with the subject matter of a mode of discourse that is to be contrasted with placing something in the normative framework constituted by the logical space of reasons. Sellars separates concepts that are intelligible only in terms of how they serve to place things in the logical space of reasons, such as the concept of knowledge, from concepts that can be employed in "empirical description". And if we read the remark as a warning against a naturalistic fallacy, we are understanding "empirical description" as placing things in the logical space of nature, to coin a phrase that is Sellarsian at least in spirit.

What would the logical space of nature be? I think we capture the essentials of Sellars's thinking if we take it that the logical space of

2. "Empiricism and the Philosophy of Mind", in Herbert Feigl and Michael Scriven, eds., *Minnesota Studies in the Philosophy of Science,* vol. 1 (University of Minnesota Press, Minneapolis, 1956), pp. 253–329, at pp. 298–9.

3. See p. 257 of "Empiricism and the Philosophy of Mind" for a formulation on these lines.

nature is the logical space in which the natural sciences function, as we have been enabled to conceive them by a well-charted, and in itself admirable, development of modern thought. We might say that to place something in nature on the relevant conception, as contrasted with placing it in the logical space of reasons, is to situate it in the realm of law. But what matters for Sellars's point is not that or any other positive characterization, but the negative claim: whatever the relations are that constitute the logical space of nature, they are *different in kind* from the normative relations that constitute the logical space of reasons. The relations that constitute the logical space of nature, on the relevant conception, do not include relations such as one thing's being warranted, or—for the general case—correct, in the light of another. That is what Sellars is saying when he insists that "empirical description" cannot amount to placing something in the logical space of reasons.

Now, supposing we accept this dichotomy of logical spaces, which logical space would be the home of the concept of experience? Of course it depends on what we mean by "experience". But suppose we want to conceive the course of a subject's experience as made up of impressions, impingements by the world on a possessor of sensory capacities. Surely such talk of impingements by the world is "empirical description"; or, to put the point in the variant terms I have introduced, the idea of receiving an impression is the idea of a transaction in nature. On Sellars's principles, then, to identify something as an impression is to place it in a logical space other than the one in which talk of knowledge—or, to keep the general case in view, talk of world-directedness, knowledgeable or not—belongs. On these principles, the logical space in which talk of impressions belongs is not one in which things are connected by relations such as one thing's being warranted or correct in the light of another. So if we conceive experience as made up of impressions, on these principles it cannot serve as a tribunal, something to which empirical thinking is answerable. Supposing that it can would just be a case of the naturalistic fallacy that Sellars warns us against—a case of taking it that "empirical description" can amount to placing things in the logical space of reasons.

I have here extracted from Sellars a line of thought that at least potentially stands in tension with a minimal empiricism. (Whether the tension is actual depends on whether empiricism needs to conceive "the tribunal of experience" as made up of impressions; I shall come back to that question (§6 below).) In the lectures that follow, it is mainly Donald Davidson who figures in the role I have here cast Sellars in: as someone whose reflection about experience disqualifies it from intelligibly constituting a tribunal. For these purposes, Sellars and Davidson are interchangeable. Sellars's attack on the Given corresponds, in a way I exploit in my first lecture, to Davidson's attack on what he calls "the third dogma of empiricism"—the dualism of conceptual scheme and empirical "content". And Davidson explicitly suggests that the thought dislodges even a minimal empiricism; he describes the third dogma of empiricism as "perhaps the last", on the ground that "if we give it up it is not clear that there is anything distinctive left to call empiricism".[4]

5. I have been suggesting that we can trace some distinctive anxieties of modern philosophy to a tension between two forces, both of which have an intelligible tendency to shape our reflection about empirical thinking, and thereby about world-directedness in general. One is the attractiveness of a minimal empiricism, which makes out that the very idea of thought's directedness at the empirical world is intelligible only in terms of answerability to the tribunal of experience, conceived in terms of the world impressing itself on perceiving subjects. The other is a frame of mind that makes it seem impossible that experience could be a tribunal. The idea of a tribunal belongs, together with the idea of what the tribunal passes its verdicts on, in what Sellars calls "the logical space of reasons"—a logical space whose structure consists in some of its occupants being, for instance, warranted or correct in the light of others. But the idea of experience, at least construed in terms of impressions, evidently belongs in a logical space of natural connections. That can easily make it seem that if we try to conceive experience as a tribunal, we must be falling into the naturalistic fallacy that Sellars depicts as a pitfall for would-be epistemologists. Suppose we are inexplicitly aware that our thinking is subject to both these forces; that makes it intelligible that we should find thought's being about the empirical world philosophically problematic.

As I said (§1 above), my aim is diagnosis, with a view to a cure. If philosophical anxiety about the very possibility of being in touch with the world can be traced to the tension between those two forces, a cure would require resolving the tension. Obviously the description I

---

4. "On the Very Idea of a Conceptual Scheme", in Donald Davidson, *Inquiries into Truth and Interpretation* (Clarendon Press, Oxford, 1984), pp. 183–98, at p. 189.

have given leaves various options available for doing that. In this book I recommend one way of resolving this tension. Here I shall briefly locate it by distinguishing it from a couple of others.

6. One option would be to renounce empiricism, at least with experience construed in terms of impressions. As I have already mentioned (§4 above), Davidson explicitly links the fate of empiricism with the fate of scheme-content dualism, which he effectively demolishes in a way that parallels Sellars's attack on the Myth of the Given. And Sellars himself works at delineating a concept of impressions that is insulated from epistemology.

I do not believe a position on these lines can be genuinely satisfying. I urge this, specifically in connection with Davidson, in the first of the lectures that make up the body of this book. Davidson's ground for giving up empiricism is, in its essentials, the claim that we cannot take experience to be epistemologically significant except by falling into the Myth of the Given, in which experience, conceived in such a way that it could not be a tribunal, is nevertheless supposed to stand in judgement over our empirical thinking. That certainly has the right shape for an argument that we *must* renounce empiricism. The trouble is that it does not show how we *can*. It does nothing to explain away the plausibility of the empiricist picture, according to which we can make sense of the world-directedness of empirical thinking only by conceiving it as answerable to the empirical world for its correctness, and we can understand answerability to the empirical world only as mediated by answerability to the tribunal of experience, conceived in terms of the world's direct impacts on possessors of perceptual capacities. If we are restricted to the positions Davidson considers, the attractions of empiricism lead only to the incoherence of the Myth of the Given. But so long as the attractions of empiricism are not explained away, that fact is only a source of continuing philosophical discomfort, not a basis for being content with abandoning empiricism, however compulsory Davidson's conception of the options makes that seem.

It is true that, on the principles that induce Davidson and Sellars to reject empiricism, empirical thinking can be seen as rationally constrained by cases of its perceptually *appearing* to a subject that things are thus and so. This might be offered as a concession to the attractions of empiricism. But the concession does not fill the gap I am pointing to; it does not explain away the attractions of empiricism, spelled out in terms of impressions. When it perceptually appears to a subject that things are thus and so, that things are thus and so is itself a case of empirical content. As long as nothing is done to undermine the plausibility of the thought that empirical content in general is intelligible only in terms of answerability to impressions, empirical content will look just as problematic in this context as it does in the context of judgements or beliefs.

7. Sellars and Davidson think we are forced to renounce empiricism, in the relevant sense, partly because they think the logical space of reasons is *sui generis,* as compared with the logical space in which Sellars sees "empirical description" as functioning, which I have identified on Sellars's behalf with the logical space of nature. That is Sellars's way of putting the claim, but Davidson has a counterpart; what figures in Sellars as the *sui generis* character of the logical space of reasons figures in Davidson as the *sui generis* character of what he calls "the constitutive ideal of rationality".[5]

This points to a second way the tension could be resolved: rejecting the dichotomy of logical spaces. If we take this course, we can accept that the concept of experience belongs in the logical space of nature, but deny that that poses any problem for empiricism. The idea is that the logical space of reasons—in which, if we are to hold on to empiricism, experience must be related to empirical thinking—is just part of the logical space of nature; the normative relations that constitute the logical space of reasons can be reconstructed out of conceptual materials whose home is the logical space that Sellars, wrongly on this view, contrasts with the logical space of reasons. This outlook figures in this book under the label "bald naturalism". Bald naturalism refuses to accept that the relations that constitute the logical space of reasons are anything but natural, in a sense of "natural" that connects with the logical space that figures in Sellars (and, with different terminology, in Davidson) on the other side of a contrast with the logical space of reasons. According to this naturalism, moves of the sort Sellars stigmatizes as committing a naturalistic fallacy are indeed natural-

---

5. See especially "Mental Events", in Donald Davidson, *Essays on Actions and Events* (Clarendon Press, Oxford, 1980), pp. 207–25; the quoted phrase is from p. 223.

istic, but not thereby shown to be fallacious. Thus we can accept that the concept of experience belongs in the logical space of nature, but that does not debar experience, so conceived, from being intelligible as a tribunal. So there is no need to explain away the attractions of empiricism.

I shall say a little more about bald naturalism shortly (§9 below), but first I want to outline the different way of resolving the tension that I recommend.

8. My alternative holds on to the thought rejected by bald naturalism, that the structure of the logical space of reasons is *sui generis,* as compared with the structure of the logical space within which natural-scientific description situates things. Even so, my alternative makes room for us to suppose, as according to Sellars and Davidson we cannot, both that the very idea of experience is the idea of something natural and that empirical thinking is answerable to experience. This requires a different way to avoid the threat of a naturalistic fallacy.

The modern scientific revolution made possible a newly clear conception of the distinctive kind of intelligibility that the natural sciences allow us to find in things. The new clarity consists largely, I claim, in an appreciation of something close to what underlies Sellars's warning of a naturalistic fallacy. We must sharply distinguish natural-scientific intelligibility from the kind of intelligibility something acquires when we situate it in the logical space of reasons. That is a way of affirming the dichotomy of logical spaces, as bald naturalism refuses to. Even so, we can acknowledge that the idea of experience is the idea of something natural, without thereby removing the idea of experience from the logical space of reasons. What makes this possible is that we need not identify the dichotomy of logical spaces with a dichotomy between the *natural* and the normative. We need not equate the very idea of nature with the idea of instantiations of concepts that belong in the logical space—admittedly separate, on this view, from the logical space of reasons—in which the natural-scientific kind of intelligibility is brought to light.

On this view, Sellars is right that the logical space in which natural-scientific investigation achieves its distinctive kind of understanding is alien to the logical space of reasons. The logical space of reasons is the frame within which a fundamentally different kind of intelligibility comes into view. And (the same point in different terms) Davidson is right that "the constitutive ideal of rationality" governs concepts that are for that reason quite special, in comparison with the conceptual apparatus of the nomothetic sciences. But it is one thing to acknowledge this—in Sellarsian terms, to single out a logical space that is to be contrasted with the logical space of reasons. It is another to equate that logical space, as Sellars at least implicitly does, with the logical space of *nature*. That is what makes it seem impossible to combine empiricism with the idea that the world's making an impression on a perceiving subject would have to be a natural happening. The mistake here is to forget that nature includes *second nature*. Human beings acquire a second nature in part by being initiated into conceptual capacities, whose interrelations belong in the logical space of reasons.

Once we remember second nature, we see that operations of nature can include circumstances whose descriptions place them in the logical space of reasons, *sui generis* though that logical space is. This makes it possible to accommodate impressions in nature without posing a threat to empiricism. From the thesis that receiving an impression is a transaction in nature, there is now no good inference to the conclusion drawn by Sellars and Davidson, that the idea of receiving an impression must be foreign to the logical space in which concepts such as that of answerability function. Conceptual capacities, whose interrelations belong in the *sui generis* logical space of reasons, can be operative not only in judgements—results of a subject's actively making up her mind about something—but already in the transactions in nature that are constituted by the world's impacts on the receptive capacities of a suitable subject; that is, one who possesses the relevant concepts. Impressions can *be* cases of its perceptually appearing—being apparent—to a subject that things are thus and so. In receiving impressions, a subject can be open to the way things manifestly are. This yields a satisfying interpretation for the image of postures that are answerable to the world through being answerable to experience.

9. The position I call "bald naturalism" figures in this book only as a competitor with the outlook I have just sketched, in the project of exorcizing some philosophical anxieties. The shared aim is to see how we need not seem obliged to set about *answering* the questions that express the anxieties. I have suggested that we can bundle the sup-

posed problems together in a question on these lines: "How is empirical content possible?" Empirical content looks problematic, in the way I aim to deal with, when one becomes inexplicitly aware of an apparent tension between empiricism and the fact that the idea of an impression is the idea of an occurrence in nature. If we can achieve a way of seeing things in which there is after all no tension there, the question, taken as a way of expressing that philosophical puzzlement, should lapse; that needs to be distinguished from its seeming to have been answered. I concern myself with bald naturalism only as sharing the wish to achieve that effect.[6]

There is a possible confusion to avoid here. Much contemporary work sets out, in a naturalistic spirit, to answer (not exorcize) questions that can be framed in the "How possible?" form, about empirical content or other aspects of mindedness. The work I mean aims to give perspicuous descriptions of the material constitution of, say, perceivers, in such a way as to make it intelligible that things composed of mere matter can possess the relevant complex of capacities. A question to which this would be an appropriate response is not a "How possible?" question of the sort I am concerned with. As I said (§2 above), a "How possible?" question of the sort I am concerned with expresses a distinctive kind of puzzlement, issuing from an inexplicit awareness of a background to one's reflection that, if made explicit, would yield an argument that the topic of the question is not possible at all. To respond to a "How possible?" question of this kind in, so to speak, engineering terms, with a perspicuous description of the requisite material constitution, would be plainly unhelpful; it would be like responding to Zeno by walking across a room. That leaves it open that investigations of the "engineering" sort might be fine for other purposes. In this book I consider bald naturalism only as a way to exorcize (not answer) the questions that give expression to that distinctively philosophical kind of puzzlement, the kind that issues from a frame of mind that, when fully explicit, would purport to display an impossibility in what the questions are asked about. Bald naturalism figures here as, I claim, a less satisfying way to do that than my alternative. I do not concern myself with those different questions and an-

---

6. The label "bald naturalism" is perhaps infelicitous for a position with a sophisticated motivation on these lines; that is what I acknowledge in the footnote on pp. 88–9. I took myself to be stuck with the label even so, since I had given it a thematic prominence in the lectures of which the book is a version.

swers, the ones that figure in inquiries into the machinery of mindedness.

I have tried to make it plausible that the anxieties I aim to exorcize
issue from the thought—often no doubt only inchoate—that the structure of the logical space of reasons is *sui generis,* as compared with
the logical framework in which natural-scientific understanding is
achieved. On this view, it emerges as unsurprising that the period in
which dealing with these supposed difficulties came to seem the dom-
inant obligation of philosophy coincides with the rise of modern science, in which natural-scientific understanding, as we are now
equipped to conceive it, was being separated out from a hitherto un-
differentiated conception of understanding in general. According to
my picture, an important element in this clarification of the proper
target of natural science was an increasingly firm awareness that we
must sharply distinguish natural-scientific understanding from the
kind of understanding achieved by situating what is understood in
the logical space of reasons; that is, precisely, that the structure of the
logical space of reasons is *sui generis,* as I have read Sellars, and in
different terms Davidson, as claiming it is.

Now bald naturalism has it that that perhaps inchoate sense of a
conceptual divide was simply wrong; it would be revealed to be wrong
by a reconstruction of the structure of the logical space of reasons in
terms that belong in the logical space of natural-scientific understanding. This claim is programmatic, but that is not my ground for finding
bald naturalism unsatisfying. The point is rather one that I mentioned
at the beginning of this Introduction (§1 above). It is easy—and not
because we are merely stupid—to be captivated by the kind of philosophy I aim to exorcize. That means that a proposed exorcism is more
satisfying to the extent that it enables us to respect, as insights, the
driving thoughts of those who take the familiar philosophical anxieties to pose real intellectual obligations (our driving thoughts when we
find ourselves beset by the anxieties), even while we unmask the supposed obligations as illusory. Now my picture is unlike bald naturalism in just that way. I acknowledge as an insight the basic conviction
that generates the anxieties, in combination with the scarcely ques-
tionable conception of impressions as occurrences in nature. In my
picture, those who take it that philosophy has to answer (rather than
exorcize) questions about how minds can be in touch with the world
are not wrong in supposing that the logical space of reasons is *sui
generis,* in just the way that seems to lead to problems about how

responsiveness to reasons can fit into the natural world. (Indeed I think that was a prime lesson our ancestors learned at the time of the rise of modern science.) We can disown an obligation to try to answer the characteristic questions of modern philosophy, without needing to deny, as bald naturalism does, that a real insight is operative in seeming to be faced with that obligation.

To make my point here, I need not pretend to have an argument that the bald naturalist programme—reconstructing the structure of the logical space of reasons in terms that belong in the logical space of natural-scientific understanding—*cannot* be executed. The point is just that the availability of my alternative and, I claim, more satisfying exorcism undercuts a philosophical motivation, the only one relevant to my concerns in this book, for supposing the programme *must* be feasible. It is not philosophically threatening to suppose there is insight in the thought that reason is not natural, in the only sense of "natural" countenanced by bald naturalism.

10. It should be clear that reflection about perceptual experience has served in this Introduction, as it does in this book, as just one example of a type. Parallel puzzlements will be prone to arise wherever we want to speak of responsiveness to reasons. "Responsiveness to reasons" is a good gloss on one notion of freedom. So the puzzlement in its general form is about how freedom, in that sense, fits into the natural world. That seems hard to comprehend if we are tempted to equate the natural with exemplifications of concepts whose home is the logical space that Sellars contrasts with the logical space of reasons. In the fifth lecture I talk briefly about another instance of the type.

Some friendly readers have taken issue with the negative attitude I profess in this book to what I call "constructive philosophy" (see, e.g., p. 95). Let me bring the point I mean to make in those terms into connection with the way I have set things out in this Introduction. What I mean by "engaging in constructive philosophy" is attempting to *answer* philosophical questions of the sort I have here singled out: "How possible?" questions whose felt urgency derives from a frame of mind that, if explicitly thought through, would yield materials for an argument that what the questions are asked about is impossible. Evidently it can seem sensible to embark on such a project only if one does not quite understand the predicament that seems to motivate it. If the frame of mind is left in place, one cannot show how whatever it is that one is asking about is possible; if the frame of mind is dislodged, the "How possible?" question no longer has the point it seemed to have. Either way, there is no prospect of answering the question as it was putatively meant. So if I am right about the character of the philosophical anxieties I aim to deal with, there is no room for doubt that engaging in "constructive philosophy", in this sense, is not the way to approach them. As I have put it, we need to exorcize the questions rather than set about answering them. Of course that takes hard work: if you like, constructive philosophy in another sense. And of course that is what I offer in this book.

Mind and World

THE LECTURES

Concepts and Intuitions

1. The overall topic I am going to consider in these lectures is the way concepts mediate the relation between minds and the world. I shall focus the discussion in terms of a familiar philosophical outlook, which Donald Davidson has described as a dualism of scheme and content.[1] That will get us quickly to Kant. One of my main aims is to suggest that Kant should still have a central place in our discussion of the way thought bears on reality.

When Davidson talks about a dualism of scheme and content, "scheme" means "conceptual scheme". If content is dualistically opposed to what is conceptual, "content" cannot mean what it often means in contemporary philosophy, namely, what is given by a "that" clause in, for instance, an attribution of a belief: just to have a label, we can call content in this modern sense "representational content". Representational content cannot be dualistically set over against the conceptual. That is obviously so, however hospitable we are to the idea that some representational content is non-conceptual. (I shall come to that issue in my third lecture.)

So why is it content that is supposed to stand over against concepts, in the dualism Davidson criticizes? We can arrive at an understanding of the terminology from the way it figures in Kant's remark "Thoughts without content are empty".[2] For a thought to be empty

---

1. "On the Very Idea of a Conceptual Scheme", in his *Inquiries into Truth and Interpretation* (Clarendon Press, Oxford, 1984), pp. 183–98. See especially p. 187, "a dualism of total scheme (or language) and uninterpreted content", and p. 189, "the dualism of conceptual scheme and empirical content".

2. *Critique of Pure Reason,* trans. Norman Kemp Smith (Macmillan, London, 1929), A51/B75.

would be for there to be nothing that one thinks when one thinks it; that is, for it to lack what I am calling "representational content". That would be for it not really to be a thought at all, and that is surely Kant's point; he is not, absurdly, drawing our attention to a special kind of thoughts, the empty ones. Now when Kant says that thoughts without content are empty, he is not merely affirming a tautology: "without content" is not just another wording for "empty", as it would be if "content" simply meant "representational content". "Without content" points to what would *explain* the sort of emptiness Kant is envisaging. And we can spell out the explanation from the other half of Kant's remark: "intuitions without concepts are blind." Thoughts without content—which would not really be thoughts at all—would be a play of concepts without any connection with intuitions, that is, bits of experiential intake. It is their connection with experiential intake that supplies the content, the substance, that thoughts would otherwise lack.

So the picture is this: the fact that thoughts are not empty, the fact that thoughts have representational content, emerges out of an interplay of concepts and intuitions. "Content" in Davidson's dualism corresponds to intuitions, bits of experiential intake, understood in terms of a dualistic conception of this interplay.

2.   This Kantian background explains why what stands over against the conceptual, in the dualism Davidson considers, is often described as the Given. In fact "dualism of scheme and Given" is a better label than "dualism of scheme and content", because it does not resonate confusingly with the idea of representational content. It also suggests a specific understanding of why the dualism is tempting.

Kant makes his remark about intuitions and concepts in the course of representing empirical knowledge as the result of a co-operation between receptivity and spontaneity, between sensibility and understanding.[3] Now we should ask why it seems appropriate to describe the understanding, whose contribution to this co-operation is its com-

---

3. To give the lead-up to the passage I have already quoted: "If the *receptivity* of our mind, its power of receiving representations in so far as it is in any wise affected, is to be entitled sensibility, then the mind's power of producing representations from itself, the *spontaneity* of knowledge, should be called the understanding. Our nature is so constituted that our *intuition* can never be other than sensible; that is, it contains only the mode in which we are affected by objects. The faculty, on the other hand, which enables us to *think* the object of sensible intuition is the understanding. To neither of these powers may a pre-

mand of concepts, in terms of spontaneity. A schematic but suggestive answer is that the topography of the conceptual sphere is constituted by rational relations. The space of concepts is at least part of what Wilfrid Sellars calls "the space of reasons".[4] When Kant describes the understanding as a faculty of spontaneity, that reflects his view of the relation between reason and freedom: rational necessitation is not just compatible with freedom but constitutive of it. In a slogan, the space of reasons is the realm of freedom.[5]

But if our freedom in empirical thinking is total, in particular if it is not constrained from outside the conceptual sphere, that can seem to threaten the very possibility that judgements of experience might be grounded in a way that relates them to a reality external to thought. And surely there must be such grounding if experience is to be a source of knowledge, and more generally, if the bearing of empirical judgements on reality is to be intelligibly in place in our picture at all. The more we play up the connection between reason and freedom, the more we risk losing our grip on how exercises of concepts can constitute warranted judgements about the world. What we wanted to conceive as exercises of concepts threaten to degenerate into moves in a self-contained game. And that deprives us of the very idea that they are exercises of concepts. Suiting empirical beliefs to the reasons for them is not a self-contained game.

The dualism of conceptual scheme and "empirical content", of

---

ference be given over the other. Without sensibility no object would be given to us, without understanding no object would be thought. Thoughts without content are empty, intuitions without concepts are blind."

4. "In characterizing an episode or a state as that [better: one] of *knowing*, we are not giving an empirical description of that episode or state; we are placing it in the logical space of reasons, of justifying and being able to justify what one says." This is from pp. 298–9 of Sellars's classic attack on the Myth of the Given, "Empiricism and the Philosophy of Mind", in Herbert Feigl and Michael Scriven, eds., *Minnesota Studies in the Philosophy of Science*, vol. 1 (University of Minnesota Press, Minneapolis, 1956), pp. 253–329. In much of the rest of these lectures, I shall be concerned to cast doubt on Sellars's idea that placing something in the logical space of reasons is, as such, to be contrasted with giving an empirical description of it. But the theme of placing things in the space of reasons is of central importance for me.

I say that the space of concepts is at least part of the space of reasons in order to leave it open, for the moment, that the space of reasons may extend more widely than the space of concepts; see the text below for this idea.

5. For a thoughtful discussion of this idea, see Robert Brandom, "Freedom and Constraint by Norms", *American Philosophical Quarterly* 16 (1979), 187–96.

scheme and Given, is a response to this worry. The point of the dualism is that it allows us to acknowledge an external constraint on our freedom to deploy our empirical concepts. Empirical justifications depend on rational relations, relations within the space of reasons. The putatively reassuring idea is that empirical justifications have an ultimate foundation in impingements on the conceptual realm from outside. So the space of reasons is made out to be more extensive than the space of concepts. Suppose we are tracing the ground, the justification, for a belief or a judgement. The idea is that when we have exhausted all the available moves within the space of concepts, all the available moves from one conceptually organized item to another, there is still one more step we can take: namely, pointing to something that is simply received in experience. It can only be pointing, because *ex hypothesi* this last move in a justification comes after we have exhausted the possibilities of tracing grounds from one conceptually organized, and so articulable, item to another.

I began with the thought that is expressed in Kant's remark: the very idea of representational content, not just the idea of judgements that are adequately justified, requires an interplay between concepts and intuitions, bits of experiential intake. Otherwise what was meant to be a picture of the exercise of concepts can depict only a play of empty forms. I have modulated into talking about how the idea of the Given figures in a thought about the grounding that entitles some empirical judgements to count as knowledgeable. But this explicitly epistemological idea is straightforwardly connected with the more general idea I began with. Empirical judgements in general—whether or not they reflect knowledge, and even whether or not they are justified at all, perhaps less substantially than knowledge requires—had better have content of a sort that admits of empirical justification, even if there is none in the present case (say in a quite unsupported guess). We could not begin to suppose that we understood how pointing to a bit of the Given could justify the use of a concept in judgement— could, at the limit, display the judgement as knowledgeable—unless we took this possibility of warrant to be constitutive of the concept's being what it is, and hence constitutive of its contribution to any thinkable content it figures in, whether that of a knowledgeable, or less substantially justifiable, judgement or any other.

This supposed requirement would bear immediately on observational concepts: concepts suited to figure in judgements that are directly responsive to experience. The supposed requirement is reflected in a familiar picture of the formation of such concepts, a picture that is a natural counterpart to the idea of the Given. The idea is that if concepts are to be even partly constituted by the fact that judgements in which they figure are grounded in the Given, then the associated conceptual capacities must be acquired from confrontations with suitable bits of the Given: that is, occasions when pointing to an ultimate warrant would have been feasible. But in any ordinary impingement on our sensibility, it would have to be a manifold Given that is presented to us. So in order to form an observational concept, a subject would have to abstract out the right element in the presented multiplicity.

This abstractionist picture of the role of the Given in the formation of concepts has been trenchantly criticized, in a Wittgensteinian spirit, by P. T. Geach.[6] I shall come back to Wittgenstein's thought about this sort of question later in this lecture (§7).

Once we have equipped ourselves with this picture of how empirical substance is infused into concepts at the ground level, the level of observational concepts, it will seem straightforward to extend the picture from there. The idea is that empirical substance is transmitted from the ground level to empirical concepts that are further removed from immediate experience, with the transmission running along channels constituted by the inferential linkages that hold a system of concepts together.

3. I have tried to explain what makes the idea of the Given tempting. But in fact it is useless for its purpose.

The idea of the Given is the idea that the space of reasons, the space of justifications or warrants, extends more widely than the conceptual sphere. The extra extent of the space of reasons is supposed to allow it to incorporate non-conceptual impacts from outside the realm of thought. But we cannot really understand the relations in virtue of which a judgement is warranted except as relations within the space of concepts: relations such as implication or probabilification, which hold between potential exercises of conceptual capacities. The attempt to extend the scope of justificatory relations outside the conceptual sphere cannot do what it is supposed to do.

6. *Mental Acts* (Routledge and Kegan Paul, London, 1957), §§6–11.

What we wanted was a reassurance that when we use our concepts in judgement, our freedom—our spontaneity in the exercise of our understanding—is constrained from outside thought, and constrained in a way that we can appeal to in displaying the judgements as justified. But when we make out that the space of reasons is more extensive than the conceptual sphere, so that it can incorporate extra-conceptual impingements from the world, the result is a picture in which constraint from outside is exerted at the outer boundary of the expanded space of reasons, in what we are committed to depicting as a brute impact from the exterior. Now perhaps this picture secures that we cannot be blamed for what happens at that outer boundary, and hence that we cannot be blamed for the inward influence of what happens there. What happens there is the result of an alien force, the causal impact of the world, operating outside the control of our spontaneity. But it is one thing to be exempt from blame, on the ground that the position we find ourselves in can be traced ultimately to brute force; it is quite another thing to have a justification. In effect, the idea of the Given offers exculpations where we wanted justifications.[7]

It can be difficult to accept that the Myth of the Given is a myth. It can seem that if we reject the Given, we merely reopen ourselves to the threat to which the idea of the Given is a response, the threat that our picture does not accommodate any external constraint on our activity in empirical thought and judgement. It can seem that we are retaining

7. In the lecture as delivered, I said "excuses" where I now say "exculpations"; Zvi Cohen pointed out that that does not make the contrast I want. What I want is an analogue to the sense in which if someone is found in a place from which she has been banished, she is exculpated by the fact that she was deposited there by a tornado. Her arriving there is completely removed from the domain of what she is responsible for; it is not that she is still responsible, but there is a basis for mitigating any sanctions.

When we are tempted by the Myth of the Given, we carefully ensure that relations across the envisaged outer boundary of the space of concepts, relations between bits of the Given and the most basic judgements of experience, can be reason-constituting; that is the point of taking the space of reasons to extend more widely than the space of concepts. But we forget to consider how things look at the new outer boundary of the space of reasons, where it makes contact with independent reality. What we wanted was to see our exercises of spontaneity as subject to a constraint imposed by the world itself, but in such a way as not to undermine the applicability of the idea of spontaneity. We wanted to be able to credit ourselves with responsible freedom, so that we are within the scope of possible justifications, all the way out to the ultimate contact between our mental life and the world. My main point in this lecture is to bring out how difficult it is to see that we can have both desiderata: both rational constraint from the world and spontaneity all the way out. The Myth of the Given renounces the second, and the Davidsonian response that I consider below (§6) renounces the first.

a role for spontaneity but refusing to acknowledge any role for receptivity, and that is intolerable. If our activity in empirical thought and judgement is to be recognizable as bearing on reality at all, there must be external constraint. There must be a role for receptivity as well as spontaneity, for sensibility as well as understanding. Realizing this, we come under pressure to recoil back into appealing to the Given, only to see all over again that it cannot help. There is a danger of falling into an interminable oscillation.

But we can find a way to dismount from the seesaw.

4.   The original Kantian thought was that empirical knowledge results from a co-operation between receptivity and spontaneity. (Here "spontaneity" can be simply a label for the involvement of conceptual capacities.) We can dismount from the seesaw if we can achieve a firm grip on this thought: receptivity does not make an even notionally separable contribution to the co-operation.

The relevant conceptual capacities are drawn on *in* receptivity. (It is important that that is not the only context in which they are operative. I shall come back to this in §5.) It is not that they are exercised *on* an extra-conceptual deliverance of receptivity. We should understand what Kant calls "intuition"—experiential intake—not as a bare getting of an extra-conceptual Given, but as a kind of occurrence or state that already has conceptual content. In experience one takes in, for instance sees, *that things are thus and so*. That is the sort of thing one can also, for instance, judge.

Of course one can be misled into supposing that one takes in that things are thus and so when things are not thus and so. But when one is not misled, one takes in how things are. It does not matter much that one can be misled. I shall not talk about it until my final lecture, and not much then.

In the view I am urging, the conceptual contents that sit closest to the impact of external reality on one's sensibility are not already, *qua* conceptual, some distance away from that impact. They are not the results of a first step within the space of reasons, a step that would be retraced by the last step in laying out justifications, as that activity is conceived within the dualism of scheme and Given. This supposed first step would be a move from an impression, conceived as the bare reception of a bit of the Given, to a judgement justified by the impression. But it is not like that: the conceptual contents that are most basic in this sense are already possessed by impressions themselves, impingements by the world on our sensibility.

This makes room for a different notion of givenness, one that is innocent of the confusion between justification and exculpation. Now we need not try to make out that the space of reasons is more extensive than the space of concepts. When we trace the ground for an empirical judgement, the last step takes us to experiences. Experiences already have conceptual content, so this last step does not take us outside the space of concepts. But it takes us to something in which sensibility—receptivity—is operative, so we need no longer be unnerved by the freedom implicit in the idea that our conceptual capacities belong to a faculty of spontaneity. We need not worry that our picture leaves out the external constraint that is required if exercises of our conceptual capacities are to be recognizable as bearing on the world at all.

5. I said (§4) that when we enjoy experience conceptual capacities are drawn on *in* receptivity, not exercised *on* some supposedly prior deliverances of receptivity. And it is not that I want to say they are exercised on something else. It sounds off key in this connection to speak of *exercising* conceptual capacities at all. That would suit an activity, whereas experience is passive.[8] In experience one finds oneself saddled with content. One's conceptual capacities have already been brought into play, in the content's being available to one, before one has any choice in the matter. The content is not something one has put together oneself, as when one decides what to say about something. In fact it is precisely because experience is passive, a case of receptivity in operation, that the conception of experience I am recommending can satisfy the craving for a limit to freedom that underlies the Myth of the Given.

Because experience is passive, the involvement of conceptual capacities in experience does not by itself provide a good fit for the idea of

---

8. Of course this is not to deny that experiencing the world involves activity. Searching is an activity; so are observing, watching, and so forth. (This sort of thing is usefully stressed by people who think we should not conceive experience as passive reception at all, such as J. J. Gibson; see, for instance, *The Senses Considered as Perceptual Systems* (George Allen and Unwin, London, 1968).) But one's control over what happens in experience has limits: one can decide where to place oneself, at what pitch to tune one's attention, and so forth, but it is not up to one what, having done all that, one will experience. This minimal point is what I am insisting on.

a faculty of spontaneity. That may make it seem that I am not really disarming the Myth of the Given, but merely rejecting the terms that pose the apparent problem it responds to. What generates the temptation to appeal to the Given is the thought that spontaneity characterizes exercises of conceptual understanding in general, so that spontaneity extends all the way out to the conceptual contents that sit closest to the impacts of the world on our sensibility. We need to conceive this expansive spontaneity as subject to control from outside our thinking, on pain of representing the operations of spontaneity as a frictionless spinning in a void. The Given seems to supply that external control. And now it may seem that when I stress that experience is passive, I am dissolving the temptation by simply denying that spontaneity extends all the way out to the content of experience, even though I claim that conceptual capacities are operative in experience.

But it is not like that. The craving for external friction in our picture of spontaneity is not something we can satisfy in that way, by simply restricting the scope of spontaneity, making it less extensive than the sphere of the conceptual.

We would not be able to suppose that the capacities that are in play in experience are conceptual if they were manifested only in experience, only in operations of receptivity. They would not be recognizable as conceptual capacities at all unless they could also be exercised in active thinking, that is, in ways that do provide a good fit for the idea of spontaneity. Minimally, it must be possible to decide whether or not to judge that things are as one's experience represents them to be. How one's experience represents things to be is not under one's control, but it is up to one whether one accepts the appearance or rejects it.[9] Moreover, even if we consider only judgements that register experience itself, which are already active in that minimal sense, we must acknowledge that the capacity to use concepts in those judgements is not self-standing; it cannot be in place independently of a capacity to use the same concepts outside that context. That is so even with the concepts that are most immediately linked to the subjective character of experience itself, the concepts of secondary qualities. Quite generally, the capacities that are drawn on in experience are recognizable as conceptual only against the background of the fact

---

9. The point here is well illustrated by familiar illusions. In the Müller-Lyer illusion, one's experience represents the two lines as being unequally long, but someone in the know will refrain from judging that that is how things are.

that someone who has them is responsive to rational relations, which link the contents of judgements of experience with other judgeable contents. These linkages give the concepts their place as elements in possible views of the world.

For example, consider judgements of colour. These judgements involve a range of conceptual capacities that are as thinly integrated into understanding of the world as any. Even so, no one could count as making even a directly observational judgement of colour except against a background sufficient to ensure that she understands colours as potential properties of things. The ability to produce "correct" colour words in response to inputs to the visual system (an ability possessed, I believe, by some parrots) does not display possession of the relevant concepts if the subject has no comprehension of, for instance, the idea that these responses reflect a sensitivity to a kind of state of affairs in the world, something that can obtain anyway, independently of these perturbations in her stream of consciousness. The necessary background understanding includes, for instance, the concept of visible surfaces of objects and the concept of suitable conditions for telling what colour something is by looking at it.[10]

Of course the concepts that can figure in the content of experience are not restricted to concepts of secondary qualities. Once we take that into account, it becomes even clearer that the passive operation of conceptual capacities in sensibility is not intelligible independently of their active exercise in judgement, and in the thinking that issues in judgement.

The conceptual capacities that are passively drawn into play in experience belong to a network of capacities for active thought, a network that rationally governs comprehension-seeking responses to the impacts of the world on sensibility. And part of the point of the idea that the understanding is a faculty of spontaneity—that conceptual capacities are capacities whose exercise is in the domain of responsible freedom—is that the network, as an individual thinker finds it governing her thinking, is not sacrosanct. Active empirical thinking takes place under a standing obligation to reflect about the credentials of the putatively rational linkages that govern it. There must be a stand-

10. For an elaboration of points of this kind, see Sellars, "Empiricism and the Philosophy of Mind", §§10–20.

ing willingness to refashion concepts and conceptions if that is what reflection recommends. No doubt there is no serious prospect that we might need to reshape the concepts at the outermost edges of the system, the most immediately observational concepts, in response to pressures from inside the system. But that no-doubt unreal prospect brings out the point that matters for my present purpose. This is that although experience itself is not a good fit for the idea of spontaneity, even the most immediately observational concepts are partly constituted by their role in something that is indeed appropriately conceived in terms of spontaneity.[11]

So we cannot simply insulate the passive involvement of conceptual capacities in experience from the potentially unnerving effects of the freedom implied by the idea of spontaneity. If we think that the way to exploit the passivity of experience is to deny that spontaneity extends all the way out to the content of experience, we merely fall back into a misleadingly formulated version of the Myth of the Given. If we try to keep spontaneity out of the picture but nevertheless talk of conceptual capacities operating in experience, the talk of conceptual capacities is mere word-play. The trouble about the Myth of the Given is that it offers us at best exculpations where we wanted justifications. That trouble shows up again here, in connection with impingements on spontaneity by the so-called conceptual deliverances of sensibility. If those impingements are conceived as outside the scope of spontaneity, outside the domain of responsible freedom, then the best they can yield is that we cannot be blamed for believing whatever they lead us to believe, not that we are justified in believing it.

I am not, then, proposing a cheap defeat of the Given, to be achieved by exploiting the fact that experience is passive so as to keep experience out of the scope of spontaneity. The view I am recommending is that even though experience is passive, it draws into operation capacities that genuinely belong to spontaneity.

6. It need not be a mere superficial oversight if someone fails to see a possibility here—if someone cannot understand how capacities that

---

11. I intend the imagery of this paragraph to be reminiscent of the well-known closing section of W. V. Quine's classic paper "Two Dogmas of Empiricism", in his *From a Logical Point of View* (Harvard University Press, Cambridge, Mass., 1961; 1st ed. 1953), pp. 20–46.

belong to spontaneity could be inextricably implicated in an operation of mere receptivity. It can be difficult to see a way out here, and the roots of the difficulty lie deep.

I want to provide a first illustration of this from Davidson himself. In a well-known paper in which he recommends a coherence approach to truth and knowledge,[12] Davidson shows a blind spot for the way out that I have described. He does not argue against it; it simply does not figure among the possibilities that he contemplates.

Davidson is clear that if we conceive experience in terms of impacts on sensibility that occur outside the space of concepts, we must not think we can appeal to experience to justify judgements or beliefs. That would be to fall into the Myth of the Given, with its confusion of justification and exculpation. The space of reasons does not extend further than the space of concepts, to take in a bare reception of the Given. So far, this is just what I have been urging.

But Davidson thinks experience can be nothing but an extra-conceptual impact on sensibility. So he concludes that experience must be outside the space of reasons. According to Davidson, experience is causally relevant to a subject's beliefs and judgements, but it has no bearing on their status as justified or warranted. Davidson says that "nothing can count as a reason for holding a belief except another belief" (p. 310), and he means in particular that experience cannot count as a reason for holding a belief.

Of course I agree with the point this train of thought starts from. But the conclusion is quite unsatisfying. Davidson recoils from the Myth of the Given all the way to denying experience any justificatory role, and the coherentist upshot is a version of the conception of spontaneity as frictionless, the very thing that makes the idea of the Given attractive. This is just one of the movements in the oscillation that I have spoken of. There is nothing to prevent it from triggering the familiar recoil in its turn. Davidson's picture depicts our empirical thinking as engaged in with no rational constraint, but only causal influence, from outside. This just raises a worry as to whether the picture can accommodate the sort of bearing on reality that empirical content amounts to, and that is just the kind of worry that can make an appeal to the Given seem necessary. And Davidson does nothing to

12. "A Coherence Theory of Truth and Knowledge", reprinted in Ernest LePore, ed., *Truth and Interpretation: Perspectives on the Philosophy of Donald Davidson* (Basil Blackwell, Oxford, 1986), pp. 307–19.

allay the worry. I think we should be suspicious of his bland confidence that empirical content can be intelligibly in our picture even though we carefully stipulate that the world's impacts on our senses have nothing to do with justification.

Of course Davidson believes that his position is a place where thought can come to rest, not a movement in an interminable oscillation. But I think he contrives to make it seem so only by going insufficiently deeply into the motivation of the Myth of the Given.

He remarks that a foundationalist conception of experience "leads to skepticism" (p. 314). Of course it is true that appealing to the Given gets us nowhere in epistemology. But it is not true that philosophical worries about scepticism arise out of the failure of the idea of the Given. And the idea of the Given is not something that comes to us in calm reflection, as if from nowhere, as a possible basis for the epistemology of empirical knowledge, so that we can cheerfully drop it when we see that it does not work. Rather, the idea of the Given is a response to a way of thinking that underlies the familiar philosophical anxiety about empirical knowledge, and that way of thinking is precisely what Davidson endorses.

We can seem to be forced into the idea of the Given; that is what happens when we are impressed by the thought that conceptual capacities belong to a faculty of spontaneity, and fall into worrying that our picture deprives itself of the possibility that exercises of concepts could be what it depicts, because it leaves out any rational constraint from outside the sphere of thought. One form that this worry takes is the fear that we have no convincing way to credit ourselves with empirical knowledge. The recoil to the Given that results from this worry—whether in its generic form (how can it be that exercises of spontaneity bear on a reality outside the sphere of thinking at all?) or in its specifically epistemological form (how can exercises of spontaneity amount to knowledge?)—is a natural response to the very sort of "coherence theory of truth and knowledge" that Davidson recommends. Such theories express precisely the unnerving idea that the spontaneity of conceptual thinking is not subject to rational constraint from outside. Coherentist rhetoric suggests images of confinement within the sphere of thinking, as opposed to being in touch with something outside it. To one who finds such imagery both appropriate and worrying, the idea of the Given can give the appearance of reinstating thought's bearing on reality. And at this point in the dialectic, it is no good pointing out that the appearance is illusory, that the idea of the Given does not fulfil its apparent promise, if the worry that can make the idea nevertheless seem inescapable remains urgent, or is even exacerbated. The effect is simply to bring out that neither of the two positions that we are being asked to choose between is satisfying.

Davidson does nothing to discourage us from taking his coherentist rhetoric in terms of confinement imagery. On the contrary, he positively encourages it. At one point he says, "Of course we can't get outside our skins to find out what is causing the internal happenings of which we are aware" (p. 312). This is, as it stands, a very unsatisfactory remark. Why should we suppose that to find out about external objects we would have to get outside our skins? (Of course we cannot do that.) And why should we suppose that we are interested in finding out what is causing internal happenings of which we are aware, rather than that we are simply interested in the layout of the environment? Of course getting outside our skins is not the same as getting outside our thoughts. But perhaps we can understand how Davidson can be so casual in this remark if we take it that our literal confinement inside our skins strikes him as an analogue to a metaphorical confinement inside our beliefs, which he is happy to let his coherentism imply. Davidson's picture is that we cannot get outside our beliefs.

Of course Davidson knows that such confinement imagery tends to prompt a recoil to the idea of the Given, the idea that truth and knowledge depend on rational relations to something outside the conceptual realm. He thinks he can allow free rein to confinement imagery, but pre-empt the recoil by arguing, within his coherentist framework, for the evidently reassuring thesis that "belief is in its nature veridical" (p. 314). Davidson argues for that thesis by connecting belief with interpretation, and urging that it is in the nature of interpretation that an interpreter must find her subjects mostly right about the world with which she can observe them causally interacting.

I do not want to dispute that argument. But I do want to raise the question how effectively it can reassure us, if we are worried about whether Davidson's coherentist picture can incorporate thought's bearing on reality. Suppose one feels the worry in this familiar form: so far as the picture goes, one might be a brain in a mad scientist's vat. The Davidsonian response seems to be that if one were a brain in a vat, it would be correct to interpret one's beliefs as being largely true beliefs about the brain's electronic environment.[13] But is that the reassurance we need if we are to be immunized against the attractions of the Given? The argument was supposed to start with the body of beliefs to which we are supposed to be confined, in our active efforts to suit our thinking to the available justifications. It was supposed to make the confinement imagery unthreatening by reassuring us that those beliefs are mostly true. But the response to the brain-in-a-vat worry works the wrong way round. The response does not calm the fear that our picture leaves our thinking possibly out of touch with the world outside us. It just gives us a dizzying sense that our grip on what it is that we believe is not as firm as we thought.[14]

I think the right conclusion is this: whatever credence we give to Davidson's argument that a body of belief is sure to be mostly true, the argument starts too late to certify Davidson's position as a genuine escape from the oscillation.

The only motivation for the Myth of the Given that figures in Davidson's thinking is a shallow scepticism, in which, taking it for granted that one has a body of beliefs, one worries about their credentials. But the Myth of the Given has a deeper motivation, in the thought that if spontaneity is not subject to rational constraint from outside, as Davidson's coherentist position insists that it is not, then we cannot make it intelligible to ourselves how exercises of spontaneity can represent the world at all. Thoughts without intuitions are empty, and the point is not met by crediting intuitions with a causal impact on thoughts; we can have empirical content in our picture only if we can acknowledge that thoughts and intuitions are rationally con-

13. We have this on the testimony of Richard Rorty; see p. 340 of his "Pragmatism, Davidson, and Truth", in LePore, ed., *Truth and Interpretation*, pp. 333–55.

14. It takes care to say precisely why the response is unsatisfying. It is not that we are being told we may be egregiously wrong about what our beliefs are about. If I protest that some belief of mine is not about electronic impulses or whatever but about, say, a book, the reply can be: "Certainly your belief is about a book—given how 'a book' as you use the phrase is correctly interpreted." The envisaged reinterpretation, to suit the hypothesis that I am a brain in a vat, affects my higher-level beliefs about what my first-level beliefs are about in a way that precisely matches its effect on my first-level beliefs. The problem is that in the argument Rorty attributes to Davidson, we ring changes on the actual environment (as seen by the interpreter and brought into the interpretation) without changing how things strike the believer, even while the interpretation is supposed to capture how the believer is in touch with her world. This strikes me as making it impossible to claim that the argument traffics in any genuine idea of being in touch with something in particular. The objects that the interpreter sees the subject's beliefs as being about become, as it were, merely noumenal so far as the subject is concerned.

nected. By rejecting that, Davidson undermines his right to the idea
that his purportedly reassuring argument starts from, the idea of a
body of beliefs. In that case his attempt to disarm the confinement
imagery does not work, and his position is exposed as a version of one
phase in the oscillation. A genuine escape would require that we avoid
the Myth of the Given without renouncing the claim that experience
is a rational constraint on thinking.

I have suggested that we can do that if we can recognize that the
world's impressions on our senses are already possessed of conceptual
content. But there is a block that prevents Davidson from seeing
any possibilities in this direction. I shall come back to this in later lectures.

7.   The Myth of the Given expresses a craving for rational constraint
from outside the realm of thought and judgement. This craving is
most familiar in connection with empirical knowledge of the world
about us: knowledge yielded by what Kant calls "outer sense".[15] But
it is instructive to see that the spatial phrase that I have just used,
"outside the realm of thought and judgement", is only metaphorical.
Exactly the same temptation arises in connection with what Kant calls
"inner sense".[16] The realm of thought and judgement includes judgements about the thinker's own perceptions, thoughts, sensations, and
the like. The conceptual capacities that are operative in such judgements must belong to spontaneity just as much as any other conceptual capacities do, and that can generate the spectre of a frictionless
spinning in a void for this region of thought too. Then, in the way that
should by now be familiar, ensuring friction, which is required for
genuine content, can seem to oblige us to take exercises of concepts in
this region to be rationally grounded in something extra-conceptual,
bare presences that are the ultimate grounds of judgements.

This description of an apparently compulsory way of thinking fits
Wittgenstein's target in the so-called Private Language Argument. If
we understand that polemic as applying a general rejection of the
Given, we make available to ourselves a sharp appreciation of its co-
gency. And perhaps we can also acquire a richer understanding of the

15. For instance at B67.
16. For instance at A22/B37. For the two phrases together in a single discussion, see the
footnote at Bxxxix–xli.

general point by considering the way it shows up in those familiar passages of Wittgenstein.[17]

I say "so-called Private Language Argument" because according to this reading the main point of the conception Wittgenstein attacks is to claim that "judgements of inner sense" are ultimately grounded on bare presences, rather than to devise a way to put the bare presences into words. If someone in the grip of the conception was convinced by an argument that language could not embrace the supposed items she insists on, she might reply that that is really just her point. If language could embrace them, that would mean they were within the conceptual sphere, and the point of acknowledging them is to acknowledge something that constrains spontaneity, which moves within that sphere, from outside. So certainly language cannot capture them; but still, it can seem necessary to insist, they are there to be pointed to as the ultimate justifications for judgements of "inner sense". The fundamental thrust of Wittgenstein's attack is not to eliminate the idea of a private language, which by itself would merely push the line of thought that he opposes to this point. Wittgenstein's attack undermines even this position, which has already given up the idea of a private language, by applying the general moral: a bare presence cannot be a ground for anything.

However, if one becomes convinced that the ultimate grounds for judgements of experience must be bits of the Given, one will naturally take oneself to be committed to the possibility of concepts that sit as closely as possible to those ultimate grounds, in the sense that their content is wholly determined by the fact that judgements involving them are warranted by the right sort of bare presence. These concepts will be the concepts that are supposed to be expressible by the words of a private language. Only one person could be the subject to whom a particular bit of the Given is given. So any concept that was constituted by a justificatory relation to a bare presence would have to be, to that extent, a private concept. It would be natural to suppose that these private concepts are acquired by abstraction from a manifold Given, as in the story about concept-formation that I mentioned ear-

---

17. I have said a little more about this reading of Wittgenstein in "One Strand in the Private Language Argument", *Grazer Philosophische Studien* 33/34 (1989), 285–303. See also my "Intentionality and Interiority in Wittgenstein", in Klaus Puhl, ed., *Meaning Scepticism* (De Gruyter, Berlin, 1991), pp. 148–69.

lier. The work of abstraction is the private ostensive definition that figures in Wittgenstein's polemic.

So situating the Private Language Argument in the context of a general rejection of the Given does not dispense us from considering the argument against private language, or at any rate against private concepts, as such. Still, I think we put those of Wittgenstein's remarks that are specifically about private language in the right light if we see them as efforts to insist on the consequences for language of the general point: that a bare presence cannot supply a justificatory input into a conceptual repertoire from outside it, the sort of thing the connection between concepts and spontaneity made us hanker for. If a concept is constituted by a justificatory linkage to a bare presence, which is what its being a private concept would amount to, then spontaneity does not extend as far as it. In fact it is really the point of the conception to exempt exercises of these supposed concepts from the responsibility that comes with spontaneity. What we have here is a version of a structure I mentioned earlier (§5), in connection with a misconception of the fact that experience is passive. Calling something to which spontaneity does not extend "a concept", and calling the linkage "rational", is fraudulent labelling: in effect, labelling a mere exculpation a justification, in the vain hope that that could make it be one.

I mentioned Geach's Wittgensteinian attack on the abstractionist account of concept-formation (§2). I have been suggesting that the Private Language Argument applies the general rejection of the Given. But it would be misleading to represent the Private Language Argument as a particular application of a more general thought. As I said, any concept that was constituted by a justificatory relation to a bare presence would have to be a private concept. Making the abstraction that would be necessary to form such a concept would be giving oneself a private ostensive definition. In effect the idea that concepts can be formed by abstraction from the Given just is the idea of private ostensive definition. So the Private Language Argument just is the rejection of the Given, in so far as it bears on the possibilities for language; it is not an application of a general rejection of the Given to a particular area. What is an application of the general point is the rejection of bare presences as what sensations and so forth are.

It makes no difference if the right occasions for performing a private ostensive definition are supposed to be signalled by other people. That is a way in which one might hope to integrate a private element, rational responsiveness to a bare presence, into a composite concept that has a public aspect, a rational linkage into a shareable conceptual repertoire, as well. Wittgenstein expresses the idea in this passage: "Or is it like this: the word 'red' means something known to everyone; and in addition, for each person, it means something known only to him? (Or perhaps rather: it *refers* to something known only to him.)"[18] If the idea of rational responsiveness to a bare presence is a confusion, this linkage into a shareable repertoire cannot save these supposedly composite concepts from being vitiated by their private ingredients. The confusion between justification and exculpation just shows up at the joint between the supposed ingredients of the composite concept.

The Myth of the Given is especially insidious in the case of "inner sense". In the case of "outer sense", the idea is that the Given mediates between the experiencing subject and an independent outer reality, of which the subject is aware through this mediation. If we reject the Given, we are not thereby abolishing the outer reality, but merely obliging ourselves not to suppose that awareness of it is mediated in that way. But the objects of "inner sense" are internal accusatives to the awareness that "inner experiences" constitute; they have no existence independently of that awareness.[19] That means that if we let bare presences into the picture, they figure as the only objects of awareness in play; they cannot figure as mediating an awareness of something else beyond them, at any rate if the mediated awareness is itself to be conceived in terms of "inner sense" at work.[20] And the result is that when we reject the Given here, we can seem to be rejecting "inner" awareness altogether. There seems to be nothing else for "inner experience" to be experience of.

How can we reject the Given without thus obliterating "inner" awareness? To give the impressions of "inner sense" the right role in justifying judgements, we need to conceive them, like the impressions of "outer sense", as themselves already possessing conceptual content; to supply the necessary limit to the freedom of spontaneity, we need

18. *Philosophical Investigations*, trans. by G. E. M. Anscombe (Basil Blackwell, Oxford, 1951), §273.

19. See P. F. Strawson, *The Bounds of Sense* (Methuen, London, 1966), pp. 100–1.

20. Not that "inner experience" cannot mediate awareness. For instance, a certain sensation might yield a mediated awareness of a certain bodily condition. But here the object of the mediated awareness is not "inner" in the Kantian sense. See the text below.

to insist that they are indeed impressions, products of receptivity. So the impressions of "inner sense" must be, like the impressions of "outer sense", passive occurrences in which conceptual capacities are drawn into operation. But if we are to respect the point about internal accusatives, we cannot conceive these passive operations of conceptual capacities exactly on the model of the impressions of "outer sense". We cannot suppose that these operations of conceptual capacities constitute awareness of circumstances that obtain in any case, and that impress themselves on a subject as they do because of some suitable relation to her sensibility. No doubt there are circumstances that obtain in any case, and figure in the aetiology of impressions of "inner sense": for instance, bodily damage in the case of feelings of pain. But if we are to respect the point about internal accusatives, we cannot suppose that such circumstances are objects of an awareness that is constituted by the impressions of "inner sense". (Although one can no doubt learn to find out about such circumstances from the impressions of "inner sense".) If we can make out that judgements of "inner sense" are about anything, it has to be that they are about the impressions of "inner sense" themselves, not about something independent of which the impressions constitute awareness.

This is a very difficult area. Wittgenstein himself sometimes seems to betray an understandable wish to duck the difficulties. What I have in mind here is the fact that he sometimes seems to toy with denying that self-ascriptions of sensation are assertions, articulations of judgements about states of affairs, at all.[21]

I have claimed that we should connect "inner experience" with conceptual capacities, so as to think about "inner sense" in parallel with "outer sense" to the fullest extent that is possible. One obvious source of difficulty about this is that creatures with no faculty of spontaneity can surely, for instance, feel pain. (Remember that "spontaneity" alludes to conceptual capacities. I am not trying to obliterate the self-moving character of merely animal life.) I shall come back to this in later lectures. My aim here has been not to wrap the matter up, but

21. For instance, p. 68 of *The Blue Book* (in *The Blue and Brown Books* [Basil Blackwell, Oxford, 1958]): "The difference between the propositions 'I have pain' and 'he has pain' is not that of 'L. W. has pain' and 'Smith has pain'. Rather it corresponds to the difference between moaning and saying that someone moans." I would not dispute what is said in the first of these sentences. But sentences like the second have suggested, at least to some commentators, a doctrine that assimilates "avowals" to other modes of expression, so as to distance them from assertions, and that strikes me as a cop-out.

only to introduce the suggestion that we should read the Private Language Argument as an attack on the Given.

8.   In this lecture, I have claimed that we are prone to fall into an intolerable oscillation: in one phase we are drawn to a coherentism that cannot make sense of the bearing of thought on objective reality, and in the other phase we recoil into an appeal to the Given, which turns out to be useless. I have urged that in order to escape the oscillation, we need a conception of experiences as states or occurrences that are passive but reflect conceptual capacities, capacities that belong to spontaneity, in operation. In the next lecture I shall start to consider some difficulties about this conception.

The Unboundedness
of the Conceptual

1. In my first lecture I talked about a tendency to oscillate between a pair of unsatisfying positions: on the one side a coherentism that threatens to disconnect thought from reality, and on the other side a vain appeal to the Given, in the sense of bare presences that are supposed to constitute the ultimate grounds of empirical judgements. I suggested that in order to escape the oscillation, we need to recognize that experiences themselves are states or occurrences that inextricably combine receptivity and spontaneity. We must not suppose that spontaneity first figures only in judgements in which we put a construction on experiences, with experiences conceived as deliverances of receptivity to whose constitution spontaneity makes no contribution. Experiences are indeed receptivity in operation; so they can satisfy the need for an external control on our freedom in empirical thinking. But conceptual capacities, capacities that belong to spontaneity, are already at work in experiences themselves, not just in judgements based on them; so experiences can intelligibly stand in rational relations to our exercises of the freedom that is implicit in the idea of spontaneity.

In this second lecture I am going to start considering problems about this conception.

It can be hard to see that there is room for such a conception. In my first lecture (§6), I introduced Davidson's coherentism to illustrate that; I suggested that Davidson's position is representative of a style of thinking within which what I am urging does not even come into view as an option. Later (starting in Lecture IV), I shall try to say something about why the conception is hard to achieve, so that we are tempted to suppose we are stuck with a choice between the original pair of positions. My aim will be to suggest that our difficulties in this area result from an intelligibly powerful influence over the cast of our thoughts, from which, however, we can liberate ourselves.

But that is not on my agenda for this lecture. I do not want to suggest that the objection I am going to consider now is itself revelatory of the deep roots of our difficulties. At best it may not be unconnected. But I do hope that discussing it will put the conception I am recommending in a clearer light.

2.   What I want to consider in this lecture is an objection on the score of idealism.

We seem to need rational constraints on thinking and judging, from a reality external to them, if we are to make sense of them as bearing on a reality outside thought at all. Davidson denies that there is any such need, and proposes that we make do with nothing but causal constraints. My suggestion has been that he can contrive to be comfortable with that only because he thinks there is no alternative, since, as he clearly realizes, the Myth of the Given is hopeless. And here, I claim, he is wrong. There is an alternative, and this fact removes the only apparent reason to deny the need for rational constraints from outside: the only apparent reason to deny that thoughts without a rational connection with intuitions would be empty.

When we try to acknowledge the need for external rational constraint, we can find ourselves supposing there must be relations of ultimate grounding that reach outside the conceptual realm altogether. That idea is the Myth of the Given, and of course the conception I have described makes no concession to it. The Myth of the Given is precisely one of the two opposing pitfalls from which the conception is intended to liberate us.

In the conception I am recommending, the need for external constraint is met by the fact that experiences are receptivity in operation. But that does not disqualify experiences from playing a role in justification, as the counterpart thought in the Myth of the Given does, because the claim is that experiences themselves are already equipped with conceptual content. This joint involvement of receptivity and spontaneity allows us to say that in experience one can take in how things are. How things are is independent of one's thinking (except, of course, in the special case in which how things are is that one thinks such-and-such). By being taken in in experience, how things anyway are becomes available to exert the required rational control, originating outside one's thinking, on one's exercises of spontaneity.

Certainly one can be misled, at least in the case of "outer experience". I have postponed any discussion of that until my final lecture. But I insist in advance that when we acknowledge the possibility of being misled, we do not deprive ourselves of "taking in how things are" as a description of what happens when one is not misled. In a particular experience in which one is not misled, what one takes in is *that things are thus and so. That things are thus and so* is the content of the experience, and it can also be the content of a judgement: it becomes the content of a judgement if the subject decides to take the experience at face value. So it is conceptual content. But *that things are thus and so* is also, if one is not misled, an aspect of the layout of the world: it is how things are. Thus the idea of conceptually structured operations of receptivity puts us in a position to speak of experience as openness to the layout of reality. Experience enables the layout of reality itself to exert a rational influence on what a subject thinks.

This image of openness to reality is at our disposal because of how we place the reality that makes its impression on a subject in experience. Although reality is independent of our thinking, it is not to be pictured as outside an outer boundary that encloses the conceptual sphere. *That things are thus and so* is the conceptual content of an experience, but if the subject of the experience is not misled, that very same thing, *that things are thus and so,* is also a perceptible fact, an aspect of the perceptible world.

Now it can seem that this refusal to locate perceptible reality outside the conceptual sphere must be a sort of idealism, in the sense in which to call a position "idealism" is to protest that it does not genuinely acknowledge how reality is independent of our thinking. If that were right, my affirmation of reality's independence would be disingenuous, mere lip-service. But though this objection is easy to understand, and even to sympathize with, it is wrong. It reflects the conviction that we have to choose between a coherentist denial that thinking and judging are subject to rational constraint from outside, on the one hand, and an appeal to the Given as what imposes the constraint, on the other. If someone takes it that those are the only options, and if she has a firmer grip on the defects of unconstrained coherentism than she has on the uselessness of the Given, then anything short of believing in the Given will strike her as slighting the independence of reality. But the point of the third option, the option I am urging, is precisely that it enables us to acknowledge that independent reality exerts a rational control over our thinking, but without falling into the confusion between justification and exculpation that characterizes the appeal to the Given.

3. I find it helpful in this connection to reflect on a remark of Wittgenstein's: "When we say, and *mean,* that such-and-such is the case, we—and our meaning—do not stop anywhere short of the fact; but we mean: *this—is—so.*"[1] Wittgenstein calls this a paradox. That is because, especially in conjunction with the fact that "thought can be of what is not the case",[2] it can prompt a reaction in which our minds boggle over what seems a miraculous power of thinking in the most general sense, in this case meaning what one says, to "catch reality in its net".[3] But Wittgenstein also says, rightly, that the remark "has the form of a truism".

We can formulate the point in a style Wittgenstein would have been uncomfortable with: there is no ontological gap between the sort of thing one can mean, or generally the sort of thing one can think, and the sort of thing that can be the case. When one thinks truly, what one thinks *is* what is the case. So since the world is everything that is the case (as he himself once wrote),[4] there is no gap between thought, as such, and the world. Of course thought can be distanced from the world by being false, but there is no distance from the world implicit in the very idea of thought.

But to say there is no gap between thought, as such, and the world is just to dress up a truism in high-flown language. All the point comes to is that one can think, for instance, *that spring has begun,* and that very same thing, *that spring has begun,* can be the case. That is truistic, and it cannot embody something metaphysically contentious, like slighting the independence of reality. When we put the point in the high-flown terms, by saying the world is made up of the sort of thing

1. *Philosophical Investigations,* §95.
2. §95 continues: "But this paradox (which has the form of a truism) can also be expressed in this way: *Thought* can be of what is *not* the case."
3. See *Philosophical Investigations,* §429: "How was it possible for thought to deal with the very object *itself?* We feel as if by means of it we had caught reality in our net."
4. *Tractatus Logico-Philosophicus,* trans. D. F. Pears and B. F. McGuinness (Routledge and Kegan Paul, London, 1961), §1.

one can think, a phobia of idealism can make people suspect we are renouncing the independence of reality—as if we were representing the world as a shadow of our thinking, or even as made of some mental stuff. But we might just as well take the fact that the sort of thing one can think is the same as the sort of thing that can be the case the other way round, as an invitation to understand the notion of the sort of thing one can think in terms of a supposedly prior understanding of the sort of thing that can be the case.[5] And in fact there is no reason to look for a priority in either direction.

If we say that there must be a rational constraint on thought from outside it, so as to ensure a proper acknowledgement of the independence of reality, we put ourselves at the mercy of a familiar kind of ambiguity. "Thought" can mean the *act* of thinking; but it can also mean the *content* of a piece of thinking: what someone thinks. Now if we are to give due acknowledgement to the independence of reality, what we need is a constraint from outside *thinking* and *judging*, our exercises of spontaneity. The constraint does not need to be from outside *thinkable contents*. It would indeed slight the independence of reality if we equated facts in general with exercises of conceptual capacities—acts of thinking—or represented facts as reflections of such things; or if we equated perceptible facts in particular with states or occurrences in which conceptual capacities are drawn into operation in sensibility—experiences—or represented them as reflections of such things. But it is not idealistic, as that would be, to say that perceptible facts are essentially capable of impressing themselves on perceivers in states or occurrences of the latter sort; and that facts in general are essentially capable of being embraced in thought in exercises of spontaneity, occurrences of the former sort.

The fact that experience is passive, a matter of receptivity in operation, should assure us that we have all the external constraint we can reasonably want. The constraint comes from outside *thinking*, but not from outside what is *thinkable*. When we trace justifications back, the last thing we come to is still a thinkable content; not something more

---

5. The *Tractatus* is often read on these lines; for a recent version, see David Pears, *The False Prison*, vol. 1 (Clarendon Press, Oxford, 1987). Opponents of the kind of reading Pears gives sometimes tend to find in the *Tractatus* a thesis of priority in the opposite direction, or at least not to distinguish their interpretations clearly from this kind of thing. (That might merit a protest of idealism.) But I doubt whether either claim of priority is to be found in the *Tractatus*.

ultimate than that, a bare pointing to a bit of the Given. But these final thinkable contents are put into place in operations of receptivity, and that means that when we appeal to them we register the required constraint on thinking from a reality external to it. The thinkable contents that are ultimate in the order of justification are contents of experiences, and in enjoying an experience one is open to manifest facts, facts that obtain anyway and impress themselves on one's sensibility. (At any rate one seems to be open to facts, and when one is not misled, one is.) To paraphrase Wittgenstein, when we see that such-and-such is the case, we, and our seeing, do not stop anywhere short of the fact. What we see is: that such-and-such is the case.

4.   Wittgenstein's aphorism can be reworked like that for any conceptual shaping of subjectivity. It is not this general possibility by itself that underwrites the image of openness. The image of openness is appropriate for experience in particular; and to bring the image into play, we need to appeal to the distinctive passivity of experience. But the general context matters for the availability of the image.

To bring out how, I want to recall something I said in my first lecture (§5), to counter a misunderstanding of the idea that conceptual capacities are passively operative in experience. The misunderstanding is to suppose that when we appeal to passivity, we insulate this invocation of the conceptual from what makes it plausible to attribute conceptual capacities in general to a faculty of spontaneity. Against this, I urged that we could not recognize capacities operative in experience as conceptual at all were it not for the way they are integrated into a rationally organized network of capacities for active adjustment of one's thinking to the deliverances of experience. That is what a repertoire of empirical concepts is. The integration serves to place even the most immediate judgements of experience as possible elements in a world-view.

We can see this even if we restrict ourselves to concepts of secondary qualities, which cannot be understood in abstraction from the subjective character of experience. What it is for something to be red, say, is not intelligible unless packaged with an understanding of what it is for something to look red. The idea of being red does not go beyond the idea of being the way red things look in the right circumstances. That has an implication that I can put like this: although judging that something is red is active, an exercise of spontaneity, it is as little removed from the passivity of experience as any judging could be. Concepts of colour are only minimally integrated into the active business of accommodating one's thinking to the continuing deliverances of experience, and hence only minimally integrated into possible views of the world. Still, they are so integrated, even if only minimally. No subject could be recognized as having experiences of colour except against a background understanding that makes it possible for judgements endorsing such experiences to fit into her view of the world. She must be equipped with such things as the concept of visible surfaces of objects, and the concept of suitable conditions for telling what something's colour is by looking at it.

Those remarks, which restate something I said in my first lecture, are about experiences and judgements that locate colours in the apparent environment. There is another kind of colour experience that we also need to make room for: the label "colour experience" can fit mere sensations, operations of "inner sense".[6] For instance, a blow to the head can cause one to "see red" without the experience's referring the "seen" colour to the apparent environment. Now I have been urging that experiences in general are states or occurrences in which conceptual capacities are passively drawn into operation. That had better hold for these "inner experiences" of colour as much as for any other experiences. And I believe we should understand the role of colour concepts in these "inner experiences" derivatively from their role in "outer experience". The concept of red gets a grip, in characterizing an "inner experience" of "seeing red", because the experience is in the relevant respect subjectively like the experience of seeing that something—some "outer" thing—is red, or at least seeming to.

It can be tempting to take things the other way round: to suppose that the "inner" role of colour concepts is autonomously intelligible, and to try to explain their "outer" role in terms of the idea that for an "outer" object to fall under a colour concept is for it to be such as to cause the appropriate visual "inner experience" in suitable viewing conditions. We can be encouraged into this by the thought that if being red and looking red are intelligible only in terms of each other, that makes it a mystery how anyone can break into this circle: a mystery we might hope to dissipate by explaining both being red and looking red in terms of the "inner" experience of "seeing red".

6. See Lecture I, §7.

But we should resist this temptation. If the "inner" role of colour concepts were a self-standing starting point, "outer experience" of colour would become impossible to comprehend. By what alchemy could an "inner experience" be transmuted into an "outer experience"? If a colour first figures, in the development of our understanding, as a feature of "inner experience", not an apparent property of objects, how could our understanding contrive to project *that* out into the world? Starting from there, we might manage to externalize at best a propensity to induce the relevant feature of "inner experience" in us. But it is quite doubtful whether the idea of possessing such a propensity adds up to the idea of being appropriately coloured: that requires precisely that our experience and thought locate something phenomenal in the external world, whereas the "propensity" conception keeps what is phenomenal in the mind.[7] And anyway the circle—the mutual dependence of the concepts of being red and looking red—is quite innocent. It is no threat, for instance, to a sane view of how colour concepts are acquired; we simply have to suppose they come only as elements in a bundle of concepts that must be acquired together.[8] So I propose to focus on the role of colour concepts, and more generally concepts of secondary qualities, in "outer experience", taking it that that is what is fundamental.

In "outer experience", a subject is passively saddled with conceptual contents, drawing into operation capacities seamlessly integrated into a conceptual repertoire that she employs in the continuing activity of adjusting her world-view, so as to enable it to pass a scrutiny of its rational credentials. It is this integration that makes it possible for us to conceive experience as awareness, or at least seeming awareness, of a reality independent of experience. We can appreciate this point by continuing to consider the way colours figure in the content of experience. Even here, where the linkages into the whole system are minimal, the relevant conceptual capacities are integrated into spontaneity at large, in a way that enables the subject to understand experiences in which those conceptual capacities are drawn into operation as

7. It is one thing to gloss being red in terms of being such as to look red, and quite another to gloss it in terms of being such as to induce a certain "inner experience" in us. Note that "red" in "looking red" expresses a concept of "outer experience" no less than does "red" in "being red", in fact the very same concept. (Sellars insists on this point in "Empiricism and the Philosophy of Mind".)

8. See Sellars, "Empiricism and the Philosophy of Mind", §§18–20.

glimpses, or at least seeming glimpses, of the world: takings in, at least seemingly, of aspects of a reality that goes beyond what is manifest in the experiences themselves. If a colour concept is drawn into operation in an experience (with the concept playing its "outer" role), the rational connections of the concept enter into shaping the content of the appearance, so that what appears to be the case is understood as fraught with implications for the subject's cognitive situation in the world: for instance, that she is confronted by an object with a facing surface illuminated in such-and-such ways.

The notion of a glimpse is distinctively visual, but we can generalize it to embrace non-visual experiences. By virtue of the way in which the conceptual capacities that are drawn into operation in an experience are rationally linked into the whole network, the subject of the experience understands what the experience takes in (or at least seems to take in) as part of a wider reality, a reality that is all embraceable in thought but not all available to this experience. The object of experience is understood as integrated into a wider reality, in a way that mirrors how the relevant concepts are integrated into the repertoire of spontaneity at large. Even in the case of colour experience, this integration allows us to understand an experience as awareness of something independent of the experience itself: something that is held in place by its linkage into the wider reality, so that we can make sense of the thought that it would be so even if it were not being experienced to be so.

We have all this, I have been insisting, even if we restrict ourselves to the way concepts of secondary qualities figure in the content of experience. And the point would not be secured for this restricted case by saying that we have to understand any particular secondary-quality experience against a background of other secondary-quality experiences, possible or actual. We cannot make a world, of which such experiences might intelligibly be glimpses, entirely out of the distinctive topics of judgements that are only minimally removed from the passivity of experience, as judgements attributing secondary qualities are.[9] We have to understand the experienceable world as a subject matter for active thinking, rationally constrained by what experience

9. This is a way of putting something Gareth Evans urges in "Things without the Mind—a Commentary upon Chapter Two of Strawson's *Individuals*", in Zak van Straaten, ed., *Philosophical Subjects: Essays Presented to P. F. Strawson* (Clarendon Press, Oxford, 1980), pp. 76–116.

reveals. The capacities that are passively drawn into operation in experience can be recognized as conceptual capacities only because we can get the idea of spontaneity to fit. And we do not genuinely get the idea of spontaneity to fit if we try to picture a practice of thinking that distances itself from actual cases of the passivity of experience only so far as to contemplate more of the same, including merely possible cases. That way, we entitle ourselves at most to the idea of an orderly sequence of "inner experiences". In fact I do not believe we entitle ourselves even to that, because we cannot make sense even of "inner experience" in the absence of a world; but it will not be clear why I say that until much later (Lecture V), and perhaps not even then. The point for now is just this: if we try to picture a mode of, say, colour experience with only this slight an integration into a practice of active thinking and judgement, it is mysterious how what we are picturing could amount to "outer experience" of colour—how the colour experienced could be experienced as a feature of an "outer" reality.

The point about how experience is rationally linked into the activity of adjusting a world-view is even clearer when we stop restricting ourselves to concepts of secondary qualities. Of course other concepts figure in experience too. It would be quite wrong to suppose that experience takes in only features of reality whose concepts are inextricably tied to concepts of modes of appearance, in the way that is exemplified by the tie between what it is to be red and what it is to look red. (As if other aspects of the world could come to mind not in experience, but only in theoretical thinking.) Experiences themselves take in more of the thinkable world than qualities that are phenomenal in that sense.

Generalized, the remark of Wittgenstein that I started from says that thinking does not stop short of facts. The world is embraceable in thought. What I have been urging is that that constitutes a background without which the special way in which experience takes hold of the world would not be intelligible. And the dependence is not only in that direction. It is not that we could first make sense of the fact that the world is thinkable, in abstraction from experience, and proceed from there to make sense of experience. What is in question could not be the thinkable world, or, to put it another way, our picture of the understanding's equipment could not be what it needs to be, a picture of a system of concepts and conceptions with substantial empirical content, if it were not already part of the picture that the system is the medium within which one engages in active thought that is rationally responsive to the deliverances of experience. Thoughts without intuitions would indeed be empty. To understand empirical content in general, we need to see it in its dynamic place in a self-critical activity, the activity by which we aim to comprehend the world as it impinges on our senses.

5. This talk of impingements on our senses is not an invitation to suppose that the whole dynamic system, the medium within which we think, is held in place by extra-conceptual links to something outside it. That is just to stress again that we must not picture an outer boundary around the sphere of the conceptual, with a reality outside the boundary impinging inward on the system. Any impingements across such an outer boundary could only be causal, and not rational; that is Davidson's perfectly correct point, and he urges that we should settle for holding that in experience the world exerts a merely causal influence on our thinking. But I am trying to describe a way of maintaining that in experience the world exerts a rational influence on our thinking. And that requires us to delete the outer boundary from the picture. The impressions on our senses that keep the dynamic system in motion are already equipped with conceptual content. The facts that are made manifest to us in those impressions, or at least seem to be, are not beyond an outer boundary that encloses the conceptual sphere, and the impingements of the world on our sensibility are not inward crossings of such a boundary. My point is to insist that we can effect this deletion of the outer boundary without falling into idealism, without slighting the independence of reality.

We find ourselves always already engaging with the world in conceptual activity within such a dynamic system. Any understanding of this condition that it makes sense to hope for must be from within the system. It cannot be a matter of picturing the system's adjustments to the world from sideways on: that is, with the system circumscribed within a boundary, and the world outside it. That is exactly the shape our picture must not take.

Of course we can initially find another thinker opaque. It may take work to make the conceptual contents of someone else's engagements with the world available to us. And in the meantime the world she engages with is surely already within our view. I have said nothing that threatens that obvious fact. What I do mean to rule out is this idea: that, when we work at making someone else intelligible, we exploit relations we can already discern between the world and something already in view as a system of concepts within which the other person thinks; so that as we come to fathom the content of the initially opaque conceptual capacities that are operative within the system, we are filling in detail in a sideways-on picture—here the conceptual system, there the world—that has been available all along, though at first only in outline. It must be an illusion to suppose that this fits the work of interpretation we need in order to come to understand some people, or that a version of it fits the way we acquire a capacity to understand other speakers of our own language in ordinary upbringing. This picture places the world outside a boundary around the system we have supposedly come to understand. That means it cannot depict anything genuinely recognizable as an understanding of a set of concepts with empirical substance. These supposed concepts could be bound up with impacts from the world only causally, not rationally (Davidson's point again); and I have been urging that that leaves their status as concepts with empirical substance, potential determinants of the content of judgements that bear on the empirical world, a mystery. (I think these considerations tell against some appeals to Davidson's notion of radical interpretation, the procedure by which one would work one's way into comprehension of a foreign language without external resources such as dictionaries and the like.)[10]

The illusion is insidious; so much so that it can entice us into aspiring to a sideways-on understanding of our own thinking, which we take to be the condition of someone else who understands us. *Some* sideways-on picture must be innocuous in the case of a thinker who is opaque to us, and then it can seem obvious that overcoming opaqueness is just filling in blanks in that sideways-on picture, leaving its orientation unchanged. But that must be wrong. The mistake is not to give proper weight to this fact: in the innocuous sideways-on picture, the person we do not yet understand figures as a thinker only in the most abstract and indeterminate way. When the specific character of her thinking starts to come into view for us, we are not filling in blanks in a pre-existing sideways-on picture of how her thought bears on the world, but coming to share with her a standpoint *within* a sys-

---

10. I have in mind Rorty's exploitation of Davidson, in "Pragmatism, Davidson, and Truth".

tem of concepts, a standpoint from which we can join her in directing a shared attention at the world, without needing to break out through a boundary that encloses the system of concepts.[11]

6. I have been talking about how the conceptual capacities that are drawn into operation in experience are integrated into spontaneity at large. I have suggested that it is this integration that makes it possible for a subject to understand an "outer" experience as awareness of something objective, something independent of the experience itself. The object of an experience, the state of affairs experienced as obtaining, is understood as part of a whole thinkable world. Since the whole is independent of this particular experience, we can use the linkage into the mostly unexperienced whole to hold the object of this particular experience in place, while we ask how things would have been if the experience had not occurred. This depends on a specific way in which concepts are integrated into spontaneity at large, a way that, as I have claimed, is minimally exemplified by colour concepts.

Now in my first lecture (§7) I said that the object of an "inner experience" does not have this independence from the experience itself. An object of "inner experience", I said, has no existence independently of the awareness that the experience constitutes.

This can put a strain on our understanding of "inner experience". It is easy to think we cannot preserve the claim that an "inner experience" has no object independent of the experience, unless we construe the objects of "inner experience" as bits of the Given, somehow constitutively related to the occurrences of their reception—that is, as "private objects". If we are persuaded by Wittgenstein's polemic against that supposed conception, we come under pressure either to deny that "inner experience" is a matter of awareness at all, which would dispense us from worrying about a relation between events in the stream of consciousness and putative objects of such events, but which looks like the embarrassing philosophical strategy of "feigning anaesthesia";[12] or else, keeping awareness in play, to give up the claim

---

11. I mean this to be reminiscent of the concept of a "fusion of horizons" exploited by Hans-Georg Gadamer in *Truth and Method* (Crossroad, New York, 1992; rev. trans. by Joel Weinsheimer and Donald Marshall), pp. 306–7.

12. I took this phrase from A. J. Ayer, p. 101 of "The Concept of a Person", in *The Concept of a Person and Other Essays* (Macmillan, London, 1964), pp. 82–128. Ayer credits the idea to C. K. Ogden and I. A. Richards.

that an object of "inner experience" is not independent of the experience. On this last view, "inner experience" is after all awareness of circumstances that obtain anyway, independently of this awareness of them. Where the relevant "inner experience" is a sensation, suitably related bodily circumstances will seem to fit the bill. This assimilates "inner experience", in so far as it constitutes awareness of something, to "outer experience"; it is just that the object of the experience is not very far out. All these positions are so unsatisfactory that one can sympathize with Wittgenstein in the inclination that at least some commentators find him succumbing to, at least sometimes: the inclination to deny that self-ascriptions of sensation and so forth give expression to judgements at all.

I think it is helpful here to exploit the fact that the concepts of "outer experience" are integrated into spontaneity at large in a specific way. We can find a different specific manner of integration for the concepts of "inner experience". Up to a point, impressions of "inner experience" are like impressions of "outer experience". They are all passive occurrences in which conceptual capacities are drawn into operation. And it is not that the conceptual capacities that are drawn into operation in "inner experience" are not integrated into spontaneity in general, or, what comes to the same thing, that the object of an "inner experience" is not understood in a way that places it as a possible element in a view of the world. That would merely prevent us from recognizing conceptual capacities here at all. But the mode of integration in this case is not such as to confer independence on the objects of awareness.

We could not credit a subject with a capacity to use, say, the concept of pain in judgements of "inner experience" if she did not understand how the circumstance that those judgements concern fits into the world at large. What that requires is that the subject must understand her being in pain as a particular case of a general type of state of affairs, *someone's* being in pain. So she must understand that the conceptual capacity drawn on in the relevant "inner experiences" is not restricted to its role in "inner experience" and judgements of "inner experience": not restricted, that is, to its first-person present-tense role.[13] This yields what we can think of as a limiting case of the struc-

13. See chap. 3 of P. F. Strawson, *Individuals: An Essay in Descriptive Metaphysics* (Methuen, London, 1959), and Gareth Evans's exploitation of Strawson's thought in chap. 7 of *The Varieties of Reference* (Clarendon Press, Oxford, 1982).

ture of awareness and object. We can understand an impression of "inner sense" in which the concept of, say, pain is drawn into play as an awareness of the circumstance that the subject is in pain. The structure of awareness and object is appropriately in place just because the subject does not conceive what it is for her to be in pain—the circumstance that is the object of her awareness—exclusively in terms of the "inner" or first-person angle on that circumstance that constitutes her awareness of it. She understands that the very same circumstance is thinkable—by someone else, or by herself at different times—otherwise than in a thought expressive of "inner experience". This gives the idea of the circumstance an independence from her awareness of it. But though her conception of the circumstance does not come at it exclusively through the awareness that is the "inner" operation of sensibility, the circumstance is nothing other than the operation of sensibility itself.

It is worth comparing objects of "inner experience", in their limiting-case substantiality, with secondary qualities of "outer experience". In one way objects of "inner experience" are less firmly rooted in objective reality than secondary qualities, but in another way they are more independent of the distinctive experience in terms of which they are identified, and so they are more substantial. On the one hand, secondary qualities are there independently of any particular experience in which their presence is revealed, whereas an object of "inner experience" is not there independently of the experience. But on the other hand, a subject understands the sensuous specificity of a secondary quality exclusively through what it is like to experience it, whereas a subject must understand that the potential objects of her "inner experience" are essentially also thinkable otherwise than from the standpoint of her experiencing them.[14]

---

14. The second half of this contrast is somewhat fragile. We might say that the sensuous specificity of an object of "inner experience" is equally understood exclusively through what it is like to experience it. It cannot be someone else's *pain* that I embrace in thought unless what I have in mind is what her experience is like for her. When I say that the circumstance of someone's being in pain is thinkable otherwise than through her "inner experience" of it, I do not mean to imply that the circumstance is thinkable in abstraction from her "inner experience" of it, for instance in behaviouristic terms. But in the case of secondary qualities there is no parallel to the play between first-person and third-person standpoints. This footnote responds to a comment by Danielle Macbeth.

7. I have been urging that, in judgements of experience, conceptual capacities are not exercised on non-conceptual deliverances of sensibility. Conceptual capacities are already operative in the deliverances of sensibility themselves. In my first lecture (§5), I suggested that it is best to disallow the question what conceptual capacities are exercised on in experience. If we talk of an exercise of conceptual capacities in this context, we put at risk our ability to insist that experience is passive; and that is the essential thing if we are to extinguish the hankering after the Given. But in disallowing the question what those conceptual capacities are exercised on, I do not disallow the question what the conceptual contents that are passively received in experience bear on, or are about. And the obvious answer, if the question is asked in that general form, is: they are about the world, as it appears or makes itself manifest to the experiencing subject, or at least seems to do so. That ought not to activate a phobia of idealism.

When we reject the Myth of the Given, we reject the idea that tracing back the ground for a judgement can terminate in pointing to a bare presence. Now this can generate some discomfort. It can seem that we are depriving ourselves of a justificatory role that it must be possible to attribute to pointing, if we are to be able to assure ourselves that our conception of thinking sufficiently acknowledges the independence of reality. It must be possible for justifications of judgements to include pointing out at features of the world, from what would otherwise risk looking like a closed circle within which our exercises of spontaneity run without friction.

But now that we are on guard against the ambiguity in phrases like "outside the sphere of thought" (§3), it is easy to deal with this. There are two different conceptions of a justificatory role for pointing in play. On the conception I am recommending, justifications can perfectly well include pointing out from the sphere of thinking, at features of the world. We fall into the Myth of the Given only if we suppose that this pointing would have to break out through a boundary that encloses the sphere of thinkable content.

8. People sometimes object to positions like the one I have been urging on the ground that they embody an arrogant anthropocentrism, a baseless confidence that the world is completely within the reach of

our powers of thinking. This looks at least akin to an accusation of idealism. Why should we be so sure of our capacity to comprehend the world if not because we conceive the world as a shadow or reflection of our thinking?[15]

But an accusation of arrogance would not stick against the position I am recommending. In my first lecture (§5) I said that the faculty of spontaneity carries with it a standing obligation to reflect on the credentials of the putatively rational linkages that, at any time, one takes to govern the active business of adjusting one's world-view in response to experience. Ensuring that our empirical concepts and conceptions pass muster is ongoing and arduous work for the understanding. It requires patience and something like humility. There is no guarantee that the world is completely within the reach of a system of concepts and conceptions as it stands at some particular moment in its historical development. Exactly not; that is why the obligation to reflect is perpetual.

There is a tendency to stop short of accepting that the obligation is perpetual. One imagines the obligation's ceasing to apply if one contemplates a state of affairs that would deserve to be called "the end of inquiry".[16] That would be a state of affairs in which inquiry, including reflective inquiry into the credentials of what at present passes for inquiry itself, is no longer necessary. It might well be argued that, even as a mere ideal of reason, this conception is suspect: what can it be if not a vestigial reflection of the unwarranted confidence in our powers that the objection complains of? But the idea of an end to inquiry is no part of the position I am recommending.

9.   In these first two lectures, I have introduced the tendency to oscillate between embracing the Myth of the Given and denying that experience has a rational bearing on thought. I have claimed that to escape this alternation, we must hold that, in experience, spontaneity is inex-

15. For this form of the accusation of idealism, see chap. 6 of Thomas Nagel, *The View from Nowhere* (Oxford University Press, New York, 1986).

16. The idea is implicit in such well-known remarks of C. S. Peirce as this: "The opinion which is fated to be ultimately agreed to by all who investigate is what we mean by the truth, and the object represented in this opinion is the real." "How to Make Our Ideas Clear", in *Writings of Charles S. Peirce*, vol. 3 (Indiana University Press, Bloomington, 1986), pp. 257–76, at p. 273; originally in *Popular Science Monthly* 12 (January 1878), 286–302.

tricably implicated in deliverances of receptivity. We must not suppose that receptivity makes an even notionally separable contribution to its co-operation with spontaneity. In this lecture I have been discussing an accusation of idealism, in the sense of a failure to acknowledge that reality is independent of thinking. This is a good context in which to raise the question how my description of the escape route relates to Kant, whose terminology I am of course exploiting.

Does Kant credit receptivity with a separable contribution to its co-operation with spontaneity? It seems that the answers "No" and "Yes" are both correct.

From the standpoint of experience, the answer is "No". If one posits an empirically separable contribution from receptivity, one commits oneself to something Given in experience that could constitute the ultimate extra-conceptual grounding for everything conceptual, and it is a way of putting a central Kantian thought to say that that idea must be rejected. For Kant, experience does not take in ultimate grounds that we could appeal to by pointing outside the sphere of thinkable content. In experience we take in, through impacts on the senses, elements in a reality that is precisely not outside the sphere of thinkable content.

But Kant also has a transcendental story, and in the transcendental perspective there does seem to be an isolable contribution from receptivity. In the transcendental perspective, receptivity figures as a susceptibility to the impact of a supersensible reality, a reality that is supposed to be independent of our conceptual activity in a stronger sense than any that fits the ordinary empirical world.

If we restrict ourselves to the standpoint of experience itself, what we find in Kant is precisely the picture I have been recommending: a picture in which reality is not located outside a boundary that encloses the conceptual sphere. It is no accident that I have been able to put what I am urging in Kantian terms. The fact that experience involves receptivity ensures the required constraint from outside thinking and judging. But since the deliverances of receptivity already draw on capacities that belong to spontaneity, we can coherently suppose that the constraint is rational; that is how the picture avoids the pitfall of the Given.

But the transcendental perspective embeds this potentially liberating picture within a peculiar version of the sideways-on view I mentioned earlier (§5), with the space of concepts circumscribed and something—the supersensible in this version, not the ordinary empirical world—outside its outer boundary. And in that frame, the liberating thought cannot take proper shape. Once the supersensible is in the picture, its radical independence of our thinking tends to present itself as no more than the independence any genuine reality must have. The empirical world's claim to independence comes to seem fraudulent by comparison. We are asked to suppose that the fundamental structure of the empirical world is somehow a product of subjectivity, in interaction with supersensible reality, which, as soon as it is in the picture, strikes us as the seat of true objectivity. But how can the empirical world be genuinely independent of us, if we are partly responsible for its fundamental structure? It does not help to be told that it is only transcendentally speaking that the fundamental structure of the empirical world is of our making.[17]

Crediting experience with ordinary empirical passivity meets our need: it ensures that when we invoke spontaneity in connection with the employment of concepts in empirical thinking, we do not condemn ourselves to representing empirical thinking as rationally unconstrained, a frictionless spinning in a void. The idea of a transcendental passivity is at best problematic anyway, in a familiar way; by Kant's own lights we are supposed to understand causation as something that operates within the empirical world. Adding this problematic idea only undermines the reassurance that empirical passivity could afford.

Kant comes within a whisker of a satisfactory escape from the oscillation. He points the way to undermining the central confusion in the Myth of the Given. According to the Myth of the Given, the obligation to be responsibly alive to the dictates of reason lapses when we come to the ultimate points of contact between thinking and reality; the Given is a brute effect of the world, not something justified by it. But in fact the obligation must be in force all the way out to reality. The world itself must exert a rational constraint on our thinking. If we suppose that rational answerability lapses at some outermost point of the space of reasons, short of the world itself, our picture ceases to

17. For a vivid expression of a dissatisfaction on these lines, see Barry Stroud's contribution to the symposium "The Disappearing 'We'" (commenting on a paper by Jonathan Lear), *Proceedings of the Aristotelian Society*, supp. vol. 58 (1984), 243–58.

depict anything recognizable as empirical judgement; we have obliter-ated empirical content altogether. If it were not for the transcendental framework, we could credit Kant with a clear formulation of that in-sight. This is how I have interpreted his almost explicit claim that thoughts without intuitions would be empty.

The idea of a faculty of spontaneity is the idea of something that empowers us to take charge of our lives. Kant points the way to a position in which we can satisfyingly apply that idea to empirical thinking: we can hold that empirical inquiry is a region of our lives in which we exercise a responsible freedom, and not let that thought threaten to dislodge our grip on the requirement that empirical think-ing be under constraint from the world itself. But the transcendental framework forces a qualification. Transcendentally speaking, our re-sponsible freedom in empirical thinking seems to fall short of the gen-uine article. It is as if Kant were saying that although an exculpation cannot do duty for a justification, and although, empirically speaking, we can have justifications for empirical judgements, still the best we can have for empirical judgements, transcendentally speaking, is ex-culpations.

This is a profoundly unsatisfactory aspect of Kant's philosophy.[18] And what I have said about it so far is much too simple, in particular in giving the impression that it would be straightforward to excise the

18. Contrast Henry E. Allison, *Kant's Transcendental Idealism: An Interpretation and Defense* (Yale University Press, New Haven, 1983). Allison defends transcendental idealism on the ground that it is the only alternative to a psychologistic phenomenalism. His basic thought is encapsulated in this passage (p. 13): "Indeed, one can claim that the fundamental issue raised by the *Critique* is whether it is possible to isolate a set of conditions of the possibility of knowledge of things . . . that can be distinguished from conditions of the pos-sibility of the things themselves. Since the former kind of condition would count as a condi-tion of things as they appear and the latter of things as they are in themselves, an affirmative answer to this question entails the acceptance of the transcendental distinction [between things as they appear and things as they are in themselves], and with it of transcendental idealism. If, on the other hand, the question is answered in the negative, as it is by the standard picture, then any purportedly 'subjective' conditions are inevitably construed in psychological terms. The subjectivistic, psychologistic, phenomenalistic reading of Kant, which is characteristic of the standard picture, is thus a direct consequence of its negative answer to this question." I agree that we should not find a psychologistic phenomenalism in Kant. (However, Allison's representative of "the standard picture", which finds a psy-chologistic phenomenalism in Kant, is Strawson's *The Bounds of Sense*, and such a reading of Strawson strikes me as absurd.) I do not agree that a negative answer to Allison's ques-tion inevitably imports psychologism. That makes no sense of the responses to Kant of Fichte and, especially, Hegel.

transcendental framework. I shall say a little more about this later (Lecture V).

I think it has to be admitted that the effect of the transcendental framework is to make Kant's philosophy idealistic in the sense I have been considering. This is quite contrary to Kant's intentions, but in spite of his staunch denials, the effect of his philosophy is to slight the independence of the reality to which our senses give us access. What is responsible for this is precisely the aspect of Kant's philosophy that struck some of his successors as a betrayal of idealism: namely, the fact that he recognizes a reality outside the sphere of the conceptual. Those successors urged that we must discard the supersensible in order to achieve a consistent idealism. In fact that move frees Kant's insight so that it can protect a commonsense respect for the independence of the ordinary world.

As I said, if we abstract from the role of the supersensible in Kant's thinking, we are left with a picture in which reality is not located outside a boundary that encloses the conceptual. What I have been urging here is that such a picture does not slight the independence of reality. The picture is not offensive to common sense, but precisely protective of it.

It is central to Absolute Idealism to reject the idea that the conceptual realm has an outer boundary, and we have arrived at a point from which we could start to domesticate the rhetoric of that philosophy. Consider, for instance, this remark of Hegel's: "In thinking, I *am free*, because I am not in an *other*."[19] This expresses exactly the image I have been using, in which the conceptual is unbounded; there is nothing outside it. The point is the same as the point of that remark of Wittgenstein's that I spent some time discussing (§§3 and 4 above): "We—and our meaning—do not stop anywhere short of the fact." I

19. *Phenomenology of Spirit*, trans. A. V. Miller (Oxford University Press, Oxford, 1977), §197 (p. 120). Robert B. Pippin, at p. 164 of *Hegel's Idealism: The Satisfactions of Self-Consciousness* (Cambridge University Press, Cambridge, 1989), reads this remark as primarily an expression of stoicism, though he says that "it is also clearly indicative of the position toward which Hegel is heading". The latter is all I need, but I would suggest that it is actually the first thing to say about the remark. The opening paragraphs of a section in the *Phenomenology* typically adumbrate "the position toward which Hegel is heading". Only later in the section does an insufficiency come to light. This remark comes in the section headed "Stoicism", but it belongs to the phase of that section that marks progress, before the emergence of something to keep the dialectical pendulum swinging.

should like to take this further, but for several reasons, of which the fact that I have said enough for one lecture is perhaps the least serious, I cannot do that now.

10.   I have been claiming that the content of experience is conceptual, and many people think that cannot be right. In my next lecture I am going to discuss that question.

Non-conceptual Content

1. I have been talking about a pair of opposing pitfalls: on the one side a coherentism that does not acknowledge an external rational constraint on thinking and therefore, I claim, cannot genuinely make room for empirical content at all; and on the other side a recoil into the Myth of the Given, which offers at best exculpations where what we need is justifications. I have urged that the way to stop oscillating between those pitfalls is to conceive empirical knowledge as a co-operation of sensibility and understanding, as Kant does. To avoid making it unintelligible how the deliverances of sensibility can stand in grounding relations to paradigmatic exercises of the understanding such as judgements and beliefs, we must conceive this co-operation in a quite particular way: we must insist that the understanding is already inextricably implicated in the deliverances of sensibility themselves. Experiences are impressions made by the world on our senses, products of receptivity; but those impressions themselves already have conceptual content.

This unqualified claim that the content of perceptual experience is conceptual will have been raising some eyebrows since my first lecture. Here I am going to defend it against some doubts.

Before I start, let me note that the issue cannot be defused as just a matter of idiosyncratic terminology on my part—as if I am merely affixing the label "conceptual" to the content of experience, although I regard the content of experience in the very way that my opponents express by saying that it is not conceptual, at least not through and through. It is essential to the picture I am recommending that experience has its content by virtue of the drawing into operation, in sensibility, of capacities that are genuinely elements in a faculty of spontaneity. The very same capacities must also be able to be exercised in judgements, and that requires them to be rationally linked into a whole system of concepts and conceptions within which their possessor engages in a continuing activity of adjusting her thinking to experience. Indeed, there can be other elements in the system that are not capable of figuring in experience at all. In my last lecture, I claimed that it is only because experience involves capacities belonging to spontaneity that we can understand experience as awareness, or apparent awareness, of aspects of the world at all. The way I am exploiting the Kantian idea of spontaneity commits me to a demanding interpretation for words like "concept" and "conceptual". It is essential to conceptual capacities, in the demanding sense, that they can be exploited in active thinking, thinking that is open to reflection about its own rational credentials.[1] When I say the content of experience is conceptual, that is what I mean by "conceptual".

2.   To focus the discussion, I am going to consider what Gareth Evans says about this question.

Evans makes the equally unqualified claim that the content of perceptual experience is non-conceptual. According to Evans, conceptual content first comes into play, in the context of perception, in judgements based on experience. When one forms a judgement on the basis of experience, one moves from non-conceptual content to conceptual content.

> The informational states which a subject acquires through perception are *non-conceptual,* or *non-conceptualized.* Judgements *based upon* such states necessarily involve conceptualization: in moving from a perceptual experience to a judgement about the world (usually expressible in some verbal form), one will be exercising basic conceptual skills. . . . The process of conceptualization or judgement takes the subject from his being in one kind of informational state (with a content of a certain kind, namely, non-conceptual content) to his being in another kind of

---

1. It is worth noting, since it helps to bring out how demanding the relevant idea of the conceptual is, that this openness to reflection implies self-consciousness on the part of the thinking subject. But I relegate the point to a footnote at this stage, since issues about self-consciousness will not be in the foreground until later (Lecture V).

cognitive state (with a content of a different kind, namely, conceptual content).[2]

These non-conceptual informational states are the results of perception's playing its role in what Evans calls "the informational system" (p. 122). The informational system is the system of capacities we exercise when we gather information about the world by using our senses (perception), receive information from others in communication (testimony), and retain information through time (memory).[3]

It is central to Evans's view that "the operations of the informational system" are "more primitive" than the rationally interconnected conceptual skills that make room for the notion of judgement and a strict notion of belief (p. 124).[4] To put the thought in the terms I have been using: the operations of the informational system are more primitive than the operations of spontaneity. This point is straightforward in the case of perception and memory, which, as Evans says, "we share with animals" (p. 124); that is, with creatures on which the idea of spontaneity gets no grip. Strikingly, he insists on the point for testimony too: "the mechanism whereby we gain information from others . . . is already operative at a stage of human intellectual development that pre-dates the applicability of the more sophisticated notion" (p. 124). His thought here is that for much of the knowledge that one has by virtue of having been exposed to statements of it, one was not in a position to understand the statements at the time.

Evans, then, identifies perceptual experiences as states of the informational system, possessing content that is non-conceptual.[5] According to Evans, conceptual capacities are first brought into operation only when one makes a judgement of experience, and at that point a different species of content comes into play. Contrast the account I have been urging. According to the picture I have been recommending, the content of a perceptual experience is already conceptual. A judgement of experience does not introduce a new kind of content,

2. *The Varieties of Reference*, p. 227 (emphasis in the original). Unless otherwise indicated, all citations from Evans in this lecture will be from this work. I want to make it clear immediately that I believe the thesis on which I shall be taking issue with Evans here is inessential to the main claims of Evans's profoundly important book. I shall come back to Evans's main claims in Lecture V (§6).

3. See pp. 122–9.

4. I shall say something about the strict notion of belief in §6.

5. It would be easy to complicate Evans's account so as to accommodate the fact that "experience" can fit occurrences as well as states.

but simply endorses the conceptual content, or some of it, that is already possessed by the experience on which it is grounded.[6]

It is important not to misconceive this divergence. In Evans's view, experiences are states of the informational system, and as such they have content that is non-conceptual. But he does not equate the idea of an experience with the idea of a perceptual informational state, produced independently of spontaneity by the operations of the informational system. On the contrary, he insists that perceptual informational states, with their non-conceptual content, "are not *ipso facto* perceptual *experiences*—that is, states of a conscious subject" (p. 157). According to Evans, a state of the perceptual informational system counts as an experience only if its non-conceptual content is available as "input to a *thinking, concept-applying, and reasoning system*" (p. 158); that is, only if its non-conceptual content is available to a faculty of spontaneity, which can rationally make or withhold judgements of experience on the basis of the perceptual state. So a non-conceptual informational state, produced by the perceptual element of the informational system in a creature that lacks a faculty of spontaneity, does not count as a perceptual experience, even though a state that does count as a perceptual experience, by virtue of its availability to spontaneity, is in itself just such a non-conceptual informational state, endowed with its non-conceptual content independently of the coming into play of the faculty of spontaneity.

3.   Near the end of my first lecture (§7), I noted a difficulty it would be natural to feel when one sets out to apply to "inner experience" the picture I have been recommending of experience in general, according to which experiences are states or occurrences in which conceptual capacities are drawn into operation. I have been claiming that it is essential to conceptual capacities that they belong to spontaneity, that is, to a faculty that is exercised in actively self-critical control of what one thinks, in the light of the deliverances of experience. But that

---

6. Note that grounding need not depend on an inferential step from one content to another. The judgement that things are thus and so can be grounded on a perceptual appearance that things are thus and so. This does not obliterate the characteristic richness of experience (especially visual experience). A typical judgement of experience selects from the content of the experience on which it is based; the experience that grounds the judgement that things are thus and so need not be exhausted by its affording the appearance that things are thus and so. Selection from among a rich supply of already conceptual content is not what Evans takes judgement to effect, a transition from one kind of content to another.

means we cannot attribute the conceptual capacities that would figure in the account of "inner experience" I have endorsed—for instance, a capacity to use the concept of pain—to many creatures of which it would be outrageous to deny that they can feel pain. It is not just active self-critical thinkers that can feel pain. Whatever it may be that is true of a creature without spontaneity when it feels pain, it cannot be that it has "inner experience", according to the picture of experience I have been recommending.

This point is obviously not peculiar to "inner experience". The application to "outer experience" is similar: "outer experience" that purports to disclose that things are thus and so is, according to the account I am recommending, a state or occurrence involving the operation of the conceptual capacities that would be actively exploited in judging that things are thus and so. In that case "outer experience" can be attributed only to a creature that could engage in such active thinking. So we have a parallel point in this case: I am committed to denying "outer experience" of features of their environment to some creatures, even though it would be outrageous to deny that they are perceptually sensitive to those features. It is not just active self-critical thinkers that are perceptually sensitive to features of their environment.

At this stage I am simply acknowledging this twin discomfort, not aiming to alleviate it; I shall make an attempt at that later (Lecture VI). One straightforward response would be to conclude that the notion of experience needs to be completely detached from anything on the lines of the notion of spontaneity. Then we would not be committed to having different stories to tell about the sentient lives of rational and non-rational animals. My point now is just that anyone who is tempted by this course cannot easily enrol Evans as an ally. In his picture as in mine, the concept of experience has a restricted use, governed by a link of a broadly Kantian sort to what is in effect the idea of spontaneity.

4. I have been concerned in these lectures with a standing threat of falling into philosophical anxiety. If we focus on the freedom implied by the notion of spontaneity, what was meant to be a picture of thinking with empirical content threatens to degenerate into a picture of a frictionless spinning in a void. To overcome that, we need to acknowledge an external constraint on the exercise of spontaneity in empirical

thinking. But now we come to the other side of the standing difficulty: we must avoid conceiving the external constraint in such a way that it could at best yield exculpations where we needed justifications. One might simply refuse to address this difficulty, by refusing to give any place, in an account of experience, to anything like the idea of spontaneity. But as I have just stressed, that is not a line that Evans takes.

To acknowledge the required external constraint, we need to appeal to receptivity. I have urged that the way to introduce receptivity without merely tipping the seesaw back to the Myth of the Given is this: we must not suppose that receptivity makes an even notionally separable contribution to its co-operation with spontaneity.

Now Evans does not respect this rule. In Evans's account of experience, receptivity figures in the guise of the perceptual element of the informational system, and his idea is that the perceptual system produces its content-bearing states independently of any operations of spontaneity. It is true that the content-bearing states that result count as experiences, in the somewhat Kantian restricted sense that Evans employs, only by virtue of the fact that they are available to spontaneity. But spontaneity does not enter into determining their content. So the independent operations of the informational system figure in Evans's account as a separable contribution made by receptivity to its co-operation with spontaneity.

In that case, the way experiences are related to conceptual capacities in Evans's picture is just the way intuitions are related to concepts in the picture of empirical knowledge that Kant, as I am reading him, displays as hopeless, at least as a picture of how things are from the standpoint of experience. It is true that Kant tries to allow a kind of correctness for a picture with that shape at the transcendental level, but Evans's account of experience is not meant to be only transcendentally correct, whatever indeed that might mean. So unless there is something wrong with the Kantian considerations I rehearsed in my first two lectures, Evans's account of experience ought to be demolished by them.

It may be hard to believe that Evans's view of experience is a version of the Myth of the Given. Evans's smoothly naturalistic account of perceptual informational states shows no sign of the epistemological obsessions that are usually operative in motivating the Myth of the Given. What usually underlies the Myth is a worry that spontaneity's involvement in our picture of empirical thought makes it mysterious how we can be picturing something that is in touch with reality at all, and there is no sign of that in Evans.

Moreover, there may seem to be a more specific problem about attributing the Myth of the Given to Evans. If experiences as Evans conceives them are intuitions without concepts, in a sense that would make his position vulnerable to the Kantian attack on the Myth of the Given, they ought to be blind. But Evans takes care to credit experiences with representational content, even independently of the availability to spontaneity in virtue of which they count as experiences. The content is non-conceptual, certainly, but one might wonder how that could warrant the image of blindness. Surely, one might think, something that is blind would have to be totally devoid of representational content?

The structure of Evans's position is comparable to the structure of a position I considered in my first lecture (§5), when I was trying to avert a misinterpretation of what I was recommending. That position purported to accept that conceptual capacities are drawn into operation in experience. But it treated the states and occurrences that it described in those terms as insulated from spontaneity. The aim was to ensure that they were not subject to the potentially unnerving effects of the freedom that the idea of spontaneity implies.

What I said about that position was that in the context of the insulation from spontaneity, the talk of concepts is mere word-play. The point of the claim that experience involves conceptual capacities is that it enables us to credit experiences with a rational bearing on empirical thinking. But the point of the strategy of insulation is that it confines spontaneity within a boundary that leaves experiences outside it. That means that the putatively rational relations between experiences, which this position does not conceive as operations of spontaneity, and judgements, which it does conceive as operations of spontaneity, cannot themselves be within the scope of spontaneity— liable to revision, if that were to be what the self-scrutiny of active thinking recommends. And that means that we cannot genuinely recognize the relations as potentially reason-constituting. We cannot put limits on the self-scrutiny of reason. If we want to be able to take it that the operations of conceptual capacities in experience impinge rationally on our thinking, as we must if they are to be recognizable as operations of conceptual capacities at all, we must acknowledge that those rational relations fall within the scope of spontaneity. And it is hard to see how we could acknowledge that while refusing to accept that the perceptual states and occurrences that lie at one end of the relations involve capacities of spontaneity in operation.

Evans's account of experience is not guilty of *that* fraudulent labelling; exactly not, since he keeps concepts out of the content of experience. But the word "content" plays just the role in Evans's account that is played in that position by the fraudulent use of the word "conceptual": that is, to make it seem that we can recognize rational relations between experiences and judgements, so that we can say, as Evans does, that judgements of experience are "based upon" experience (p. 227), even though these relations are supposed to hold across a boundary that encloses spontaneity. The same point should apply here too. If these relations are to be genuinely recognizable as reason-constituting, we cannot confine spontaneity within a boundary across which the relations are supposed to hold. The relations themselves must be able to come under the self-scrutiny of active thinking.

Evans's position has a deceptively innocent look. It can seem obvious that a possessor of one piece of representational content, whether conceptual or not, can stand in rational relations, such as implication or probabilification, to a possessor of another. But with spontaneity confined, we lose the right to draw the conclusion, as a matter of routine, that one term in such a relation can be someone's reason for another. If experience is pictured as input to spontaneity from outside, then it is another case of fraudulent labelling to use the word "content" for something we can even so take experience to have, in such a way that reason-constituting relations can intelligibly hold between experiences and judgements. The label serves to mask the fact that the relations between experiences and judgements are being conceived to meet inconsistent demands: to be such as to fit experiences to be reasons for judgements, while being outside the reach of rational inquiry.[7]

I am claiming that although Evans does take care to credit experiences with content, that does not save them from being intuitions in a sense that entitles us to apply the Kantian tag to them: since they are

---

7. Why can we not acknowledge that the *relations* between experience and judgements have to be rational, and therefore within the scope of spontaneity, without being thereby committed to a concession about experience itself? I have claimed that it is hard to see how this combination could work, but as long as Evans's position looks innocent it will seem quite easy. Rather than radically recasting this lecture from the form in which I delivered it, I postpone further discussion of this matter to the Afterword.

without concepts, they are blind. And actually there is an interpretation of that claim under which Evans would not dispute it. It was
wrong to suggest that experiences as he conceives them cannot possibly be blind, since he equips them with content. It makes all the difference that the content is supposed to be non-conceptual.

How should we cash out the image of blindness? To say that an
experience is not blind is to say that it is intelligible to its subject as
purporting to be awareness of a feature of objective reality: as a seeming glimpse of the world. And Evans himself insists that that can be so
only against the background of an understanding of how perception
and reality are related, something sufficient to sustain the idea that the
world reveals itself to a perceiving subject in different regions and aspects, in a way that depends on the subject's movement through the
world.[8] Such a background can be in place only for a subject with a
self-conscious conception of how her experience relates to the world,
and we cannot make sense of that in the absence of conceptual capacities in a strong sense, a faculty of spontaneity.[9]

So when Evans says that experiences, considered in themselves,
have non-conceptual content, he is not thereby pre-empting my suggestion that experiences as he conceives them are blind, because they
are intuitions without concepts. What makes it intelligible, in his view,
that the eyes of empirical thought are opened is not the claim that,

8. See p. 176: "Any subject at all capable of thought about an objective spatial world
must conceive of his normal experiences as simultaneously due to the way the world is and
his changing position in it. . . . The capacity to think of oneself as located in space, and
tracing a continuous path through it, is necessarily involved in the capacity to conceive the
phenomena one encounters as independent of one's perception of them—to conceive the
world as something one 'comes across'." See also p. 222: "Any thinker who has an idea of
an objective spatial world—an idea of a world of objects and phenomena which can be
perceived but which are not dependent on being perceived for their existence—must be able
to think of his perception of the world as being simultaneously due to his position in the
world, and to the condition of the world at that position. The very idea of a perceivable,
objective, spatial world brings with it the idea of the subject as being *in* the world, with the
course of his perceptions due to his changing position in the world and to the more or less
stable way the world is." Evans elaborates this thought in "Things without the Mind". The
thought is central to Strawson's reading of Kant; see chap. 2 of *The Bounds of Sense,* especially p. 104.

9. In "Things without the Mind" Evans argues that the idea of an object of experience
"cannot stand on its own, stand without any surrounding theory" (p. 88). The required
theory is a theory of the conditions under which something perceptible is actually perceived
(pp. 88–9). If we make sense of the Kantian notion of spontaneity, we must surely suppose
that the possession of spontaneity marks the difference between creatures that can intelligibly be thought to have such a theory, even if only implicitly, and creatures that cannot.

even considered in abstraction from any connection with spontaneity, experiences have (non-conceptual) content. It is the claim that that content is available to spontaneity: that it is a candidate for being integrated into the conceptually organized world-view of a self-conscious thinker. I am only stressing an aspect of Evans's own view when I say that, according to him, the item that an experience is, considered in itself (in abstraction from the availability to spontaneity in virtue of which it acquires the title "experience"), is blind.

This would be all right if we could make sense of the potential for rational linkage with a world-view that is supposed to make the item an experience, something that is not blind. But although crediting the items that experiences are with content, independently of their availability to spontaneity, gives the appearance of making room for this connection, I have urged that when the content is said to be non-conceptual, the appearance stands revealed as illusory.

I am not saying there is something wrong with just any notion of non-conceptual content. It would be dangerous to deny, from a philosophical armchair, that cognitive psychology is an intellectually respectable discipline, at least so long as it stays within its proper bounds. And it is hard to see how cognitive psychology could get along without attributing content to internal states and occurrences in a way that is not constrained by the conceptual capacities, if any, of the creatures whose lives it tries to make intelligible. But it is a recipe for trouble if we blur the distinction between the respectable theoretical role that non-conceptual content has in cognitive psychology, on the one hand, and, on the other, the notion of content that belongs with the capacities exercised in active self-conscious thinking—as if the contentfulness of our thoughts and conscious experiences could be understood as a welling-up to the surface of some of the content that a good psychological theory would attribute to goings-on in our cognitive machinery.[10]

10. For a clear and engaging exposition of this welling-up picture, see Daniel Dennett, "Toward a Cognitive Theory of Consciousness", in his *Brainstorms: Philosophical Essays on Mind and Psychology* (Bradford Books, Montgomery, Vt., 1978), pp. 149–73. Dennett suggests that the role of content at the personal level is to be understood in terms of our access to some of the content that figures in a sub-personal story about our internal machinery. I think Dennett's own discussion strongly suggests that something is wrong with this picture: it leads Dennett into the highly implausible claim that perceptual awareness is a matter of presentiments or premonitions, differing from what are ordinarily so called only in that they are not isolated (see pp. 165–6). I discuss this in "The Concept of Perceptual Experience", *Philosophical Quarterly* 44 (1994), 190–205.

5. Why does Evans think he has to locate experiences outside the sphere of the conceptual? If his position is indeed a case of lapsing into the Myth of the Given, it is a special case. As I said, it does not issue from the usual epistemological motivation, the recoil from a picture that threatens to leave empirical thinking out of touch with reality, and so not recognizable as empirical thinking at all.

One consideration that impresses Evans is the determinacy of detail that the content of experience can have. He claims that this detail cannot all be captured by concepts at the subject's disposal. "Do we really understand the proposal that we have as many colour concepts as there are shades of colour that we can sensibly discriminate?"[11] Others besides Evans have taken this kind of consideration to require crediting experience with non-conceptual content. This formulation includes people who do not follow Evans in relegating the content of experience completely to the non-conceptual, but aim to accommodate the phenomenological point Evans makes here by saying that the content of experience is *partly* non-conceptual.[12]

When Evans suggests that our repertoire of colour concepts is coarser in grain than our abilities to discriminate shades, and therefore unable to capture the fine detail of colour experience, what he has in mind is the sort of conceptual capacities that are associated with colour expressions like "red", "green", or "burnt sienna". Such words and phrases express concepts of bands on the spectrum, whereas Evans's thought is that colour experience can present properties that correspond to something more like lines on the spectrum, with no discernible width.

But why should we accept that a person's ability to embrace colour within her conceptual thinking is restricted to concepts expressible by words like "red" or "green" and phrases like "burnt sienna"? It is possible to acquire the concept of a shade of colour, and most of us have done so. Why not say that one is thereby equipped to embrace shades of colour within one's conceptual thinking with the very same determinateness with which they are presented in one's visual experience, so that one's concepts can capture colours no less sharply than one's experience presents them? In the throes of an experience of the kind that putatively transcends one's conceptual powers—an experi-

---

11. *The Varieties of Reference*, p. 229. Obviously colour figures here as representative of a number of features of experience.

12. Christopher Peacocke takes this view in recent work; for an overview see *A Study of Concepts* (MIT Press, Cambridge, Mass., 1992).

ence that *ex hypothesi* affords a suitable sample—one can give linguistic expression to a concept that is exactly as fine-grained as the experience, by uttering a phrase like "that shade", in which the demonstrative exploits the presence of the sample.

We need to be careful about what sort of conceptual capacity this is. We had better not think it can be exercised only when the instance that it is supposed to enable its possessor to embrace in thought is available for use as a sample in giving linguistic expression to it. That would cast doubt on its being recognizable as a conceptual capacity at all. Consider undertaking to give expression to a thought in a way that exploits the availability of a sample, by saying (possibly to oneself) something like "My visual experience represents something as being of *that* shade". Suppose we try to hold that this attempted expression of a thought contains an expression of a colour concept that is restricted to this occasion of utterance. This looks like Wittgenstein's case of the person who says "I know how tall I am", putting his hand on top of his head to prove it.[13] The putative thought—"I am *this* tall", "It looks to me as if something is of *that* shade"—is being construed so as to lack the distance from what would determine it to be true that would be necessary for it to be recognizable as a thought at all.

We can ensure that what we have in view is genuinely recognizable as a conceptual capacity if we insist that the very same capacity to embrace a colour in mind can in principle persist beyond the duration of the experience itself. In the presence of the original sample, "that shade" can give expression to a concept of a shade; what ensures that it is a concept—what ensures that thoughts that exploit it have the necessary distance from what would determine them to be true—is that the associated capacity can persist into the future, if only for a short time, and that, having persisted, it can be used also in thoughts about what is by then the past, if only the recent past.[14] What is in play here is a recognitional capacity, possibly quite short-lived, that sets in with the experience. It is the conceptual content of such a recognitional capacity that can be made explicit with the help of a sample, something that is guaranteed to be available at the time of the experience with which the capacity sets in. Later in the life of the capacity it can

13. *Philosophical Investigations*, §279.
14. Obviously people differ in the retentiveness of their memory for precise shades. No doubt it can be cultivated, as a memory for flavours is cultivated by aspiring connoisseurs of food or wine.

be given linguistic expression again, if the course of experience is favourable; that is, if experience again, or still, presents one with a suitable sample. But even in the absence of a sample, the capacity goes on being exploitable as long as it lasts, in thoughts based on memory: thoughts that are not necessarily capable of receiving an overt expression that fully determines their content.

If such recognitional capacities are conceptual, Evans's question does not have the answer he thinks it does. It is true that we do not have ready, in advance of the course our colour experience actually takes, as many colour concepts as there are shades of colour that we can sensibly discriminate. But if we have the concept of a shade, our conceptual powers are fully adequate to capture our colour experience in all its determinate detail.

What reason could there be for refusing to accept that such recognitional capacities are conceptual? They seem perfectly suited to figure in an understanding of how experience takes hold of aspects of the world, on the lines I sketched in my first two lectures. I claimed that we can make sense of this image of experience taking hold of the world, or being open to it, if we suppose that experience involves the operation of capacities that are conceptual, in the sense that they are rationally integrated into spontaneity at large. Evans's phenomenological point is that the world as experience takes hold of it is more finely grained than we could register by appealing only to conceptual capacities expressible by general colour words and phrases. Now it is true that the fine-grained capacities I have appealed to have a special character, which is marked by how demonstrative expressions would have to figure in linguistic expressions of them. But why should that prevent us from recognizing them as rationally integrated into spontaneity in their own way, so that they can simply take their place in my general framework? Why, in fact, are they not so much as considered in Evans's argument, and in the appeal by many others to the consideration about fineness of grain that drives Evans's argument?[15]

---

15. Peacocke is an exception; see *A Study of Concepts*, pp. 83–4. But notice that even though Peacocke there in effect acknowledges that fineness of grain is no threat to the thesis that the content of experience is conceptual, he is not above claiming, in an earlier passage, an advantage for his different view in the fact that "writers on the objective content of experience have often remarked that an experience can have a finer-grained content than can be formulated by using concepts possessed by the experiencer" (p. 67). If this claim that writers have often made is false, why should accommodating it be an advantage for Peacocke's view?

The very identity of one of these possibly short-term recognitional capacities is tied to a particular case of the kind of impact on sensibility that is supposed to be captured by the associated concept. A capacity to embrace a shade within one's thinking (as *that* shade, we can say in favourable circumstances) is initiated by the figuring of an instance of the shade in one's experience.[16] There is no saying which capacity it is in abstraction from the activating experience itself. That is how these capacities permit the fine-grained sensuous detail that figures in the actual course of visual life to be taken up into the conceptual content of visual experience.

This means that from the standpoint of a dualism of concept and intuition, these capacities would seem hybrids. There is an admixture of intuition in their very constitution, and that might explain why they do not even figure as candidates for being recognized as conceptual. But if that is why Evans's thinking takes the course it does, it is obviously damaging. Evans is trying to enforce a distance between the conceptual, on the one hand, and the world's impact on the senses, on the other. If it is assumed in advance that the role of intuition in their constitution prevents us from counting these capacities as (purely) conceptual, the distance is being presupposed, not argued for. And obviously this ground for refusing to accept that these capacities are conceptual is equally illicit for those who use the fine-grained character of experience to recommend a mixed position, in which the content of experience is partly conceptual and partly non-conceptual.

Evans thinks intuition and concept, dualistically conceived, need to be shared out between experience and judgement. Proponents of the mixed position differ from Evans in thinking intuition and concept can be juxtaposed in experience. In so far as the claim that intuitions, conceived as non-conceptual, must figure in experience is based on the argument from fineness of grain, this mixed position shares its shakiness of foundation with Evans's view. Moreover, by simply juxtaposing the two species of content in experience, the mixed position makes it difficult for itself to accommodate the strong point of Evans's view,

---

16. In another sense, the capacity to have that particular shade in mind is a standing one, which requires no more than possession of the concept of a shade together with the subject's standing powers of discrimination. Experience raises this standing potential to a degree of actuality; the capacity to have that shade in mind as *that* shade is actually operative in the experience, and potentially operative subsequently in thoughts that exploit recall of the experience.

the Kantian insight that we need to appeal to conceptual capacities in order to make it intelligible that experience is not blind.[17]

6. A second consideration that Evans appeals to is that states of the informational system are, as he puts it, "belief-independent" (p. 123). The content of a perceptual experience cannot be explained as the content of an appropriate actual belief, since there may be no belief with a suitable content; a familiar visual illusion continues to present its illusory appearance even though the subject does not believe that things are as they look. Some people try to preserve a definitional connection between informational content and belief content, while acknowledging this point, by suggesting that the content of an experience can be captured as something that the experience gives its subject "a *prima facie* inclination to believe" (p. 124). Evans responds (ibid.): "I cannot help feeling that this gets things the wrong way round. It is as well to reserve 'belief' for the notion of a far more sophisticated cognitive state: one that is connected with (and, in my opinion, defined in terms of) the notion of *judgement,* and so, also, connected with the notion of *reasons.*" That is, to put it in the terms I have been using: we should reserve the idea of belief for something that can be understood only in the context of the idea of spontaneity, the idea of an active undertaking in which a subject takes rational control of the shape of her thinking. Not that all one's beliefs are the result of actively making up one's mind. But there is a point in reserving the title of belief for a kind of cognitive state that is essentially within the scope of one's powers of actively making up one's mind; even in the case of a belief that one simply finds oneself with, the question of one's entitlement to it can always be raised. We can sum up what Evans is suggesting about belief by saying that belief is a disposition to make judgements, and judging is essentially an act of spontaneity.

Evans is here insisting that the active business of making up one's mind is the proper context in which to place conceptual capacities, and that is something I have been urging throughout these lectures.

17. The main lines of what I say in this section date from a seminar I gave in Oxford in 1986 (with Colin McGinn). But my thinking on these issues has since been enriched by discussions with Sonia Sedivy, who independently arrived at similar thoughts, in reaction to the Sellarsian idea that the sensuous specificity of perceptual experience needs to be accounted for in terms of impressions as opposed to concepts. See her 1990 University of Pittsburgh dissertation, "The Determinate Character of Perceptual Experience".

But he uses the point as an argument that the content of experience cannot be conceptual, and by my lights that betrays a blind spot. The point does not tell against the conception of experience I have been recommending: a conception according to which capacities that belong to spontaneity are already operative in receptivity, rather than working on something independently supplied to them by receptivity. Evans does not argue against that conception; it simply does not figure among the possibilities he contemplates.

Someone who holds that the content of experience is conceptual, and who places the idea of the conceptual in the right context, must register a link between the conceptual capacities that she takes to be at work in perception and the active exercise of spontaneity in judgements. Evans considers only one way in which one might try to register the link: namely, by identifying experiences with dispositions to make judgements. The idea would be that these dispositions are realized in actual judgements only when an "other things being equal" clause is satisfied. That is how the position accommodates the fact that experience is "belief-independent": other things fail to be equal in the presence of known illusions, and in any other circumstances in which there is experience without the associated belief.

Evans objects that this picture falsifies the phenomenology of perception (p. 229): "The proposal is implausible, because it is not the case that we simply find ourselves with a yen to apply some concept—a conviction that it has application in the immediate vicinity. Nothing could more falsify the facts of the situation." The picture interposes a distance between experience itself and the active employment of concepts in judgement, a distance that is supposed to be bridged by the idea of dispositions. Evans's protest is that, even so, the picture connects the content of experience too closely to active thinking for it to be able to do justice to experience. Suppose the "other things being equal" clause is satisfied, and there is an inclination to apply some concept in judgement. This inclination does not just inexplicably set in. If one does make a judgement, it is wrung from one by the experience, which serves as one's reason for the judgement. In a picture in which all there is behind the judgement is a disposition to make it, the experience itself goes missing.

This is very perceptive, and I think it is devastating to the suggestion that we can bring experience within the scope of a faculty of spontaneity by conceiving experiences as dispositions to make judgements.

But the point does not touch the position I am recommending. According to the position I am recommending, conceptual capacities are already operative in experience itself. It is not that actual operations of conceptual capacities first figure only in actualizations of dispositions to judge, with which experiences are identified—so that experience is connected with concepts only by way of a potentiality. Having things appear to one a certain way is already itself a mode of actual operation of conceptual capacities.

This mode of operation of conceptual capacities is special because, on the side of the subject, it is passive, a reflection of sensibility. In the context of that claim, it takes work to ensure that the capacities are recognizable as genuinely conceptual capacities—that the invocation of the conceptual is not mere word-play. What is needed is that the very same capacities can also be exploited in active judgements. And what secures this identification, between capacities that are operative in appearances and capacities that are operative in judgements, is the way appearances are rationally linked into spontaneity at large: the way appearances can constitute reasons for judgements about objective reality—indeed, do constitute reasons for judgements in suitable circumstances ("other things being equal").

Now this link between experience and spontaneity is similar in some ways to the link that is effected, in the position Evans attacks, by conceiving experiences as dispositions to judge. But the link I envisage, unlike that one, is a link that connects experiences to judgements as reasons for them. That means my picture does not have the feature that Evans complains of: that when there is an inclination to make a judgement of experience, the inclination seems to float mysteriously free of the situation, taking on the look of an unaccountable conviction that some concept "has application in the immediate vicinity". On the contrary, when one does have such a conviction, my picture allows it to be satisfactorily grounded in how things appear to one.

In my first lecture (§6), I suggested that Davidson's coherentism reflects an obstacle in the way of seeing that operations of conceptual capacities can be passive. The same obstacle seems to be at work in Evans's argument from the fact that experience is "belief-independent". In fact Davidson and Evans represent the two horns of a dilemma posed by that obstacle. If one fails to see that conceptual capacities can be operative in sensibility itself, one has two options: either, like Davidson, to insist that experience is only causally related to empirical thinking, not rationally; or else, like Evans, to fall into the Myth of the Given, and try to credit experience, conceived as extra-conceptual, with rational relations to empirical thinking. Davidson holds that the Myth of the Given can be avoided only by denying that experience is epistemologically significant. Evans, for good reasons, cannot stomach that denial, and he shows that he shares Davidson's view of the possibilities by accordingly embracing a form of the Myth of the Given. My point is that we need not confine ourselves within this framework of possibilities. I shall return to this in the next lecture.

7. I have already mentioned a third consideration Evans appeals to. This is the fact that we share perception (like memory) with "animals" (p. 124); that is, with creatures that cannot be credited with conceptual capacities, in the demanding sense Evans and I agree on.

This brings me back to the area of the twin discomforts I mentioned some time ago (§3). Both Evans and I are committed to there being different stories to tell about perceptual goings-on in creatures with spontaneity and in creatures without it. In the one case we can apply the notion of experience, in a strict sense that connects it with conceptual capacities, and in the other case we cannot. But it may seem that Evans's position makes this implication less embarrassing, because the position supplies us with something we can conceive as straightforwardly common to the two cases: namely, states of the informational system, with their non-conceptual content.

We can shake this impression somewhat by considering the third element of the informational system, the testimony system. According to Evans, we have knowledge derived from operations of the testimony system that took place before we were in a position to understand the linguistic performances in question. So the testimony system is, in itself, "more primitive" than understanding. And that is a partial parallel to the fact that we share perception and memory with mere animals. Now suppose our sharing perception with creatures that lack spontaneity were a good reason for crediting our perceptual experience with content that is not conceptual, on the ground that if we said that the content of our experience is conceptual, that would put this kind of content out of reach of those other perceivers. In that case, by parity of reasoning, the partially parallel fact about the primitive operations of the testimony system should be a good reason for supposing that non-conceptual content is involved in our mature dealings

with the testimony system, when we do understand the linguistic performances we witness. But understanding language is surely a matter
of conceptual capacities if anything is. So what is the role of these
conceptual capacities in our mature dealings with the testimony system, if the content involved is non-conceptual? A straightforward parallel to Evans's picture of the role of conceptual capacities in experience would be this: the conceptual capacities exercised in
understanding a linguistic performance do not enter into determining
the content with which one takes oneself to be presented, but serve
only to account for one's access to that content, which is independently determined by the operations of the informational system. But
that is surely a quite unattractive idea.

   If we share perception with mere animals, then of course we have
something in common with them. Now there is a temptation to think
it must be possible to isolate what we have in common with them by
stripping off what is special about us, so as to arrive at a residue that
we can recognize as what figures in the perceptual lives of mere animals. That is the role that is played in Evans's picture by informational states, with their non-conceptual content. But it is not compulsory to attempt to accommodate the combination of something in
common and a striking difference in this factorizing way: to suppose
our perceptual lives include a core that we can also recognize in the
perceptual life of a mere animal, and an extra ingredient in addition.
And if we do take this line, there is no satisfactory way to understand
the role of the supposed core in our perceptual lives. We are confronted with the dilemma whose horns are embraced by Davidson and
Evans, each of them, I claim, deceived in the thought that his position
is satisfactory.

   We can avoid the dilemma. We do not need to say that we have
what mere animals have, non-conceptual content, and we have something else as well, since we can conceptualize that content and they
cannot. Instead we can say that we have what mere animals have,
perceptual sensitivity to features of our environment, but we have it in
a special form. Our perceptual sensitivity to our environment is taken
up into the ambit of the faculty of spontaneity, which is what distinguishes us from them.

   I think we ought ultimately to be able to take something on those
lines in our stride. But perhaps such formulations begin to uncover the
character of the obstacle I have been alluding to: the intelligibly pow-

erful influence over the cast of our thinking that tends to obliterate the very possibility of the right picture. The difficulty comes out in questions like this: how can spontaneity permeate our lives, even to the extent of structuring those aspects of them that reflect our naturalness—those aspects of our lives that reflect what we share with ordinary animals? The thought is that the freedom of spontaneity ought to be a kind of exemption from nature, something that permits us to elevate ourselves above it, rather than our own special way of living an animal life. I shall come back to these issues in the next lecture.

Reason and Nature

1. So far, I have been concerned with difficulties we can fall into, in our reflection about empirical judgement and knowledge, if we try to accommodate the point that Kant makes by talking of spontaneity.

To accept that point is to acknowledge that judging is an active employment of capacities that empower us to take charge of our thinking. But that threatens us with oscillating between two unpalatable alternatives. The initial threat is that we lose a connection between empirical thinking and independent reality, a connection that there must be if what is in question is to be recognizable as bearing on independent reality at all. The idea of spontaneity is an idea of freedom, and that threatens to make what was meant to be empirical thinking degenerate, in our picture, into a frictionless spinning in a void. Recoiling from that, we are tempted to suppose we can reinstate friction between thought and the world by making out that justifications of empirical judgements stop at objects of pure ostension, uncontaminated by conceptualization. But when we think this alternative through, we realize that these supposed stopping points for justification cannot intelligibly serve as a subject's reasons for her judgements. Now we are tempted to recoil back into renouncing the need for friction.

I have been urging that we must conceive experiences as states or occurrences in which capacities that belong to spontaneity are in play in actualizations of receptivity. Experiences have their content by virtue of the fact that conceptual capacities are operative in them, and that means capacities that genuinely belong to the understanding: it is essential to their being the capacities they are that they can be exploited in active and potentially self-critical thinking. But when these capacities come into play in experience, the experiencing subject is passive, acted on by independent reality. When experience makes conceptual content available to one, that is itself one's sensibility in operation, not understanding putting a construction on some pre-conceptual deliverances of sensibility. At least with "outer experience", conceptual content is already borne by impressions that independent reality makes on one's senses. This allows us to acknowledge an external constraint on the freedom of spontaneity without falling into incoherence. So we can exorcize the spectre of frictionless spinning, which deprives us of anything recognizable as empirical content.

The position I am urging appeals to receptivity to ensure friction, like the Myth of the Given, but it is unlike the Myth of the Given in that it takes capacities of spontaneity to be in play all the way out to the ultimate grounds of empirical judgements. That is what enables us to reinstate friction without undermining the very idea of ultimate grounds, as the Myth of the Given does.

I have suggested (Lecture I, §6; Lecture III, §§6, 7) that there is a difficulty in the way of accepting this conception, one whose roots must lie deep. We can appreciate this by comparing the views of Davidson and Evans, as I did at the end of the last lecture. Both Davidson and Evans aim to accommodate the point of Kant's talk of spontaneity. Neither of them is tempted by a bald naturalism that would opt out of this area of philosophy altogether, by denying that the spontaneity of the understanding is *sui generis* in the way suggested by the link to the idea of freedom. But they do not so much as consider the possibility that conceptual capacities might be already operative in actualizations of sensibility. It is not that they argue that there is no such possibility; it simply does not figure in their thinking. And the result of this absence is that they are faced by the choice I have described. So long as a passive operation of conceptual capacities is not in view as an option, one cannot even try to cast experience as a rational constraint on empirical thinking without falling into the Myth of the Given. But that is to picture what are supposed to be ultimate justifications in a way that makes it unintelligible that they might exert rational influence at all. And now the only alternative is to stop trying to make out that empirical thinking is rationally constrained by experience. I have been urging that this is intolerable: within this conception of the possibilities, there is no way to credit thought with friction against independent reality, but we must have that if we are to have empirical content in our picture at all. There is no comfortable resting place here, and something deep must be influential in persuading Davidson and Evans, in their different ways, to the contrary.

Davidson embraces a version of one horn of this dilemma, the renunciation of rational control from independent reality. He thinks a merely causal, not rational, linkage between thinking and independent reality will do, as an interpretation of the idea that empirical content requires friction against something external to thinking. But it will not do. Thoughts without intuitions would be empty, as Kant almost says; and if we are to avert the threat of emptiness, we need to see intuitions as standing in rational relations to what we should think, not just in causal relations to what we do think. Otherwise the very idea of what we think goes missing. The items that were meant to be thoughts are still without intuitions in the relevant sense, and so empty. Davidson manages to be comfortable with his coherentism, which dispenses with rational constraint on thinking from outside it, only because he does not see that emptiness is the threat. He thinks the only point of wanting a rational connection between intuitions and thoughts is reassurance that we are justified in endorsing the thoughts, as if we could take it for granted in any case that they are thoughts, that they possess content. But if we do not let intuitions stand in rational relations to them, it is exactly their possession of content that is put in question. When Davidson argues that a body of beliefs is sure to be mostly true, he helps himself to the idea of a body of beliefs, a body of states that have content. And that means that, however successfully the argument might work on its own terms, it comes too late to neutralize the real problem for this horn of the dilemma.

Evans embraces a version of the other horn of the dilemma. Like Davidson, Evans takes experiences to be extra-conceptual (in themselves, we have to add in Evans's case). But unlike Davidson, Evans thinks experiences can both be extra-conceptual and constitute a rational constraint on the operations of spontaneity. He thinks judgements can be "based upon" experiences even though experiences are external to spontaneity. Evans is right, as against Davidson, in the implicit belief that motivates this view: if thoughts are not to be empty, that is, if they are to be thoughts at all, they must be rationally responsive to intuitions. But Evans's position cannot be made to cohere. Davidson is right, as against Evans, that if experiences are extra-conceptual, they cannot be what thoughts are rationally based on.

When Evans invokes non-conceptual content, that serves merely to mask the fact that by excluding experiences from the province of spontaneity, he has made it impossible to see how an experience could be someone's reason for a paradigmatic exercise of spontaneity such as a judgement.

So the situation is as follows. Given an assumption that Davidson and Evans share, they are confined to the pair of positions between which they choose. And each has what looks like a completely cogent argument against the other.

2.   Now I want to start uncovering the presumably deep-rooted mental block that produces this uncomfortable situation. This is a task I have had hanging over me since my first lecture.

Evans offers a number of grounds for holding that the content of our perceptual experiences is non-conceptual. One of them, which I discussed briefly at the end of my last lecture (§7), is the fact that we share perception with creatures that lack conceptual capacities, in the demanding sense Evans accepts: we share perception with creatures incapable of active and self-critical thinking.

I insisted that this point cannot dislodge the picture I have been urging, in which spontaneity permeates our perceptual dealings with the world, all the way out to the impressions of sensibility themselves. It cannot compel us to substitute Evans's picture, in which the spontaneity that is distinctive of our perceptual lives is extra to a part of the truth about us, our sensibility, that must be independent of spontaneity, since it is common to us and more primitive perceivers. What we share with dumb animals is perceptual sensitivity to features of the environment. We can say there are two species of that, one permeated by spontaneity and another independent of it. This accommodates the combination of likeness and difference between us and dumb animals, but not as Evans does, by factorizing the truth about us into independent components corresponding to the respects of likeness and difference. And it is just as well that this alternative is available, since Evans's factorizing move takes us back to the dilemma I began by elaborating.

So comparing ourselves with dumb animals cannot require us to separate sensibility from understanding, to exclude intuitions from the scope of spontaneity. But as I suggested at the end of my last lecture, the comparison can put us on the way to seeing why it is so easy to think the separation is compulsory. It can begin to explain why we tend to miss the very possibility that conceptual capacities, in the demanding sense, might be operative in actualizations of our sensibility.

Dumb animals are natural beings and no more. Their being is entirely contained within nature. In particular, their sensory interactions with their environment are natural goings-on. Now we are like dumb animals in that we, too, are perceptually sensitive to our environment. Sentience is a feature of their animal life, and it should be something animal in our case too. The sentience of dumb animals is one way in which their animal being, their purely natural being, actualizes itself, and our sentience, as an aspect of our animal life, should equally be one way in which our natural being actualizes itself. (Even if we are willing to suppose that our being is not purely natural, it is at least partly natural.)

But it can seem impossible to reconcile the fact that sentience belongs to nature with the thought that spontaneity might permeate our perceptual experience itself, the workings of our sensibility. How could the operations of a bit of mere nature be structured by spontaneity, the freedom that empowers us to take charge of our active thinking? If we see no possibility here, we are forced to suppose intuitions must be constituted independently of the understanding, by the senses responding naturally to the world's impacts on them. And then we are in the space of options that Davidson and Evans locate themselves in.

3. What is at work here is a conception of nature that can seem sheer common sense, though it was not always so; the conception I mean was made available only by a hard-won achievement of human thought at a specific time, the time of the rise of modern science. Modern science understands its subject matter in a way that threatens, at least, to leave it disenchanted, as Weber put the point in an image that has become a commonplace. The image marks a contrast between two kinds of intelligibility: the kind that is sought by (as we call it) natural science, and the kind we find in something when we place it in relation to other occupants of "the logical space of reasons", to repeat a suggestive phrase from Wilfrid Sellars.[1] If we identify nature with what

---

1. See Lecture I, §2. Of course depictions of nature are linked by relations of justification. The point is that there are no such linkages in what is depicted.

natural science aims to make comprehensible, we threaten, at least, to empty it of meaning. By way of compensation, so to speak, we see it as the home of a perhaps inexhaustible supply of intelligibility of the other kind, the kind we find in a phenomenon when we see it as governed by natural law.[2] It was an achievement of modern thought when this second kind of intelligibility was clearly marked off from the first. In a common mediaeval outlook, what we now see as the subject matter of natural science was conceived as filled with meaning, as if all of nature were a book of lessons for us; and it is a mark of intellectual progress that educated people cannot now take that idea seriously, except perhaps in some symbolic role.[3]

Now if we conceive the natural as the realm of law, demarcating it by the way its proper mode of intelligibility contrasts with the intelligibility that belongs to inhabitants of the space of reasons, we put at risk the very idea that spontaneity might characterize the workings of our sensibility as such. The faculty of spontaneity is the understanding, our capacity to recognize and bring into being the kind of intelligibility that is proper to meaning. We disclose this kind of intelligibil-

2. The crucial contrast here is between the internal organization of the space of reasons and the internal organization of nature, on a conception that modern natural science invites us to hold. This contrast echoes the Kantian contrast between the realm of freedom and the realm of nature. It sets the agenda for much post-Kantian philosophy, and it is central to Sellars's thinking.

In the text, I avoid a gloss that some of Sellars's followers put on what stands opposed to the space of reasons: Rorty, for instance, speaks on Sellars's behalf of a distinction between the logical space of reasons and the logical space of "causal relations to objects" (*Philosophy and the Mirror of Nature* [Princeton University Press, Princeton, 1979], p. 157). I think this reflects a disputable picture of how modern natural science most fundamentally organizes its subject matter: one that Russell protested against in his essay "On the Notion of Cause", in Bertrand Russell, *Mysticism and Logic* (George Allen and Unwin, London, 1917), pp. 132–51 in the 1963 paperback edition. Russell suggested that the idea of causation should be replaced, in the role of basic organizing principle for the world as viewed by natural science, with something like the idea of law-governed processes. So the right contrast for the space of reasons is not the space of causes but, as in my text, the realm of law. (This leaves untouched the fact, which I exploited in my Sellarsian explanation of why the Myth of the Given is a myth [Lecture I, §3], that a *merely* causal relation cannot do duty for a justificatory relation.)

It is not just that this reading of the contrast is wrong about science; it is also disputable in its implication that the idea of causal connections is restricted to thinking that is *not* framed by the space of reasons. On my reading, the contrast leaves it possible for an area of discourse to be in the logical space of causal relations to objects without thereby being shown not to be in the logical space of reasons. Contrary to what Rorty's contrast implies, reasons might *be* causes.

3. See chap. 1 of Charles Taylor, *Hegel* (Cambridge University Press, Cambridge, 1975).

ity by placing things in a logical space that is *sui generis,* by comparison with the realm of law. But sensibility, as I said, is part of our nature, part of what we share with mere animals. If that means its operations are what they are by virtue of their positions in the realm of law, it can seem incoherent to suppose that they might be shaped by concepts. That would imply that their being what they are is also a matter of positions in the contrasting logical space.

Moreover, we had better not aspire to put the lost enchantment back into the merely natural world. According to the picture I have been recommending, our sensibility yields states and occurrences with conceptual content. That enables us to see an experiencing subject as open to facts. The conceptual sphere does not exclude the world we experience. To put it another way: what we experience is not external to the realm of the kind of intelligibility that is proper to meaning. (See Lecture II.) But in so far as what we experience includes merely natural facts, this can look like a call to regress into a pre-scientific superstition, a crazily nostalgic attempt to re-enchant the natural world.

Let me stress that the issue here cannot be confined to our understanding of one another, something that must involve "space of reasons" intelligibility. If we acquiesce in the disenchantment of nature, if we let meaning be expelled from what I have been calling "the merely natural", we shall certainly need to work at bringing meaning back into the picture when we come to consider human interactions. But it is not just in our comprehension of language, and in our making sense of one another in the other ways that belong with that, that conceptual capacities are operative. I have urged that conceptual capacities, capacities for the kind of understanding whose correlate is the kind of intelligibility that is proper to meaning, are operative also in our perception of the world apart from human beings. The question is how we can take that view without offering to reinstate the idea that the movement of the planets, or the fall of a sparrow, is rightly approached in the sort of way we approach a text or an utterance or some other kind of action.

4. As I remarked (§1), neither Evans nor Davidson is tempted by what I called "a bald naturalism": a style of thinking that would simply dismiss the fuss I have made over spontaneity. In effect, they hold that we cannot understand the idea of spontaneity naturalistically, if

"naturalistically" is used in accordance with the conception of nature I have been describing.

That conception obviously raises a question about the status of spontaneity, and I am going to distinguish three styles of response.

First, there is bald naturalism, which aims to domesticate conceptual capacities within nature conceived as the realm of law. This approach need not deny that conceptual capacities belong to a faculty of spontaneity, a faculty that empowers us to take charge of our lives. But the idea is that if there is any truth in talk of spontaneity, it must be capturable in terms whose fundamental role lies in displaying the position of things in nature so conceived. Perhaps we should grant that the relations that constitute the structure of the space of reasons, relations of justification and the like, are not visibly there, as such, in nature as the paradigmatic natural sciences depict it. But according to this approach, we can reconstruct the structure of the space of reasons out of conceptual materials that already belong in a natural-scientific depiction of nature. And then modes of thought that place their subject matter in the space of reasons, for instance, reflection that brings spontaneity into view as such, can after all count as natural-scientific too. No doubt they are not paradigmatically natural-scientific, but only because it takes work to show how their distinctive concepts serve to place things in nature.

In the most straightforward version of this approach, the task is to *reduce* the structure of the space of reasons to something that is already unproblematically natural on the relevant conception. But I do not want to limit the approach to such reductionism. What matters is just that ideas whose primary home is the space of reasons are depicted as, after all, serving to place things in nature in the relevant sense. On these lines, we can equate nature with the realm of law, but deny that nature so conceived is utterly disenchanted. The claim is that, even so conceived, naturalness does not exclude the intelligibility that belongs to meaning.

Opponents of this kind of naturalism hold that the contrast that poses our difficulties, the contrast of logical spaces, is genuine. The structure of the space of reasons stubbornly resists being appropriated within a naturalism that conceives nature as the realm of law. So if something's way of being natural is its position in the realm of law, what is natural, as such, cannot be anything but disenchanted. I want to distinguish two ways in which this can be elaborated: the second and third of the three styles of response to the question about the status of spontaneity.

One is the way of thinking that I have recommended. Even though the logical space that is the home of the idea of spontaneity cannot be aligned with the logical space that is the home of ideas of what is natural in the relevant sense, conceptual powers are nevertheless operative in the workings of our sensibility, in actualizations of our animal nature, as such. As I have acknowledged, this can seem to express a nostalgia for a pre-scientific world-view, a call for a re-enchantment of nature. And certainly it requires that we resist the characteristically modern conception according to which something's way of being natural is its position in the realm of law.

The third approach diverges in just that respect. What I have in mind here is a way of thinking that is almost explicit in Davidson.

Davidson opposes a baldly naturalistic domestication of, in effect, the idea of spontaneity. He urges that concepts of "propositional attitudes" make sense only as governed by a "constitutive ideal of rationality".[4] In the terms I have been using, the claim comes to this: the fundamental point of those concepts is to subserve the kind of intelligibility that is proper to meaning, the kind of intelligibility we find in something when we place it in the space of reasons.[5] On that basis Davidson argues that we cannot reduce those concepts to concepts governed by a different "constitutive ideal", or, to put it in Sellarsian terms, concepts whose home is a different logical space. Specifically, and again putting it in the terms I have been using: the intellectual role of those spontaneity-related concepts cannot be duplicated in terms of concepts whose fundamental point is to place things in the realm of law.

So far, this is something like common ground for opposition to bald naturalism. What is distinctive about Davidson's approach is an ontological claim: the very things that satisfy the *sui generis* concepts, the concepts whose applicability signals the presence of spontaneity, are

4. See "Mental Events", in his *Essays on Actions and Events* (Clarendon Press, Oxford, 1980), pp. 207–25; especially pp. 221–3.

5. I am taking Davidson's thought to concern what I have been calling, in Kantian terms, "the spontaneity of the understanding". I base this on the obvious convergence between Davidson's invocation of "the constitutive ideal of rationality", to explain what is special about the conceptual apparatus he is concerned with, and the Sellarsian image of the space of reasons, which I have exploited to gloss Kant's idea of spontaneity.

already in principle available to an investigation whose concern is the realm of law. The constitutive focus on the two kinds of intelligibility separates two batches of conceptual equipment, but it does not separate their subject matter. Davidson makes this ontological claim specifically about events: every event, even those that fall under the concepts that subserve "space of reasons" intelligibility, can in principle be made intelligible in terms of the operations of natural law.

Davidson's purpose here is to make room for holding that the satisfiers of the *sui generis* concepts stand in causal relations, to one another and to other things, without threatening the thesis that causal relations hold only between occupants of the realm of law. Given that thesis, satisfiers of the *sui generis* concepts can be causally linked only if they are also occupants of the realm of law; and Davidson says they are, even though they are not revealed as such by their satisfaction of the *sui generis* concepts.[6] But we come closer to my concerns if we consider a counterpart purpose, in which the thesis that causal relations hold between occupants of the realm of law is replaced by the thesis that to be natural is to have a position in the realm of law. In this context, the point of the ontological claim would be to make room for holding that the satisfiers of the *sui generis* concepts are items in nature, even though their satisfaction of the *sui generis* concepts does not disclose their positions in the realm of law.

I do not (here at least) want to question the truth of the ontological claim. I just want to note how this approach excludes the conception of experience I have recommended. So long as we do not dispute that something's way of being natural is its place in the realm of law, the fact that sensibility is natural works together with the fact that the concept of spontaneity functions in the space of reasons, so as to rule out the possibility that spontaneity might permeate the operations of sensibility as such—at least if we set our faces against a baldly naturalistic integration of the space of reasons within the realm of law. According to the ontological thesis, the items that instantiate the *sui generis* spontaneity-related concepts have a location in the realm of law. But the concepts are *sui generis* precisely in that it is not by virtue of their location in the realm of law that things instantiate those con-

---

6. So a reason can be a cause, though it is not by virtue of its rational relationships that it stands in causal relations.

cepts. So if we go on equating something's place in nature with its location in the realm of law, we are debarred from holding that an experience has its conceptual content precisely as whatever natural phenomenon it is.

It is common ground that impressions of sense are manifestations of sentient life and hence natural phenomena. The strategy I am considering ensures that it cannot be as the natural phenomena they are that impressions are characterizable in terms of spontaneity. Their place in nature is their location in the quite different structure of the realm of law. So actualizations of a natural capacity of sensibility, considered as such, can only be intuitions on a dualistic conception: products of disenchanted nature operating independently of spontaneity. And that locks us into the framework of possibilities that Davidson and Evans move in. I have argued that this is intolerable.

5.   I have distinguished three conceptions of how spontaneity relates to nature. If one is intolerable, we are left with the other two.

One alternative is to revert to bald naturalism. It should be beginning to emerge how that can be attractive, not just because it conforms to a scientism that shapes much contemporary thinking, but also because it offers what can seem to be the only escape from a philosophical impasse. I have been exploiting the appearance of a forced choice between the Myth of the Given and a coherentism that renounces external rational constraints on thinking. A tempting diagnosis of this philosophical difficulty traces it to the idea that we cannot have thought in our picture unless we secure an application for *sui generis* notions of rational justification and the like: notions that function in their own logical space, which is alien to the structure of the realm of law. If we can discard that idea, this whole sea of philosophy can subside. Bald naturalism tells us not to go on being nagged by these anxieties; instead we should set about saving whatever is worth saving in our conception of ourselves, by reconstructing it in terms of conceptual equipment that is already unproblematically naturalistic.

The only other option is to see our way to accepting what I have been urging: that a concept of spontaneity that is *sui generis*, in the way that threatens to pose the problem, can nevertheless enter into characterizing states and occurrences of sensibility as such—as the actualizations of our nature that they are. Bald naturalism blames the trouble on the idea that spontaneity is *sui generis,* but that is not the only possible target of suspicion. There is also the naturalism that equates nature with the realm of law. We need that background to make it appear that we can acknowledge a *sui generis* character for spontaneity only by locating ourselves in the framework of possibilities that Davidson and Evans move in.

It would be a cheat, a merely verbal manoeuvre, to object that naturalism about nature cannot be open to question. If we can rethink our conception of nature so as to make room for spontaneity, even though we deny that spontaneity is capturable by the resources of bald naturalism, we shall by the same token be rethinking our conception of what it takes for a position to deserve to be called "naturalism".

6. The rethinking requires a different conception of actualizations of our nature. We need to bring responsiveness to meaning back into the operations of our natural sentient capacities as such, even while we insist that responsiveness to meaning cannot be captured in naturalistic terms, so long as "naturalistic" is glossed in terms of the realm of law.

It can easily seem that there is no space to move here. Setting our faces against bald naturalism, we are committed to holding that the idea of knowing one's way about in the space of reasons, the idea of responsiveness to rational relationships, cannot be reconstructed out of materials that are naturalistic in the sense that we are trying to supersede. This can easily seem to commit us to a rampant platonism.[7] It can seem that we must be picturing the space of reasons as an autonomous structure—autonomous in that it is constituted independently of anything specifically human, since what is specifically human is surely natural (the idea of the human is the idea of what pertains to a certain species of animals), and we are refusing to naturalize the requirements of reason. But human minds must somehow be able to latch on to this inhuman structure. So it looks as if we are picturing human beings as partly in nature and partly outside it. What

---

7. I use the lower case to stress that I mean the label "platonism" in something like the sense that it bears in the philosophy of mathematics. I imply no connection with Plato, beyond the general resemblance in imagery that underlies the use of the term in the mathematical context. I shall say something against connecting the position with Plato in Lecture VI (§1).

we wanted was a naturalism that makes room for meaning, but this is no kind of naturalism at all.[8]

But there is a way out. We get this threat of supernaturalism if we interpret the claim that the space of reasons is *sui generis* as a refusal to naturalize the requirements of reason. But what became available at the time of the modern scientific revolution is a clear-cut understanding of the realm of law, and we can refuse to equate that with a new clarity *about nature*. This makes room for us to insist that spontaneity is *sui generis,* in comparison with the realm of law, without falling into the supernaturalism of rampant platonism.

To reassure ourselves that our responsiveness to reasons is not supernatural, we should dwell on the thought that it is our lives that are shaped by spontaneity, patterned in ways that come into view only within an inquiry framed by what Davidson calls "the constitutive ideal of rationality". Exercises of spontaneity belong to our mode of living. And our mode of living is our way of actualizing ourselves as animals. So we can rephrase the thought by saying: exercises of spontaneity belong to our way of actualizing ourselves as animals. This removes any need to try to see ourselves as peculiarly bifurcated, with a foothold in the animal kingdom and a mysterious separate involvement in an extra-natural world of rational connections.

This does not require that we blur the contrast between the space of reasons and the realm of law. To see exercises of spontaneity as natural, we do not need to integrate spontaneity-related concepts into the structure of the realm of law; we need to stress their role in capturing patterns in a way of living. Of course there would be no contrast here if the idea of lives and their shapes belonged exclusively or primarily within the logical space of the realm of law, but there is no reason to suppose that that is so.

7. The best way I know to work into this different conception of what is natural is by reflecting on Aristotle's ethics.

For Aristotle, virtue of character in the strict sense is distinct from a merely habitual propensity to act in ways that match what virtue

---

8. Davidsonian monism is no help here. It is no comfort to reflect that all the items we speak of figure in nature, if we are still stuck with truths about some of them that look supernatural. The problem posed by the contrast between the space of reasons and the realm of law, in the context of a naturalism that conceives nature as the realm of law, is not ontological but ideological.

would require.[9] Virtue of character properly so called includes a specifically shaped state of the practical intellect: "practical wisdom", in the standard English translation.[10] This is a responsiveness to some of the demands of reason (though that is not Aristotle's way of putting it). The picture is that ethics involves requirements of reason that are there whether we know it or not, and our eyes are opened to them by the acquisition of "practical wisdom". So "practical wisdom" is the right sort of thing to serve as a model for the understanding, the faculty that enables us to recognize and create the kind of intelligibility that is a matter of placement in the space of reasons.

Modern readers often credit Aristotle with aiming to construct the requirements of ethics out of independent facts about human nature.[11] This is to attribute to Aristotle a scheme for a naturalistic foundation for ethics, with nature playing an archaic version of the role played by disenchanted nature in modern naturalistic ethics. Given the prevalence of readings on these lines, it is difficult to get Aristotle's picture into view in the way I want, as a model for a radical rethinking of nature. Read like this, Aristotle's picture of ethical understanding counts rather as a peculiar sort of bald naturalism.

But I think this kind of reading is a historical monstrosity. This reassuring role for nature can seem to make sense only as a response to a kind of anxiety about the status of reasons—ethical reasons in this case—that is foreign to Aristotle. What underlies the anxiety is precisely the conception of nature that I have represented as distinctively modern. When the kind of intelligibility that belongs to the realm of law is clearly demarcated, the other side of the coin is an appreciation that the structure of the space of reasons is special by comparison. And there is an intelligible tendency to set up the study of nature as the very exemplar of what it is to investigate how things are. Thus, when nature threatens to extrude the space of reasons, philosophical worries are generated about the status of rational connections, as something that we can be right or wrong about. One response to these

---

9. *Nicomachean Ethics* 6.13.

10. That of Sir David Ross, *The Nicomachean Ethics of Aristotle* (Oxford University Press, London, 1954). Terence Irwin's translation (Hackett, Indianapolis, 1985) has "intelligence". (Aristotle's word is *"phronēsis"*.)

11. For a reading of this sort, see chap. 3 of Bernard Williams, *Ethics and the Limits of Philosophy* (Harvard University Press, Cambridge, Mass., 1985). There is something similar in chap. 9 of Alasdair MacIntyre, *After Virtue* (Duckworth, London, 1981).

worries is to resist the extrusion in the manner of bald naturalism, leaving the conception of nature unquestioned but insisting that after all the putative rational requirements that we want to defend can be founded on, or constructed out of, independent facts of nature. If I am right about the genesis of the worries, it must be anachronistic to read something like this into Aristotle.[12]

If a person conceives her practical situation in terms provided for her by a specific ethical outlook, that will present her with certain apparent reasons for acting. On a better understanding of Aristotle's picture, the only standpoint at which she can address the question whether those reasons are genuine is one that she occupies precisely because she has a specific ethical outlook. That is a standpoint from which those seeming requirements are in view as such, not a foundational standpoint at which she might try to reconstruct the demandingness of those requirements from scratch, out of materials from an independent description of nature.

Aristotle scarcely even considers that doubts might arise about the specific ethical outlook he takes for granted.[13] On the reading I am attacking, this shows confidence that he could validate the demands of that ethical outlook by appealing to nature. But I think it shows his immunity to our metaphysical anxieties; he is simply not vulnerable to the sort of worries such a conception would address. It may also show

12. Compare the worries of epistemology as we know it, which are widely acknowledged to be distinctively modern. At root the point is the same. Sellars traced the anxieties of modern epistemology to the fact that the idea of knowledge is the idea of a position in a justificatory network; this was the context in which he mentioned the space of reasons. Anxiety about knowledge, of the familiar modern kind, results when that fact is juxtaposed with the threatened extrusion of the space of reasons from nature. It is not that the idea of knowledge as a position in the space of reasons was new—as if it was not until around the seventeenth century that people hit on the thought that becomes so pregnant in modern epistemology, that knowledge is a normative status. But before the modern era, the idea that knowledge is a normative status was not felt to stand in tension with, say, the idea that knowledge might be the result of an exercise of natural powers. A naturalism that responds to this tension by setting out to ground the normative connections that constitute the space of reasons, after all, within nature, conceived in the very way that threatens the tension, is quite different from a naturalism like Aristotle's, which never feels a tension here, and has no need for imagery of grounding or foundations. (I discuss this further in "Two Sorts of Naturalism", forthcoming in a Festschrift for Philippa Foot edited by Rosalind Hursthouse and Gavin Lawrence.)

13. He shows no interest in addressing such doubts; he stipulates that he is addressing only people in whom that ethical outlook has been inculcated (*Nicomachean Ethics* 1.4, 1095b4–6).

something less interesting: a tendency to smugness, for which we can easily correct.

Like any thinking, ethical thinking is under a standing obligation to reflect about and criticize the standards by which, at any time, it takes itself to be governed. (For this point applied to empirical thinking, see Lecture I, §5; Lecture II, §6.) Aristotle may be less than duly sensitive to the obligation in the case of ethics, but it is implicit in the very idea of a shaping of the intellect, and that is what "practical wisdom" is. Now it is a key point that for such reflective criticism, the appropriate image is Neurath's, in which a sailor overhauls his ship while it is afloat. This does not mean such reflection cannot be radical. One can find oneself called on to jettison parts of one's inherited ways of think-ing; and, though this is harder to place in Neurath's image, weaknesses that reflection discloses in inherited ways of thinking can dictate the formation of new concepts and conceptions. But the essen-tial thing is that one can reflect only from the midst of the way of thinking one is reflecting about. So if one entertains the thought that bringing one's current ethical outlook to bear on a situation alerts one to demands that are real, one need not be envisaging any sort of vali-dation other than a Neurathian one. The thought is that this applica-tion of one's ethical outlook would stand up to the outlook's own reflective self-scrutiny.

No doubt the self-scrutiny of an ethical outlook can take note of independent facts about the layout of the realm of law, when they are relevant. But that is not to say that we can reconstruct the idea of genuine ethical demands on us from materials that are naturalistic in that sense. The idea of getting things right in one's ethical thinking has a certain autonomy; we need not conceive it as pointing outside the sphere of ethical thinking itself.

Of course the fact that a thought passes muster so far, in reflective examination of a way of thinking from within, does not guarantee that it is acceptable. The way of thinking, including its implicit stan-dards for self-scrutiny, may have hitherto unnoticed defects, such as parochialism or reliance on bad prejudice.[14] But we can only make honest efforts to eliminate the sorts of defects we know our thinking risks, and perhaps to expand our conception of ways things might go

---

14. "Bad prejudice" is not a pleonasm. For the idea that prejudice, so far from being necessarily a bad thing, is a condition for understanding, see Gadamer, *Truth and Method*, pp. 277–85.

wrong, so as to be on guard against other potential sources of error. The best we can achieve is always to some extent provisional and inconclusive, but that is no reason to succumb to the fantasy of an external validation.

If we enrich it, then, to include a proper place for reflectiveness, Aristotle's picture can be put like this. The ethical is a domain of rational requirements, which are there in any case, whether or not we are responsive to them. We are alerted to these demands by acquiring appropriate conceptual capacities. When a decent upbringing initiates us into the relevant way of thinking, our eyes are opened to the very existence of this tract of the space of reasons. Thereafter our appreciation of its detailed layout is indefinitely subject to refinement, in reflective scrutiny of our ethical thinking. We can so much as understand, let alone seek to justify, the thought that reason makes these demands on us only at a standpoint within a system of concepts and conceptions that enables us to think about such demands, that is, only at a standpoint from which demands of this kind seem to be in view.

In my second lecture (§4), I talked about a sideways-on picture of understanding and the world, a picture that places reality outside a boundary enclosing the conceptual. A scientistic naturalism encourages a version of that picture, in which what is outside the boundary is the realm of law. And if conceiving reality as the realm of law leaves it disenchanted, what is outside the boundary can contain no demands of reason or the like. Hence the very idea of sensitivity to real demands of reason looks spooky, unless we can reconstruct it from materials that are naturalistic in the relevant sense.

This picture tries to cast the realm of law in a naturalized version of the role Kant gives to the supersensible. But this is not how to correct what is unsatisfactory in Kant's thinking about the supersensible: keeping its basic shape, and merely naturalizing what lies outside the conceptual. This way we lose the insight that Kant spoils by putting it in the framework of his talk of the supersensible; we lose what we discern through obstacles in Kant, a way to make sense of empirical thinking as rationally answerable to the reality that it aims to be about. And if we lose that, we put in question the very possibility of empirical thinking. This kind of naturalism tends to represent itself as educated common sense, but it is really only primitive metaphysics.

The way to correct what is unsatisfactory in Kant's thinking about the supersensible is rather to embrace the Hegelian image in which the conceptual is unbounded on the outside. I have urged (Lecture II, §8) that that is precisely not threatening to common sense, to the conviction that the world is independent of our thinking.

In any case, this pseudo-Kantian naturalism has nothing to do with Aristotle. It responds to a philosophical anxiety whose sources post-date Aristotle by a couple of millennia. In Aristotle's conception, the thought that the demands of ethics are real is not a projection from, or construction out of, facts that could be in view independently of the viewer's participation in ethical life and thought, so that they would be available to a sideways-on investigation of how ethical life and thought are related to the natural context in which they take place.[15] The fact that the demands bear on us is just, irreducibly, itself. It is something that comes into view only within the kind of thinking that conceives practical situations in terms of such demands.

In crediting this self-standing character to ethical demands and thoughts about them, the outlook I am attributing to Aristotle looks like a kind of platonism. But it is not what I called "rampant platonism" (§6). We fall into rampant platonism if we take it that the structure of the space of reasons is *sui generis,* but leave in place the equation of nature with the realm of law. That makes our capacity to respond to reasons look like an occult power, something extra to our being the kind of animals we are, which is our situation in nature. But in Aristotle's conception, the rational demands of ethics are not alien to the contingencies of our life as human beings. Even though it is not supposed that we could explain the relevant idea of demandingness in terms of independently intelligible facts about human beings, still ordinary upbringing can shape the actions and thoughts of human beings in a way that brings these demands into view.

15. According to the kind of reading I am disputing, Aristotle attributes this foundational status to facts about what it would be for a human life to be fulfilling. But the notion of a fulfilling life figures in Aristotle in a way that is already ethical through and through. The relevant motivations are shaped by concerns that are already ethical. (See *Nicomachean Ethics* 1.7, 1098a16–17.)

A different candidate to ground demands of reason is social interactions, conceived as describable without presupposing a context structured by just such demands, those ones or others that would replace them in our thinking after better reflection. I shall say something about this sort of position in the next lecture.

To focus the way this conception can serve as a model for us, consider the notion of *second nature*. The notion is all but explicit in Aristotle's account of how ethical character is formed.[16] Since ethical character includes dispositions of the practical intellect, part of what happens when character is formed is that the practical intellect acquires a determinate shape. So practical wisdom is second nature to its possessors. I have been insisting that for Aristotle the rational demands of ethics are autonomous; we are not to feel compelled to validate them from outside an already ethical way of thinking. But this autonomy does not distance the demands from anything specifically human, as in rampant platonism. They are essentially within reach of human beings. We cannot credit appreciation of them to human nature as it figures in a naturalism of disenchanted nature, because disenchanted nature does not embrace the space of reasons. But human beings are intelligibly initiated into this stretch of the space of reasons by ethical upbringing, which instils the appropriate shape into their lives. The resulting habits of thought and action are second nature.

This should defuse the fear of supernaturalism. Second nature could not float free of potentialities that belong to a normal human organism. This gives human reason enough of a foothold in the realm of law to satisfy any proper respect for modern natural science.

The point is clearly not restricted to ethics. Moulding ethical character, which includes imposing a specific shape on the practical intellect, is a particular case of a general phenomenon: initiation into conceptual capacities, which include responsiveness to other rational demands besides those of ethics. Such initiation is a normal part of what it is for a human being to come to maturity, and that is why, although the structure of the space of reasons is alien to the layout of nature conceived as the realm of law, it does not take on the remoteness from the human that rampant platonism envisages. If we generalize the way Aristotle conceives the moulding of ethical character, we arrive at the notion of having one's eyes opened to reasons at large by acquiring a second nature. I cannot think of a good short English expression for this, but it is what figures in German philosophy as *Bildung*.

16. See Book 2 of *Nicomachean Ethics*. For an excellent discussion, see M. F. Burnyeat, "Aristotle on Learning to Be Good", in Amélie Oksenberg Rorty, ed., *Essays on Aristotle's Ethics* (University of California Press, Berkeley, 1980), pp. 69–92.

8. In these lectures so far, I have taken perceptual experience as an object lesson, in order to describe a kind of predicament we tend to fall into when we think about aspects of the human condition. I promised to try to uncover a deep-rooted but, as we can come to realize, non-compulsory influence on our thinking that accounts for the predicament. I have now introduced my candidate for that role: the naturalism that leaves nature disenchanted. We tend to be forgetful of the very idea of second nature. I am suggesting that if we can recapture that idea, we can keep nature as it were partially enchanted, but without lapsing into pre-scientific superstition or a rampant platonism. This makes room for a conception of experience that is immune to the philosophical pitfalls I have described.

We need to recapture the Aristotelian idea that a normal mature human being is a rational animal, but without losing the Kantian idea that rationality operates freely in its own sphere. The Kantian idea is reflected in the contrast between the organization of the space of reasons and the structure of the realm of natural law. Modern naturalism is forgetful of second nature; if we try to preserve the Kantian thought that reason is autonomous within the framework of that kind of naturalism, we disconnect our rationality from our animal being, which is what gives us our foothold in nature. The upshot is a temptation to drop the Kantian thought and naturalize our rationality in the manner of bald naturalism. I have described that as opting out of this region of philosophy. If we want to combine avoiding the problems with a more substantial acknowledgement of them, we need to see ourselves as animals whose natural being is permeated with rationality, even though rationality is appropriately conceived in Kantian terms.

What I am suggesting could be put in terms of a task for philosophy, to effect a reconciliation. That may make it seem that I am holding out for a conception of philosophy that Richard Rorty has tried to represent as outmoded.[17] But I do not feel threatened by Rorty's objections, for two reasons. First, the need for reconciliation that I envisage arises at a particular period in the history of ideas, one in which our thought tends, intelligibly, to be dominated by a naturalism that constricts the idea of nature. My suggestion does not involve an idea that Rorty persuasively attacks, that there is a timeless set of obligations for philosophy. Second, the task I envisage is not the one that

17. See *Philosophy and the Mirror of Nature*.

Rorty deconstructs, the reconciling of subject and object, or thought and world. My proposal is that we should try to reconcile reason and nature, and the point of doing that is to attain something Rorty himself aspires to, a frame of mind in which we would no longer seem to be faced with problems that call on philosophy to bring subject and object back together. If we could achieve a firm hold on a naturalism of second nature, a hold that could not be shaken by any temptation to lapse back into ordinary philosophical worries about how to place minds in the world, that would not be to have produced a bit of constructive philosophy of the sort Rorty aims to supersede. In Wittgenstein's poignant phrase, it would be to have achieved "the discovery that gives philosophy peace".[18]

18. *Philosophical Investigations,* §133.

Action, Meaning, and the Self

1. I have been discussing how to accommodate the point of Kant's remark "Thoughts without content are empty, intuitions without concepts are blind". According to the view I have recommended, conceptual capacities are in one sense non-natural: we cannot capture what it is to possess and employ the understanding, a faculty of spontaneity, in terms of concepts that place things in the realm of law. But spontaneity is inextricably implicated in receptivity, and our capacities of receptivity, our senses, are part of our nature. So in another sense conceptual capacities must be natural. Otherwise, if we acknowledge that the idea of spontaneity works in a *sui generis* conceptual framework, we commit ourselves to picturing the deliverances of sensibility as intuitions without concepts. That leaves us oscillating between, on the one hand, a coherentism that makes no sense of how thoughts could fail to be empty and, on the other hand, a vain appeal to bare presences. This awkward choice looks like the only alternative to a bald naturalism, a way of thinking that would not even let these philosophical difficulties get started.

It can be hard to see any way out, short of denying that the idea of spontaneity works in a *sui generis* conceptual framework. Sensibility is one of our natural powers. How can spontaneity be non-natural, in any sense, and yet be inextricably implicated when our sensory capacities are activated?

But in my last lecture I suggested that the difficulty is illusory. Our nature is largely second nature, and our second nature is the way it is not just because of the potentialities we were born with, but also because of our upbringing, our *Bildung*. Given the notion of second nature, we can say that the way our lives are shaped by reason is natural, even while we deny that the structure of the space of reasons can be integrated into the layout of the realm of law. This is the partial re-enchantment of nature that I spoke of.

This is not to lapse into a rampant platonism. In rampant platonism, the structure of the space of reasons, the structure in which we place things when we find meaning in them, is simply extra-natural. Our capacity to resonate to that structure has to be mysterious; it is as if we had a foothold outside the animal kingdom, in a splendidly non-human realm of ideality. But thanks to the notion of second nature, there is no whiff of that here. Our *Bildung* actualizes some of the potentialities we are born with; we do not have to suppose it introduces a non-animal ingredient into our constitution. And although the structure of the space of reasons cannot be reconstructed out of facts about our involvement in the realm of law, it can be the framework within which meaning comes into view only because our eyes can be opened to it by *Bildung*, which is an element in the normal coming to maturity of the kind of animals we are. Meaning is not a mysterious gift from outside nature.

These considerations should undermine one attraction of what I have called "bald naturalism". If we refuse to naturalize spontaneity within the realm of law, it can seem that we are trapped in the philosophical impasse I began with, the forced choice between coherentism and the Myth of the Given. But the refusal to naturalize spontaneity does not generate the impasse all by itself. There is also the naturalism that equates disclosing how something fits into nature with placing it in the realm of law. Apart from that naturalism, we would not have to conclude that since the operations of sensibility are, as such, natural goings-on, considered in themselves they can only be intuitions without concepts. So once the idea of second nature is in place, the impasse need no longer look like a recommendation for bald naturalism. We can claim both that the notion of spontaneity functions in a conceptual framework that is alien to the structure of the realm of law, and that it is needed for describing actualizations of natural powers as such. If nature had to be identified with the realm of law, that combination would be incoherent. But once we allow that natural powers can include powers of second nature, the threat of incoherence disappears.[1]

1. Perhaps "bald naturalism" is not a good label for a position adopted on the grounds I consider here. Someone who thought on these lines would be alive to the case for supposing

2. In order to introduce the attractions of a relaxed naturalism, I have exploited philosophical difficulties about perceptual experience. But this focus was not essential; the difficulties exemplify a type.

I have stressed that experience is passive (Lecture I, §5). In that respect the position I have been recommending coincides with the Myth of the Given. The passivity of experience allows us to acknowledge an external control over our empirical thinking, if passivity will cohere with an involvement of spontaneity. But it is difficult to see how the combination is possible; my last lecture aimed to uncover the source of the difficulty.

Now the difficulty concerns not the passivity of experience as such, but its naturalness. The problem is that operations of sensibility are actualizations of a potentiality that is part of our nature. When we take sensing to be a way of being acted on by the world, we are thinking of it as a natural phenomenon, and then we have trouble seeing how a *sui generis* spontaneity could be anything but externally related to it. But passivity is not part of the very idea of what it is for a natural potentiality to be actualized. So we should be able to construct a train of thought about actualization of active natural powers, duplicating the difficulties I have exploited in the case of passive natural powers.

Consider, say, the capacity to move one of one's limbs, as it appears in the framework of a naturalism that leaves nature disenchanted. I have been discussing the way such a naturalism distances a *sui generis* spontaneity from a subject's enjoyment of sensibility, given that sensibility is a natural capacity. In a parallel way, it distances a *sui generis* spontaneity from exercises of the power to move one's limbs, given that that power is natural. The result is a similar difficulty in our reflection about bodily action.

Kant says "Thoughts without content are empty, intuitions without concepts are blind". Similarly, intentions without overt activity are idle, and movements of limbs without concepts are mere happenings, not expressions of agency. I have urged that we can accommodate the point of Kant's remark if we accept this claim: experiences are actualizations of our sentient nature in which conceptual capacities are in-

---

that the structure of the space of reasons is *sui generis*, alien to the structure of the realm of law, but would suppose that all the same it cannot be so, on pain of philosophical impasse. Here naturalism is motivated by a reflective avoidance of unprofitable philosophy. My label "bald naturalism" better fits an unreflective scientism: not a principled avoidance of unprofitable philosophy, but a way of thinking that does not explicitly appreciate what threatens to lead to it. Perhaps people who think like this should be congratulated on their immunity, but it ought not to be mistaken for an intellectual achievement.

extricably implicated. The parallel is this: intentional bodily actions are actualizations of our active nature in which conceptual capacities are inextricably implicated.

But just as a naturalism that disenchants nature excludes the understanding from actualizations of our sentient nature as such, so here it excludes our mastery of concepts from what ought to be recognizable as actualizations of our active nature as such: goings-on in which natural things, like limbs, do natural things, like moving. And this exclusion has characteristic results when we reflect about action. Shut out from the realm of happenings constituted by movements of ordinary natural stuff, the spontaneity of agency typically tries to take up residence in a specially conceived interior realm. This relocation of spontaneity may be seen as a renunciation of naturalism, or the interior realm may be conceived as a special region of the natural world.[2] Either way, this style of thinking gives spontaneity a role in bodily action only in the guise of inner items, pictured as initiating bodily goings-on from within, and taken on that ground to be recognizable as intentions or volitions. The bodily goings-on themselves are events in nature; in the context of a disenchanting naturalism, combined with a conviction that the conceptual is *sui generis,* that means that they cannot be imbued with intentionality.[3] They are actualizations of natural powers, and for that reason they can figure in this style of thinking only as mere happenings. (No doubt they can be singled out from mere happenings at large, but only in that they are the effects of those interior operations of spontaneity.)

2. The second option, with its counterpart in philosophical reflection about other aspects of the mental, fits Cartesian philosophy of mind, at least on a certain familiar reading (the one given currency by Gilbert Ryle in *The Concept of Mind* [Hutchinson, London, 1949]). We can understand Cartesian philosophy of mind, on that reading, as reflecting an inchoate awareness of what only later comes into focus as the *sui generis* character of the space of reasons. It is intelligible that at an early stage in the formation of the conception of placement in nature by comparison with which the space of reasons is *sui generis*—the conception that, when it comes into focus, is seen as excluding what is done by concepts that function in the space of reasons—there should be an inclination to suppose that what is special about those concepts is that they place their satisfiers in a special tract of nature, with nature understood according to a rudimentary form of the very conception that sets up the strain.

3. Like anything else, they can conform to a specification, which might give the content of an intention. But on this view intention cannot be more intimately involved in movements of an agent's limbs than it is in, say, some fallings of trees. In both cases, we can have an event conforming to a specification framed by an agent, and occurring in consequence of the framing of the specification. Intention has only an external bearing on the event itself.

This withdrawal of agency from nature, at any rate from the ordinary nature in which the movements of our bodies occur, strains our hold on the idea that the natural powers that are actualized in the movements of our bodies are powers that belong to us as agents. Our powers as agents withdraw inwards, and our bodies with the powers whose seat they are—which seem to be different powers, since their actualizations are not doings of ours but at best effects of such doings—take on the aspect of alien objects. It comes to seem that what we do, even in those of our actions that we think of as bodily, is at best to direct our wills, as it were from a distance, at changes of state in those alien objects.[4] And this is surely not a satisfactory picture of our active relation to our bodies. Just as the exclusion of spontaneity from sentient nature obliterates anything we can recognize as empirical content, so here the withdrawal of spontaneity from active nature eliminates any authentic understanding of bodily agency.

Here too, we can return to sanity if we can recapture the Aristotelian idea that a normal mature human being is a rational animal, with its rationality part of its animal, and so natural, being, not a mysterious foothold in another realm. The way to do that is to realize that our nature is largely second nature.[5]

3. In my last lecture (§7) I claimed that Aristotle's ethics contains a model case of a naturalism that would not stand in the way of a satisfactory conception of experience (and of action, I can now add). The position is a naturalism of second nature, and I suggested that we can equally see it as a naturalized platonism. The idea is that the dictates of reason are there anyway, whether or not one's eyes are opened to them; that is what happens in a proper upbringing. We need not try to understand the thought that the dictates of reason are objects of an enlightened awareness, except from within the way of thinking such an upbringing initiates one into: a way of thinking

4. "At best" because such a picture is unstable. What are supposed to be willings are distanced from any occurrence in ordinary nature, in a way that ultimately undermines the very idea of willing.

5. My aim in these remarks about agency is only to bring out that the philosophical anxieties I have been exploiting are general: the application to experience is just one case. Much more could be said about the application to action. In particular, I think the way certain bodily goings-on *are* our spontaneity in action, not just effects of it, is central to a proper understanding of the self as a bodily presence in the world, something that comes to the fore later in this lecture (§5). But I shall not expand on that.

that constitutes a standpoint from which those dictates are already in view.

This naturalized platonism is quite distinct from rampant platonism. In rampant platonism, the rational structure within which meaning comes into view is independent of anything merely human, so that the capacity of our minds to resonate to it looks occult or magical. Naturalized platonism is platonistic in that the structure of the space of reasons has a sort of autonomy; it is not derivative from, or reflective of, truths about human beings that are capturable independently of having that structure in view. But this platonism is not rampant: the structure of the space of reasons is not constituted in splendid isolation from anything merely human. The demands of reason are essentially such that a human upbringing can open a human being's eyes to them.

Now rampant platonism figures as a pitfall to avoid in Wittgenstein's later writings about meaning and understanding.[6] And I think naturalized platonism is a good way to understand what Wittgenstein is driving at there.

I want to stress how different this is from many readings of Wittgenstein. Many readers implicitly attribute to Wittgenstein a philosophical stance that I described in my last lecture (§7): a stance in which one finds a spookiness in the very idea that requirements of reason are there for subjects to have their eyes opened to them, unless the idea can be reconstructed out of independent facts. This poses a philosophical task, and the thought is that Wittgenstein points to a way of executing it by appealing to social interactions, described in a way that does not presuppose the material to be reconstructed.[7]

If we try to construct something that can pass for possession of meaning, the kind of intelligibility that is constituted by placement in

---

6. Rampant platonism is clearly operative in the idea of a "superlative fact" (*Philosophical Investigations*, §192), which Wittgenstein registers as an idea that one can be tempted into when one reflects on "how meaning [something] can determine the steps in advance" (§190). In Wittgenstein's presentation of the syndrome, the supposed "superlative fact" tends to be pictured in terms of a super-mechanism, like an ordinary mechanism except that it is made of some inconceivably rigid material; see §97.

7. See Saul A. Kripke, *Wittgenstein on Rules and Private Language* (Basil Blackwell, Oxford, 1982). Crispin Wright has an independent and partly similar reading. Both start from Wittgenstein's rejecting the mythology of rampant platonism. Kripke's Wittgenstein concludes that there is nothing that constitutes our sensitivity to the requirements that

the space of reasons, in this communitarian or "social pragmatist" style, we cannot see meaning as autonomous. Indeed, that is the point of this kind of reading: the sense of spookiness reflects the conviction that any platonism about meaning, any position that credits meaning with autonomy, must be a rampant platonism, with its characteristic trafficking in the occult. When the autonomy of meaning is renounced on these grounds, that puts in question a seemingly commonsense conception of the objectivity of the world, the reality that our command of meaning enables us to think and talk about. If there is nothing to the normative structure within which meaning comes into view except, say, acceptances and rejections of bits of behaviour by the community at large, then how things are—how things can be said to be with a correctness that must partly consist in being faithful to the meanings one would exploit if one said that they are thus and so—cannot be independent of the community's ratifying the judgement that things are thus and so. The most clear-sighted proponents of this sort of reading explicitly embrace this consequence on Wittgenstein's behalf.[8]

I think the consequence is intolerable, but I am not going to work at justifying that assessment. What I want to bring out now is a point about the philosophical orientation of this sort of approach: it is out of tune with something central to Wittgenstein's own conception of what is to be done in philosophy, namely, his "quietism", his rejection of any constructive or doctrinal ambitions.[9] I believe that ensures that this sort of approach must miss Wittgenstein's point.

Modern philosophy has taken itself to be called on to bridge dualistic gulfs, between subject and object, thought and world. This style of approach to meaning sets out to bridge a dualism of norm and nature. The claim might be that this is a deeper dualism, the source of

meaning places on us; instead, we must understand the role of that idea in our lives in terms of our participation in a community. Wright reads the same materials as gesturing towards a substantive account of what constitutes our grasp of meaning. (Only gesturing: Wittgenstein's "official" renunciation of substantive philosophical theory, his "quietism", prevents him from acknowledging that he is in the business of constructive philosophy.) See Wright's "Critical Notice of Colin McGinn, *Wittgenstein on Meaning*", *Mind* 98 (1989), 289–305.

8. See Wright's discussion of "ratification-transcendence", in chap. 11 of *Wittgenstein on the Foundations of Mathematics* (Duckworth, London, 1980).

9. Wright is self-conscious about this; his response is to deplore Wittgenstein's affirmations of "quietism".

the familiar dualisms of modern philosophy. So far, so good; this fits the picture I have been urging. But what is debatable is how we ought to respond to the deeper dualism.

Ordinary modern philosophy addresses its derivative dualisms in a characteristic way. It takes its stand on one side of a gulf it aims to bridge, accepting without question the way its target dualism conceives the chosen side. Then it constructs something as close as possible to the conception of the other side that figured in the problems, out of materials that are unproblematically available where it has taken its stand. Of course there no longer seems to be a gulf, but the result is bound to look more or less revisionist. (How revisionist depends on how urgent the original apparent problems were: how firmly entrenched was the way of thinking that gave the appearance of an uncrossable chasm.) Phenomenalism is a good example of a philosophical construction with this traditional shape; it aims to overcome anxiety about a gap between experience and the world by constructing the world out of experience, still conceived in just the way that gives rise to the anxiety.

This putatively Wittgensteinian style of approach to meaning approaches its deeper dualism in exactly that way. The impetus to the approach is that one finds a spookiness in norms if they are conceived platonistically. This reflects looking at norms from nature's side of the duality of norm and nature; nature is equated with the realm of law, and that poses the familiar threat of disenchantment. Now any platonism has the effect that norms are on the far side of a gulf, and that sets a philosophical task with a familiar shape: to build as close a likeness as possible to what threatened to seem out of reach, using only materials that are reassuringly present on the hither side of the threatening gulf. The aim is that the gulf should disappear. If our construction lacks features that what posed the problem seemed to possess, that is a revisionism that was only to be expected.

This is one more spasm of ordinary modern philosophy, touting itself as the last; not what Wittgenstein aspires to, which is that we should see through the apparent need for ordinary philosophy. And that is not just a quirk of Wittgenstein's self-conception, to be set aside while we proceed to read him as just another ordinary philosopher. The aspiration is not fantastic. The naturalism of second nature that I have been describing is precisely a shape for our thinking that would leave even the last dualism not seeming to call for constructive philosophy. The bare idea of *Bildung* ensures that the autonomy of meaning is not inhuman, and that should eliminate the tendency to be spooked by the very idea of norms or demands of reason. This leaves no genuine questions about norms, apart from those that we address in reflective thinking about specific norms, an activity that is not particularly philosophical. There is no need for constructive philosophy, directed at the very idea of norms of reason, or the structure within which meaning comes into view, from the standpoint of the naturalism that threatens to disenchant nature. We need not try to get meaning into view from that standpoint.

Of course the category of the social is important. *Bildung* could not have its place in the picture if that were not so. But the point is not that the social constitutes the framework for a construction of the very idea of meaning: something that would make the idea safe for a restrictive naturalism, the sort that threatens to disenchant nature. Wittgenstein says, "Commanding, questioning, recounting, chatting, are as much part of our natural history as walking, eating, drinking, playing".[10] By "our natural history", he must mean the natural history of creatures whose nature is largely second nature. Human life, our natural way of being, is already shaped by meaning. We need not connect this natural history to nature as the realm of law any more tightly than by simply affirming our right to the notion of second nature.

I am crediting Wittgenstein with an "ism", naturalized platonism. Am I myself flouting his insistence that he is not in the business of offering philosophical doctrine? No. Recall what I said at the end of the last lecture (§8) about Rorty and "the discovery that gives philosophy peace". "Naturalized platonism" is not a label for a bit of constructive philosophy. The phrase serves only as shorthand for a "reminder", an attempt to recall our thinking from running in grooves that make it look as if we need constructive philosophy.[11]

4. At the end of my second lecture (§8), I said that if we take Kant's conception of experience out of the frame he puts it in, a story about a transcendental affection of receptivity by a supersensible reality, it

10. *Philosophical Investigations*, §25.
11. Cf. *Philosophical Investigations*, §127.

becomes just what we need. Outside that frame, Kant's conception is a satisfactory way to avoid our dilemma, the apparently forced choice between the Myth of the Given and a coherentism that renounces external constraints on thinking. But the frame spoils the insight, because the radical mind-independence of the supersensible comes to seem exemplary of what any genuine mind-independence would be, and then when Kant purports to attribute mind-independence to the ordinary empirical world, as it figures in his thinking, that looks merely disingenuous. I left hanging the question why Kant locates his attempt at the necessary insight in this unsatisfactory context.

Now there are familiar features of Kant's thinking that can help explain why he is attracted by the idea of an unknowable supersensible reality, apparently in violation of his own standards for what makes sense. The transcendental framework gives the appearance of explaining how there can be knowledge of necessary features of experience. And Kant thinks acknowledging the supersensible is a way to protect the interests of religion and morality. This last point, indeed, relates quite directly to my question. There are pressures within ethical thinking that tend to distort ethics into what Bernard Williams distinguishes as "the morality system".[12] One feature of "the morality system" is an appearance that one could be genuinely responsible only for exercises of a completely unconditioned freedom. That can help explain why Kant is prone to suppose genuine spontaneity would have to be wholly unconstrained. The best we could have in experience, empirically conceived, is a naturally constrained spontaneity. That would be bound to look second-rate in comparison with the unconditioned freedom that moral responsibility is supposed to require.

But none of these explanations operates within Kant's thinking about experience itself. These extraneous considerations, the interests of philosophy itself, religion, and morality, can take us some distance towards understanding why Kant's thinking about experience distorts its own best insight, but surely they cannot be the whole explanation.

We can construct an internal explanation in terms of the pressures of modern naturalism. No doubt the notion of *Bildung* is at Kant's disposal, but not as the background for a serious employment of the idea of second nature. For Kant, the idea of nature is the idea of the

12. See chap. 10 of *Ethics and the Limits of Philosophy*.

realm of law, the idea that came into focus with the rise of modern science. Consider Kant's response to Hume. Hume had responded with excessive enthusiasm to the disenchanting effect of modern naturalism; he thought nature had to be denied not only the intelligibility of meaning but also the intelligibility of law. Against Hume, Kant aims to regain for nature the intelligibility of law, but not the intelligibility of meaning. For Kant, nature is the realm of law and therefore devoid of meaning. And given such a conception of nature, genuine spontaneity cannot figure in descriptions of actualizations of natural powers as such.

The point here is one of some delicacy. For Kant, the ordinary empirical world, which includes nature as the realm of law, is not external to the conceptual. In view of the connection between the conceptual and the kind of intelligibility that belongs to meaning, I have suggested that defending that Kantian thought requires a partial reenchantment of nature. (See Lecture IV, §§3, 4.) But it does not require us to rehabilitate the idea that there is meaning in the fall of a sparrow or the movement of the planets, as there is meaning in a text. It is a good teaching of modernity that the realm of law is as such devoid of meaning; its constituent elements are not linked to one another by the relations that constitute the space of reasons. But if our thinking about the natural stops at an appreciation of that point, we cannot properly comprehend the capacity of experience to take in even the meaningless occurrences that constitute the realm of law. We cannot satisfactorily splice spontaneity and receptivity together in our conception of experience, and that means we cannot exploit the Kantian thought that the realm of law, not just the realm of meaningful doings, is not external to the conceptual. The understanding—the very capacity that we bring to bear on texts—must be involved in our taking in of mere meaningless happenings.[13]

Kant's lack of a pregnant notion of second nature explains why the right conception of experience cannot find a firm position in his thinking. But it does not explain how, even so, he comes so close to the right conception. At this point I think we must simply marvel at his insight, especially in view of how the transcendental framework prevents the insight from taking proper form. And it is not that the transcendental framework is a gratuitous afterthought. In the absence of a

13. I am responding here to comments by Robert Brandom and Michael Lockwood.

pregnant notion of second nature, the insight can appear only in that distorted form.

If we conceive intuitions as products of disenchanted nature, and spontaneity as non-natural, the closest we can get to the conception we need is the Davidsonian position I discussed in my last lecture (§4): spontaneity characterizes what are in fact operations of sentient nature, but it does not characterize them as such. That leaves us in our familiar dilemma: either we must see our way to supposing that, even so, operations of sentient nature can stand in rational relations to thought (the Myth of the Given), or we must accept that sensibility has no epistemological significance at all (a radical coherentism). In effect Kant sees that this choice is intolerable. So spontaneity must structure the operations of our sensibility as such. Since he does not contemplate a naturalism of second nature, and since bald naturalism has no appeal for him, he cannot find a place in nature for this required real connection between concepts and intuitions. And in this predicament, he can find no option but to place the connection outside nature, in the transcendental framework.

Kant is peculiarly brilliant here. Even though he has no intelligible way to deal with it, he manages to hold on to the insight that a merely notional connection of concepts with intuitions will not do. That forces him into a way out that is unintelligible by his own lights. The real connection has to be that spontaneity is involved in the transcendental affection of receptivity by the supersensible. And now the good thought that our sensibility opens us to a reality that is not external to the conceptual can show up only in a distorted form, as if the ordinary empirical world were constituted by appearances of a reality beyond.

Alongside this strain to which Kant's thinking is subject, when he tries to find a place for the essential insight about experience in the lethal environment of a naturalism without second nature, we should note another historical influence: the rise of Protestant individualism. That brings with it a loss or devaluation of the idea that immersion in a tradition might be a respectable mode of access to the real. Instead it comes to seem incumbent on each individual thinker to check everything for herself. When particular traditions seem ossified or hidebound, that encourages a fantasy that one should discard reliance on tradition altogether, whereas the right response would be to insist that a respectable tradition must include an honest responsiveness to reflective criticism.

What results from this devaluation of tradition is an outlook in which individual reason is sovereign. And that is hard to combine with the idea that reason might be operative in states or occurrences of sheer passivity, which would make it indebted to the world. So what starts as a loss of the idea that reason might owe its being to a place in a tradition shows up as a strain on the idea that reason might owe anything to impacts from the world. I shall say a little more about the significance of tradition in my final lecture.

5. If we could equip Kant with the idea of second nature, that would not only free his insight about experience from the distorting effect of the framework he tries to express it in; it would also allow the connection between self-consciousness and consciousness of the world, which figures in an equivocal way in his thinking, to take a satisfactory shape.

In the Transcendental Deduction, Kant seems to offer a thesis on these lines: the possibility of understanding experiences, "from within", as glimpses of objective reality is interdependent with the subject's being able to ascribe experiences to herself; hence, with the subject's being self-conscious.[14]

Now it would be satisfying if the self that is in question here were, in the end at least, the ordinary self. But it is hard to make that cohere with what Kant actually says. When he introduces the self-consciousness that he argues to be correlative with awareness of objective reality, he writes of the "I think" that must be able "to accompany all my representations".[15] In the Paralogisms of Pure Reason, he claims that if we credit this "I" with a persisting referent, the relevant idea of identity through time is only formal. It has nothing to do with the substantial identity of a subject who persists as a real presence in the world she perceives.[16] The subjective temporal continuity that is a

14. For this reading of the Transcendental Deduction, see pp. 72–117 of Strawson, *The Bounds of Sense.*

15. *Critique of Pure Reason,* B131.

16. A363: "The identity of the consciousness of myself at different times is . . . only a formal condition of my thoughts and their coherence, and in no way proves the numerical identity of my subject."

counterpart to experience's bearing on objective reality shrinks to the continuity of a mere point of view, not, apparently, a substantial continuant.[17]

Kant has a reason for the thesis of the Paralogisms, that only a formal idea of persistence through time is available for the "I" in the "I think" that can "accompany all my representations". He thinks anything else would commit him to a Cartesian conception of the ego.

Consider Locke's account of what a person is: "a thinking intelligent being, that has reason and reflection, and can consider itself as itself, the same thinking thing, in different times and places".[18] Locke is talking about what he calls "consciousness"; we might call it "self-consciousness". "Consciousness" can hold together, in a single survey, states and occurrences that are temporally separated; they are conceived as belonging to the career of a continuant, a thinking thing. To put the point in Kant's terms: in the "I think" that can "accompany all my representations", the reference of the "I" is understood as reaching into the past and future. But Kant's point in the Paralogisms is that the flow of what Locke calls "consciousness" does not involve applying, or otherwise ensuring conformity with, a criterion of identity.[19] In the continuity of "consciousness" through time, there is what appears to be knowledge of an identity, the persistence of an object over a period; part of the content of the flow of "consciousness" is the idea of a persisting referent for the "I" in the "I think" that can "accompany all my representations". But when a subject makes this application of the idea of persistence, she needs no effort to ensure that her attention stays fixed on the same thing. For a contrast, consider keeping one's thought focused on an ordinary object of perception over a period. That requires the ability to keep track of things, a skill whose exercise we can conceive as a practical substitute for the explicit application of a criterion of identity. Continuity of "consciousness" involves no analogue to this, no keeping track of the persisting self that nevertheless seems to figure in its content.[20]

17. See Quassim Cassam, "Kant and Reductionism", *Review of Metaphysics* 43 (1989), 72–106, especially pp. 87–8.

18. *An Essay concerning Human Understanding*, ed. P. H. Nidditch (Clarendon Press, Oxford, 1975), 3.27.9.

19. This is Strawson's reading of the Paralogisms: *The Bounds of Sense*, pp. 162–70.

20. For an elaboration on these lines of the point Strawson finds in Kant, see Evans, *The*

Now suppose we assume that, in providing for the content of this thought of a persisting self, we must confine ourselves within the flow of "consciousness" itself. If the topic of the thought is a substantial continuant, what its continuing to exist consists in must be peculiarly simple. The notion of persistence applies itself effortlessly; there is nothing to it except the flow of "consciousness" itself. This looks like a recipe for arriving at the conception, or supposed conception, of the referent of "I" that figures in Descartes.

That is essentially Kant's account of how the Cartesian conception of the ego arises. And it can easily seem that we had better draw Kant's conclusion: the idea of persistence that figures in the flow of "consciousness" had better be only formal. If we allowed that it is an idea of substantial persistence, the continuing to exist of an objective item, we would be committed to understanding self-consciousness as awareness of a Cartesian ego.

But as I have stressed, this depends on assuming that when we provide for the content of this idea of persistence, we must confine ourselves within the flow of "consciousness". And this assumption is not sacrosanct. Indeed, it is deeply suspect; I think it is the real root of the Cartesian conception. If we discard it, we make room for supposing that the continuity of the "I think" involves a substantial persistence, without implying that the continuant in question is a Cartesian ego. We can say that the continuity of "consciousness" is intelligible only as a subjective take on something that has more to it than "consciousness" itself contains: on the career of an objective continuant, with which the subject of a continuous "consciousness" can identify itself. It is true that the continuity within the subjective take does not involve keeping track of a persisting thing, but this effortlessness does not require us to agree with Kant that the idea of identity here is only formal. Even "from within", the subjective take is understood as situated

---

Varieties of Reference, p. 237. Evans (or more probably his editor) seems to slip when he suggests that the point can be captured in terms of the idea of "immunity to error through misidentification", which he exploits elsewhere (pp. 179–91), in connection with perceptually based demonstrative thinking. We have "immunity to error through misidentification" when a predication is not attached to its subject by way of a judgement of identity. But as Evans points out on p. 236, "identification-freedom" in that sense is consistent with a judgement's depending on keeping track of its object, the very thing he denies in the case of self-consciousness. Keeping track serves as it were instead of an "identification component", in what underlies continuing demonstrative thought about objects of perception. The point about the self is a peculiarly strong form of "identification-freedom".

in a wider context; so there can be more content to the idea of persistence it embodies. The wider context makes it possible to understand that the first person, the continuing referent of the "I" in the "I think" that can "accompany all my representations", is also a third person, something whose career is a substantial continuity in the objective world: something such that other modes of continuing thought about it would indeed require keeping track of it. That is a way of putting the gist of Gareth Evans's brilliant treatment of self-identification, which builds on P. F. Strawson's brilliant reading of the Paralogisms.[21]

I think something on these lines is the right frame for the Kantian thought that self-awareness and awareness of the world are interdependent. And there may be hints of this in Kant.[22] But I do not see how it can be his official view. If we situate self-consciousness in a wider context, we can avoid the Cartesian ego, without needing to say that the idea of a persisting self that figures in the continuity of "consciousness" is merely formal. But that is exactly what Kant thinks he has to say. It looks as if Kant leaves in place the suspect assumption that when we set out to provide for the content of the idea of a persisting self, we may not go outside the flow of "consciousness". Only so can it seem that to avoid the Cartesian ego, he needs to adjust the content of the idea of persistence. If I am right about the assumption, Kant's diagnosis of Cartesian thinking does not go to the root.

The result of Kant's move is that the subjective continuity he appeals to, as part of what it is for experience to bear on objective reality, cannot be equated with the continuing life of a perceiving animal. It shrinks, as I said, to the continuity of a mere point of view: something that need not have anything to do with a body, so far as the claim of interdependence is concerned.

This is quite unsatisfying. If we begin with a free-standing notion of an experiential route through objective reality, a temporally extended point of view that might be bodiless so far as the connection between subjectivity and objectivity goes, there seems to be no prospect of building up from there to the notion of a substantial presence in the world. If something starts out conceiving itself as a merely formal re-

---

21. *The Varieties of Reference*, chap. 7. Evans's thinking here can be seen as an elaboration of Strawson's remark, in his reading of the Paralogisms (*The Bounds of Sense*, p. 165): "'I' can be used without criteria of subject-identity and yet refer to a subject because, even in such a use, the links with those criteria are not severed."

22. This is what Strawson finds, at least in germ, in the Paralogisms.

ferent for "I" (which is already a peculiar notion), how could it come to appropriate a body, so that it might identify itself with a particular living thing? Perhaps we can pretend to make sense of the idea that such a subject might register a special role played by a particular body in determining the course of its experience. But that would not provide for it to conceive itself, the subject of its experience, as a bodily element in objective reality—as a bodily presence in the world.

If Kant's connection between self-awareness and awareness of the world is to leave it open to us to regain the idea that the subjects of our experience are our ordinary selves, then the merely formal persistence of the I, in the "I think" that can "accompany all my representations", had better be only an abstraction from the ordinary substantial persistence of the living subject of experience.[23] It had better not be something free-standing, which we might hope to build on in reconstructing the persistence of the ordinary self. But this does not seem to fit Kant's conception of what he is doing. Kant takes himself to be laying bare a necessary connection that is knowable *a priori*.[24] And it would be hard to make the idea of an abstraction from the persistence of the ordinary self cohere with the temporal connotations he gives to *"a priori"*, as when he suggests that transcendental self-consciousness "precedes all data of intuitions" (A107).

It is not surprising if Kant cannot get his thinking into the right light. Why can there not be a free-standing idea of formal subjective continuity? The answer is this: the idea of a subjectively continuous series of states or occurrences in which conceptual capacities are implicated in sensibility—or, more generally, the idea of a subjectively continuous series of exercises of conceptual capacities of any kind, that is, the idea of a subjectively continuous series of "representations", as Kant would say—is just the idea of a singled out tract of a life. The idea of a subjectively continuous series of "representations" could no more stand alone, independent of the idea of a living thing in whose life these events occur, than could the idea of a series of digestive events with its appropriate kind of continuity. But in the absence of a serious notion of second nature, this exploitation of the concept of life, which is a quintessentially natural phenomenon, to make sense

23. See Strawson's appeal to abstraction at pp. 103–4 of *The Bounds of Sense*.

24. See, for instance, *Critique of Pure Reason*, A116: "We are conscious *a priori* of the complete identity of the self in respect of all representations which can ever belong to our knowledge, as being a necessary condition of the possibility of all representations."

of a unity within the domain of spontaneity, which by Kant's lights has to be non-natural, is not within Kant's grasp.

Kant's aim is to exorcize Cartesian temptations about the self, and he gets to the very brink of success. He wants to acknowledge the peculiarities of self-awareness that encourage Cartesian philosophy, but without letting them seem to show that the object of self-aware-ness is a Cartesian ego. But he thinks the only alternative is a transcen-dental self-awareness, something that has no object substantially pres-ent in the world. If we insist on supplying this self-awareness with an object, we can locate the object in the world only geometrically, as a point of view. This avoids the familiar Cartesian problems about the relation between a peculiar substance and the rest of reality. But it leaves us with what look like descendants of those problems. If we start from a putative sense of self as at most geometrically in the world, how can we work up from there to the sense of self we actually have, as a bodily presence in the world? (When I say that that is what self-awareness is, I am not implying that one's bodily presence in the world is always borne in on one in self-awareness.)[25] Kant's insight would be able to take satisfactory shape only if he could accommo-date the fact that a thinking and intending subject is a living animal. But with his firm conviction that conceptual powers are non-natural, in the sense that equates nature with the realm of law, and with his lack of a seriously exploitable notion of second nature, he is debarred from accommodating that fact.

6. Kant sometimes associates the idea of the conceptual especially with generality.[26] That can suggest that we should explain the relation of concepts to intuitions in terms of the relation of predicates to sub-jects.[27]

This might seem to reveal a Kantian shape in a certain trend in re-

25. Cases of sensory deprivation bring out that one's bodily being need not always im-press itself on one. In "The First Person" (in Samuel Guttenplan, ed., *Mind and Language* [Clarendon Press, Oxford, 1975], pp. 45–65), G. E. M. Anscombe exploits that fact to argue that "the use of 'I' as subject" (as distinguished by Wittgenstein from "the use as object"; *The Blue and Brown Books*, pp. 66–7) functions independently of a sense of one-self as a bodily presence in the world. Anscombe concludes that "the use of 'I' as subject" should not be taken to refer, on pain of a Cartesian conception of what it refers to. But the argument is flawed in just the same way as the argument of the Paralogisms.

26. See, for instance, A320/B377.

27. This thought is central to Strawson's reading of the First Critique. See *The Bounds of Sense*, pp. 20, 72.

cent thinking about singular reference. There was a time when the standard view of reference was inspired by Russell's Theory of Descriptions. The idea was that whenever a thought is directed at a particular object, part of its content is given by a specification of the object in general terms: conceptual terms, the equation I am considering would lead us to say. The trend is to recoil from this.[28] There are kinds of object-directedness in thoughts that cannot easily be made to fit that mould. For instance, a perceptual demonstrative thought surely homes in on its object not by containing a general specification, with the object figuring in the thought as what fits the specification, but by virtue of the way this sort of thinking exploits the perceptible presence of the object itself. If the conceptual is equated with the predicative, this resistance to the general application of the Theory of Descriptions takes the form of saying that in the cases that warrant the resistance, singular reference is, or rests on, an extra-conceptual relation between thinkers and things.[29] So the picture is that the conceptual realm does have an outside, which is populated by particular objects. Thought makes contact with objects, from its location within the conceptual realm, by exploiting relations such as perception, which are conceived as penetrating the outer boundary of the conceptual.

This picture fits a contemporary view of singular reference that perhaps deserves to be counted as an orthodoxy. As I said, it can seem to be Kantian. But in fact it is not Kantian at all. In Kant, the conceptual realm has no outside; not unless we shift to the transcendental story, and nobody thinks the objects that, say, demonstrative thoughts focus on are noumenal. And in any case, the picture is really incoherent, unless "conceptual" is serving as a mere synonym for "predicative". Circumscribing the conceptual realm can seem to make interesting sense only if the circumscribed realm is singled out as the realm of

28. Influential early proponents of this trend include Saul A. Kripke, "Naming and Necessity", in Donald Davidson and Gilbert Harman, eds., *Semantics of Natural Language* (Reidel, Dordrecht, 1972), pp. 253–355, 763–9, reissued as a monograph by Basil Blackwell, Oxford, 1980; and Keith S. Donnellan, "Proper Names and Identifying Descriptions", ibid., pp. 356–79. See also, predating the trend, Ruth Barcan Marcus, "Modalities and Intensional Languages", *Synthese* 27 (1962), 303–22.

29. For a striking exposition of a position on these lines, long predating the works usually cited as initiating the contemporary trend, see Geach, *Mental Acts*, §15. For a more recent expression of the idea that the relation between thought and individual things, in the relevant sorts of case, is extra-conceptual, see Tyler Burge, "Belief *De Re*", *Journal of Philosophy* 74 (1977), 338–62.

thought. This picture has predications in the conceptual realm, but thought supposedly has to break out of the conceptual to make contact with the objects of which predications are to be made. And that leaves no room for a coherent conception of how a predication, located within the circumscribed conceptual realm, could be brought into connection with an object.

Given this conception of the anti-Russellian revolution, it is easy to sympathize with counter-revolutionary partisans of the generalized Theory of Descriptions, such as John Searle.[30] If this picture is the only recourse for someone who wants to be able to conceive thought as focusing on particulars otherwise than by way of specifications, it would be better to give up wanting that, and go back to the task of trying to spell out the unobvious specifications by way of which, after all, the sorts of thought that trigger the recoil must make contact with their objects.

In my third lecture I attacked Gareth Evans's view that the content of perceptual experience is non-conceptual. That was for purposes somewhat remote from Evans's fundamental concern, which is with singular reference. Indeed, I do not believe Evans's appeal to a non-conceptual content for perception is central to his thinking about singular reference. It is easy to recast Evans's main contentions, even about perceptual demonstrative thought, without mentioning non-conceptual content.

Evans's master thought is that Frege's notion of sense, which Frege introduces in terms of modes of presentation, can accommodate the sorts of connection between thinkers and particular objects that have been recognized to make trouble for the generalized Theory of Descriptions.[31] The detail of Evans's work spells this out case by case. It explains the various ways in which thoughts focus on particular objects, always by placing thinking in its proper context, the thinker's competent self-conscious presence in the

---

30. See chap. 8 of *Intentionality* (Cambridge University Press, Cambridge, 1983). I discuss Searle's view of singular thought in "Intentionality *De Re*", in Ernest LePore and Robert Van Gulick, eds., *John Searle and His Critics* (Basil Blackwell, Oxford, 1991), pp. 215–25. See also my "Singular Thought and the Extent of Inner Space", in Philip Pettit and John McDowell, eds., *Subject, Thought, and Context* (Clarendon Press, Oxford, 1986), pp. 137–68, for a more extensive consideration of the issues that are in play here.

31. So it is quite wrong to lump Frege in with Russell as a target for the recoil from the generalized Theory of Descriptions.

world.[32] If we want to identify the conceptual realm with the realm of thought, the right gloss on "conceptual" is not "predicative" but "belonging to the realm of Fregean sense". (The stupid idea that those come to the same thing is unfortunately still widespread.) Evans's achievement is to show how we can avoid an apparently forced choice between, on the one hand, the implausibilities of the generalized Theory of Descriptions, which are increasingly palpable despite the rearguard efforts of philosophers like Searle, and, on the other, the incoherence of the pseudo-Kantian picture, in which thought has to break out of its own proper sphere in order to make contact with particulars otherwise than by specification. By invoking Frege, Evans makes it clear how the non-specificatory relations between thinkers and objects that proponents of the latter picture rightly insist on need not be conceived as carrying thought outside an outer boundary of the conceptual realm.

I think describing Evans's thinking like this reveals it to be deeply right, at least in general outline. It is common for philosophers to think they can dismiss Evans's position, without attention to the wider context I have placed it in, on the ground that they find its implications counter-intuitive. This just reveals the depressing extent to which his ground-breaking work has not been understood. That such work can be so little appreciated is a mark of degeneracy in our philosophical culture.

32. I stress this to bring out how important Strawson's Kant is for the main lines of Evans's thinking in *The Varieties of Reference*. Strawson's influence goes far beyond where it is visible on the surface.

Rational and Other Animals

1. I have been considering the tendency to oscillate between two unpalatable positions: a coherentism that loses the bearing of empirical thought on reality altogether and a recoil into a vain appeal to the Given. I have proposed a diagnosis of this tendency: it reflects an intelligible distortion undergone by the Aristotelian idea that normal mature human beings are rational animals. Animals are, as such, natural beings, and a familiar modern conception of nature tends to extrude rationality from nature. The effect is that reason is separated from our animal nature, as if being rational placed us partly outside the animal kingdom. Specifically, the understanding is distanced from sensibility. And that is the source of our philosophical impasse. In order to escape it, we need to bring understanding and sensibility, reason and nature, back together.

One way to avoid the dilemma is to leave unquestioned the conception of nature that threatens to extrude reason from nature, but to reconceive reason in naturalistic terms, on a corresponding understanding of what it is for a term to be naturalistic. This position is what I have been calling "bald naturalism". It allows us to conceive ourselves as rational animals, but I think the conception is not Aristotle's. Admittedly, though, bald naturalism is like Aristotelian thinking in that it does not address the philosophical worries I have been considering, but simply refuses to feel them.

The threat is that an animal endowed with reason would be metaphysically split, with disastrous consequences for our reflection about empirical thinking and action. I have claimed that we can avoid the threat even while we maintain, unlike bald naturalism, that the structure of the space of reasons is *sui generis,* in comparison with the organization of the realm of law. The spontaneity of the understanding cannot be captured in terms that are apt for describing nature on that conception, but even so it can permeate actualizations of our animal nature. If we can see our way to accepting that, we can avoid the philosophical difficulties while fully appreciating what makes them gripping.

In Aristotle's conception of human beings, rationality is integrally part of their animal nature, and the conception is neither naturalistic in the modern sense (there is no hint of reductiveness or foundationalism) nor fraught with philosophical anxiety. What makes this possible is that Aristotle is innocent of the very idea that nature is the realm of law and therefore not the home of meaning. That conception of nature was laboriously brought into being at the time of the modern scientific revolution.

I am not urging that we should try to regain Aristotle's innocence. It would be crazy to regret the idea that natural science reveals a special kind of intelligibility, to be distinguished from the kind that is proper to meaning. To discard that part of our intellectual inheritance would be to return to mediaeval superstition. It is right to set a high value on the kind of intelligibility we disclose in something when we place it in the realm of law, and to separate it sharply from the intelligibility we disclose in something when we place it in the space of reasons.

But instead of trying to integrate the intelligibility of meaning into the realm of law, we can aim at a postlapsarian or knowing counterpart of Aristotle's innocence. We can acknowledge the great step forward that human understanding took when our ancestors formed the idea of a domain of intelligibility, the realm of natural law, that is empty of meaning, but we can refuse to equate that domain of intelligibility with nature, let alone with what is real.

The notion of second nature needs no particular emphasis in the context of Aristotle's innocence, but it takes on a special significance in this attempt to achieve a knowing counterpart. We are looking for a conception of our nature that includes a capacity to resonate to the structure of the space of reasons. Since we are setting our faces against bald naturalism, we have to expand nature beyond what is countenanced in a naturalism of the realm of law. But the expansion is limited by the first nature, so to speak, of human animals, and by plain facts about what happens to human animals in their upbringing. We are not irresponsibly cutting the concept of nature loose from the realm of law, as we would be if we pretended that the capacity postulated by rampant platonism, a capacity to resonate to structures of reason constituted in utter isolation from anything human, might count as a natural capacity of human minds.

Rampant platonism has what intelligibility it has as a desperate attempt to keep meaning, conceived as able to come into view only within a *sui generis* logical space, while acquiescing in the disenchantment of nature. It is not so much as intelligible that a prelapsarian thinker might feel that temptation. My naturalized version of platonism is not usually in the picture, and what I am calling "rampant platonism" is usually called just "platonism". But if I am right about its historical context, naming the position after Plato must do him an injustice.

2. A typical form of modern philosophy confronts a familiar predicament. It takes itself to be called on to explain how, starting from independently available data of consciousness, we work out into a justified confidence that there is an objective world. In a part of his thinking that I discussed in my last lecture (§5), Kant aims to supersede that conception of philosophy's task. He tries to make it plausible that the very idea of data for consciousness is interdependent with the idea that at least some states and occurrences of consciousness constitute glimpses of an objective world. In that case, it makes no sense to think we might start with contents of minds and build up to objective reality. Kant does not have occasion to consider the inverted form of traditional philosophy that I mentioned in my last lecture (§3) in connection with some readings of Wittgenstein: that is, a philosophy in which the project is to start with the natural world and make a place in it for minds and their contents. But I think he would be similarly dismissive of that.

I suggested that Kant's insight could take satisfactory form only in the context of a naturalism of second nature, a conception that Kant himself does not achieve. Kant wants subjects of experience and intentional action to be already, just as such, in possession of objective reality. He wants exercises of conceptual powers to be intelligible only as undertaken by subjects who do not need philosophy to regain the world for them. But since he lacks a pregnant notion of second nature, and has no inclination to naturalize spontaneity within the realm of law, the best he can provide in the way of an experiencing and acting subject is the merely formal referent he allows to "I", in the "I think" that must be able to "accompany all my representations". Such a subject could not be something substantially present in the world; it is at best a point of view. That means, I suggested, that Kant cannot succeed in his admirable aim, to supersede traditional philosophy. Cartesian thinking confronts familiar difficulties about how to relate a subjective substance to objective reality, and Kant's conception is beset by what look like descendants of those difficulties. If we start with a referent for "I" that is only geometrically in the world, it seems impossible to build up to a substantial presence, an embodied perceiver and agent.

Things look different if we equip Kant with a seriously exploitable notion of second nature. Now we can give a satisfactory form to the insight he is straining after. We can conceive exercises of capacities that belong to spontaneity as elements in the course of a life. An experiencing and acting subject is a living thing, with active and passive bodily powers that are genuinely her own; she is herself embodied, substantially present in the world that she experiences and acts on. This is a framework for reflection that really stands a chance of making traditional philosophy obsolete.

In that recapitulation of something I said in my last lecture, I have described a philosophical project: to stand on the shoulders of the giant, Kant, and see our way to the supersession of traditional philosophy that he almost managed, though not quite. The philosopher whose achievement that description best fits is someone we take almost no notice of, in the philosophical tradition I was brought up in, although I have mentioned him a couple of times before: namely, Hegel.[1]

3. I have urged that experience can be conceived as openness to the world (Lectures I and II). I promised to return to the fact that experience can mislead us (Lecture I, §4; Lecture II, §2). There is a tendency to conclude that even a non-misleading experience cannot genuinely be a case of openness to reality. In that case we cannot exploit the

1. In view of how I exploited Strawson's reading of Kant in my last lecture, this remark implies that Strawson's Kant is more Hegel than Kant. For a reading of Hegel that takes very seriously Hegel's own idea that his philosophy completes a Kantian project, see Robert B. Pippin, *Hegel's Idealism*.

image of openness in the way I have suggested, so as to bypass the anxieties of traditional epistemology. The objection might be put like this. "You grant that experience can be misleading. That is to grant that what you are pleased to call 'glimpses of the world' can be subjectively indistinguishable from states or occurrences that cannot be glimpses of the world, since they would lead one astray if one took them at face value. So surely the problems of traditional epistemology are just as pressing as they ever were. In your terminology, they come out like this: how can one know that what one is enjoying at any time is a genuine glimpse of the world, rather than something that merely seems to be that?"

But this misses the point. An objection on these lines would be appropriate if I were aiming to answer traditional sceptical questions, to address the predicament of traditional philosophy. That is the predicament in which we are supposed to start from some anyway available data of consciousness, and work up to certifying that they actually yield knowledge of the objective world. Of course if that is our predicament, we need to answer the traditional sceptical questions before we can talk of openness to the world. But my talk of openness is a rejection of the traditional predicament, not an attempt to respond to it.

Traditional epistemology accords a deep significance to the fact that perception is fallible. It is supposed to show something like this: however favourable a perceiver's cognitive stance may be, we cannot make sense of subjective states of affairs constituted by a subject's letting the layout of the objective world reveal itself to her. As the objector insists, something that is not a glimpse of reality, since the subject would be misled if she took it at face value, can be subjectively indistinguishable (at least at the time) from experiences that are veridical. That is supposed to show that the genuinely subjective states of affairs involved in perception can never be more than what a perceiver has in a misleading case.

This strains our hold on the very idea of a glimpse of reality. If we are confined to such materials when we build a conception of the best cognitive stance perception could yield, the most we can aspire to is something like this: an explicably veridical presentiment of some fact about the layout of the environment.[2] We cannot have the fact itself

---

2. In fact we cannot even have that; empirical content as such (even as possessed by mere presentiments) is intelligible only in a context that allows us to make sense of direct rational constraint on minds from the world itself.

impressing itself on a perceiver. This seems off key, phenomenologically at least, and we can resist it if we can so much as comprehend the idea of a direct hold on the facts, the sort of position that the image of openness conveys. It is true that we could not establish that we are open to facts in any given case; at any rate not to the satisfaction of a determined sceptic, who can always insist on exploiting fallibility to give bite to the question how we know the present case is one of the non-misleading ones. But that is beside the point. It would matter if it showed that the very idea of openness to facts is unintelligible, and it does not show that. For my present purposes, the sheer intelligibility of the idea is enough. If the idea is intelligible, the sceptical questions lack a kind of urgency that is essential to their troubling us, an urgency that derives from their seeming to point up an unnerving fact: that however good a subject's cognitive position is, it *cannot* constitute her having a state of affairs directly manifest to her. There is no such fact. The aim here is not to answer sceptical questions, but to begin to see how it might be intellectually respectable to ignore them, to treat them as unreal, in the way that common sense has always wanted to.

Insisting on the image of openness is a way to give vivid expression to this point: there is no good argument from fallibility to what I call "the highest common factor conception" of our subjective position— the idea that even when things go well, cognitively speaking, our subjective position can only be something common between such cases and cases in which things do not go well. That is a way of putting the traditional picture of our epistemic predicament. It is not compulsory, and the fact of fallibility cannot make it so. Traditional epistemology cannot be vindicated by the sheer possibility of asking, "How do you know that what you are enjoying is a genuine glimpse of the world?", as was suggested by the objection at the beginning of this section. If someone insists on asking that, on some particular occasion, an appropriate response might start like this: "I know why you think that question is peculiarly pressing, but it is not." If the question still stands, nothing particularly philosophical is called for in answering it.[3]

---

3. I discuss the "highest common factor conception" in "Criteria, Defeasibility, and Knowledge", *Proceedings of the British Academy* 68 (1982), 455–79; and in "Singular Thought and the Extent of Inner Space".

4. We can put part of the Kantian thesis that I discussed in my last lecture, and recalled earlier in this one (§2), like this: the objective world is present only to a self-conscious subject, a subject who can ascribe experiences to herself; it is only in the context of a subject's ability to ascribe experiences to herself that experiences can constitute awareness of the world. Now that takes us back to a restriction I drew attention to in my third lecture (§3). It is the spontaneity of the understanding, the power of conceptual thinking, that brings both the world and the self into view. Creatures without conceptual capacities lack self-consciousness and—this is part of the same package—experience of objective reality.

I acknowledged that this restriction raises a question about the perceptual capacities of mere animals. Mere animals do not come within the scope of the Kantian thesis, since they do not have the spontaneity of the understanding. We cannot construe them as continually reshaping a world-view in rational response to the deliverances of experience; not if the idea of rational response requires subjects who are in charge of their thinking, standing ready to reassess what is a reason for what, and to change their responsive propensities accordingly. It follows that mere animals cannot enjoy "outer experience", on the conception of "outer experience" I have recommended. And that can seem to commit me to the Cartesian idea that brutes are automata.

The thought here is a form of one I found in Evans (Lecture III, §7). It is a plain fact that we share perception with mere animals. Partly on that basis, Evans suggests that when we make judgements about the perceptible world, we must be converting experiential content of a kind we share with mere animals, so that it must be non-conceptual, into conceptual form. When I discussed this in my third lecture, I had in place some of the Kantian framework that disallows Evans's conclusion. My claim was that when Evans argues that judgements of experience are based on non-conceptual content, he is falling into a version of the Myth of the Given, which is one side of the useless oscillation from which Kant tries to rescue us. And we now have another angle on why Evans's conclusion will not fit into a Kantian framework: why the framework precludes supposing that sensibility by itself yields content that is less than conceptual but already world-involving. In the absence of spontaneity, no self can be in view, and by the same token, the world cannot be in view either.

What about the fear that this implies an obvious falsehood: that mere animals are not genuinely sentient? To deal with this, I want to borrow from Hans-Georg Gadamer a remarkable description of the difference between a merely animal mode of life, in an environment, and a human mode of life, in the world.[4] For my purposes, the point of this is that it shows in some detail how we can acknowledge what is common between human beings and brutes, while preserving the difference that the Kantian thesis forces on us.

In mere animals, sentience is in the service of a mode of life that is structured exclusively by immediate biological imperatives. That is not to imply that the life is restricted to a struggle to keep the individual and the species going. There can be immediate biological imperatives that are at most indirectly connected with survival and reproduction: for instance, the impulse to play, which is found in many animals.[5] But without falling into that kind of restrictiveness, we can recognize that a merely animal life is shaped by goals whose control of the animal's behaviour at a given moment is an immediate outcome of biological forces. A mere animal does not weigh reasons and decide what to do. Now Gadamer's thesis is this: a life that is structured only in that way is led not in the world, but only in an environment. For a creature whose life has only that sort of shape, the milieu it lives in can be no more than a succession of problems and opportunities, constituted as such by those biological imperatives.

When we acquire conceptual powers, our lives come to embrace not just coping with problems and exploiting opportunities, constituted as such by immediate biological imperatives, but exercising spontaneity, deciding what to think and do. A naturalism of second nature allows us to put it like that; we can take in our stride something that is problematic in the context of a different sort of naturalism, that these exercises of freedom are elements in our lives, our careers as living and therefore natural beings. Of course it had better not be that our being in charge of our lives marks a transcendence of biology; that looks like a version of the rampant platonist fantasy. But we do not fall into rampant platonism if we say the shape of our lives is no longer determined by immediate biological forces. To acquire the

4. See *Truth and Method*, pp. 438–56, especially pp. 443–5.

5. I say "at most indirectly", and it is not clear that there is always even an indirect connection. That depends on such questions as whether playing can be completely accounted for in terms of, for instance, the honing of skills that are normally called on for survival.

spontaneity of the understanding is to become able, as Gadamer puts it, to "rise above the pressure of what impinges on us from the world" (*Truth and Method,* p. 444)—that succession of problems and opportunities constituted as such by biological imperatives—into a "free, distanced orientation" (p. 445). And the fact that the orientation is free, that it is above the pressure of biological need, characterizes it as an orientation to the world. For a perceiver with capacities of spontaneity, the environment is more than a succession of problems and opportunities; it is the bit of objective reality that is within her perceptual and practical reach. It is that for her because she can conceive it in ways that display it as that.[6]

When I say that for a creature with a merely animal life the milieu in which it lives can be no more than a succession of problems and opportunities, I am not saying that it *conceives* its environment in those terms. That would be to try to attribute to mere animals a full-fledged subjectivity, involving a conceptually mediated orientation that ought, as such, to count as an orientation to the world, even though we restrict the concepts in question to concepts things satisfy in virtue of how they relate to biological imperatives, which is to acknowledge that the orientation lacks the freedom and distance that would be required for it to be an orientation to the world at all. The point of the distinction between living merely in an environment and living in the world is precisely that we need not credit mere animals with a full-fledged subjectivity, an orientation to the world, at all, not even one that is restricted in that way. This is not to imply that features of the environment are nothing to a perceiving animal. On the contrary, they can be problems or opportunities for it, as I have been saying. The point is just that we must distinguish that from saying that the animal conceives the features as problems or opportunities.

This talk of what features of the environment are for an animal expresses an analogue to the notion of subjectivity, close enough to ensure that there is no Cartesian automatism in our picture. Exactly not: we need to appeal to an animal's sensitivity to features of its environment if we are to understand its alert and self-moving life, the

6. Gadamer's topic, in the passage I am exploiting, is the role of language in disclosing the world to us; it is language, he claims, that makes the "free, distanced orientation" possible. I postpone any discussion of the connection between language and the spontaneity of the understanding until the sketchy remarks at the end of this lecture; meanwhile I adapt Gadamer's remarks to my purposes.

precise way in which it copes competently with its environment. But by putting the notion of sensitivity to this or that in the context of the idea of inhabiting an environment, we ensure that we need not try to credit a mere animal with an orientation to the world, even the world as conceptualized in purely behaviour-related ways. To register how far we are from the Kantian structure, we might say that what is in question here is proto-subjectivity rather than subjectivity.

In a merely animal mode of life, living is nothing but responding to a succession of biological needs. When Gadamer describes the contrast as a "free, distanced orientation", the note of emancipation from the need to produce behaviour can suggest the idea of the theoretical. And certainly one thing that is absent from any sane conception of a merely animal mode of life is a disinterestedly contemplative attitude, towards the world at large or towards something in particular in it. But the point is not just that with spontaneity the activities of life come to include theorizing as well as acting. The lack of freedom that is characteristic of merely animal life is not enslavement to the practical as opposed to the theoretical, but enslavement to immediate biological imperatives. Emancipation into the "free, distanced orientation" brings intentional bodily action on to the scene no less than theoretical activity. The picture of full-fledged subjectivity that is in play here is not a picture of that dubiously intelligible kind of thing, an observer and thinker that does not act in the world it observes and thinks about.

Gadamer's account of how a merely animal life, lived in an environment, differs from a properly human life, lived in the world, coincides strikingly with some of what Marx says in his 1844 manuscript on alienated labour.[7] (Gadamer does not note the parallel.) This convergence should help to exorcize the idea of the passive observer.[8] For Marx, of course, a properly human life is nothing if not active: it involves the productive making over of "nature, the sensuous exterior world" (p. 135). If productive activity is properly human, it can in principle range freely over the world. This contrasts with merely animal life. As in Gadamer's description, merely animal life is a matter of dealing with a series of problems and opportunities that the environ-

---

7. I shall cite from the translation of David McLellan, in *Karl Marx: Early Texts* (Basil Blackwell, Oxford, 1972), pp. 133–45.

8. The convergence is surely not a coincidence. It reflects a Hegelian influence on both texts.

ment throws up, constituted as such by biologically given needs and drives. Marx complains memorably of a dehumanization of humanity in wage slavery. The part of human life that should be most expressive of humanity, namely, productive activity, is reduced to the condition of merely animal life, the meeting of merely biological needs. And although it is freedom that gives its distinctively human character to human life, wage slavery restricts freedom to the merely animal aspects of what are thus only incidentally human lives. "Man (the worker) only feels himself freely active in his animal functions of eating, drinking, and procreating, at most also in his dwelling and dress, and feels himself an animal in his human functions" (pp. 137–8).

Marx sums up his vision of what a properly human life would be in a striking image: without alienation, "the whole of nature" is "the inorganic body of man" (p. 139).[9] We can point up the convergence with Gadamer by glossing the image like this: the world is where a human being lives, where she is at home. Contrast the relation of an environment to an animal life. An environment is essentially alien to a creature that lives in it; it is the source of "the pressure of what impinges on [the animal] from the world". Not that a merely animal life is a constant struggle, whereas a distinctively human life is peculiarly easy. In Marx as in Gadamer, the point is not that a properly human life is easy but rather that it is distinctively free. And that is the same fact as that it is lived in the world, as opposed to consisting in coping with an environment.

Of course we must not understand the contrast between possessing the world and merely inhabiting an environment in terms of the absurd notion that when one comes to possess the world one stops having an environment—as if being human exempted one from having to be somewhere in particular. And of course it is already open to a mere animal to leave its present environment, in the straightforward sense of going somewhere else. That is one response to the pressures imposed on an animal by its present environment: insufficient food, no sexual partners, various sorts of threat. Coming to possess the world is in part acquiring the capacity to conceptualize the facts that underlie this already available behavioural possibility, so that one conceives the present environment as the region of the world within one's pres-

9. He adds "in so far as it is not itself a human body". Of course my ordinary (organic) body is part of nature; the striking thought is that the rest of nature is, in a different way, my body also.

ent sensory and practical reach: as where one happens to be, in contrast with other places where one might be.

And of course there is more than that to coming to possess the world. For instance, possessing the world shows also in the pointless knowable detail that one's current environment typically makes available to one. Consider the richness of a normal adult human being's visual field, which is far beyond anything that could matter for a capacity to cope with merely animal needs. Marx says man is unique in producing "according to the laws of beauty" (p. 140), and the point he is making in that remark shows up also here, in a distinctive feature of our consciousness. Our very experience, in the aspect of its nature that constitutes it as experience of the world, partakes of a salient condition of art, its freedom from the need to be useful.

5. As I noted in my third lecture (§3), the potential embarrassment I have been discussing does not stop with the denial that mere animals have "outer experience". They cannot have "inner experience" either, on the conception of "inner experience" I have recommended. This generates a parallel worry that I am obliterating their sentience. But if the considerations that can be summed up in the label "proto-subjectivity" can disarm the worry as it arises in the case of "outer experience", they should be no less capable of disarming it as it arises in the case of "inner experience".

As Gadamer describes merely animal lives, they are made up of coping with the "pressures" imposed on them by the environment. I have been insisting that if we refuse to find an orientation to the world in such a life, that does not commit us to denying that it includes a proto-subjective perceptual sensitivity to features of the environment. And such a life has just as much room for, say, pain or fear. Perceptual sensitivity to the environment need not amount to awareness of the outer world; I have been defending the claim that awareness of the outer world can be in place only concomitantly with full-fledged subjectivity. Somewhat similarly, feelings of pain or fear need not amount to awareness of an inner world. So we can hold that an animal has no inner world without representing it as insensate and affectless.

Sensations, emotional states, and the like are there for our subjectivity in an inner world. To talk in those terms is to employ the idea of objects of experience, present in a region of reality. In my second lecture (§5), I suggested that we should understand this application of the idea of objects of experience as a limiting case, because here the objects of awareness do not exist independently of the awareness. So the idea of the inner world is a limiting case of the idea of a region of reality. In these actualizations of our sensibility, as in others, conceptual capacities are passively drawn into operation, in this case in a first-person and present-tense mode. But we can recognize the relevant conceptual capacities as operative here only because these operations of them embody an understanding that they are not restricted to the first-person and present-tense mode: the very same circumstances of which these motions of our conceptual powers constitute awareness are also thinkable otherwise than in the first-person present. That is what entitles us to apply the structure of awareness and object: since the circumstances are understood to be essentially such as to admit of that alternative angle on them, we can conceive the first-person angle on them as a case of awareness of something, even though the object of this awareness is really nothing over and above the awareness itself.

Now it would be absurd to try to fit this complexity of structure, which is needed to sustain the idea that the inner world is a region of reality, into a description of a merely animal way of living. And it would not meet the point if we tried saying that sensations and emotional states are present to the proto-subjectivity of a mere animal. It would be hopeless to claim that sensations and emotional states are there for a mere animal in the way problems and opportunities thrown up by the environment are there for it. That would be to suggest that when we refuse to credit mere animals with an inner world, we could compensate by crediting them with an inner something else (we could hardly say "inner environment"), somehow analogous to the outer environment they are alive to in the way that is central to their proto-subjectivity. "Inner environment" does not make sense, and it does not seem plausible that we could force sense into the suggestion by careful choice of a different noun. But in any case nothing I have said about the inner world prevents us from acknowledging that mere animals can feel pain and fear.

Only for a full-fledged subjectivity can what it is to feel pain or fear amount to a limiting-case awareness of a degenerately substantial inner state of affairs. The limiting case of the structure of awareness and object is in place only because of how the awareness is structured by understanding. But nothing in the concepts of pain or fear implies that they can get a grip only where there is understanding, and thus full-fledged subjectivity. There is no reason to suppose that they can be applied in a non-first-person way only to something capable of applying them to itself in a first-person way.

6. At this point I want to stress again something I said in my third lecture (§4). I am rejecting a picture of a mere animal's perceptual sensitivity to its environment: a picture in which the senses yield content that is less than conceptual but already such as to represent the world. What I am rejecting is a picture of what perceptual states and occurrences are *for an animal*. I have said nothing about how things look when someone tackles scientific questions about how an animal's *perceptual machinery* works. And it is hard to see how those questions could be addressed without exploiting an idea of content that represents the world but cannot be conceptual in the demanding sense I have been using, since no animal's perceptual machinery (not even ours) possesses the spontaneity of understanding. I do not mean to be objecting to anything in cognitive science.

What I do mean to be rejecting is a certain philosophical outlook, one that could be expressed like this, if its proponents would consent to use my terms: delineating the contours of a subjectivity and delineating the contours of a proto-subjectivity are two tasks of much the same kind; they differ only in that they involve two different modes of orientation to the world, and so two different sorts of content. According to this outlook, both tasks call for saying how the world strikes a perceiver. (Among other things: we should also need to characterize other aspects of subjectivity, or proto-subjectivity, such as sensations or emotions.) It is just that in one kind of case the content involved in the world's striking the perceiver in a certain way is nonconceptual.

For a vivid example of this philosophical outlook, consider the importance Thomas Nagel attributes to the question "What is it like to be a bat?"[10] Think first about a different question: what would it be like if we had a sensory capacity for echo-location? That question challenges our imagination in a striking way. We have to project our imagination into an alternative possible world in which our subjectivity is in part differently constituted, and the question is challenging

---

10. "What Is It Like to Be a Bat?", in Nagel's *Mortal Questions* (Cambridge University Press, Cambridge, 1979), pp. 165–80.

because we have no sensory basis for this imaginative extrapolation. Now compare the question Nagel actually asks: what is it like for bats to do their echo-locating? Nagel's idea is that this presents just the same challenge to the imagination, but now in a form that makes our failure to meet it not a failure to conceptualize a mere possibility, but a failure to get our minds around part of the layout of the actual world. In my terms, this is to treat what is only a proto-subjectivity as if it were a full-fledged subjectivity. Nagel's picture is that bats have a full-fledged subjectivity whose shape is beyond the reach of our concepts.

I do not believe the question what it is like to be a bat should seem any more intractable than the question what it is like to be a dog or a cat, where there are no senses that we do not share. To answer such questions, we need an account of the biological imperatives that structure the lives of the creatures in question, and an account of the sensory capacities that enable them to respond to their environment in ways that are appropriate in the light of those biological imperatives. Saying that bats can locate prey or cave walls by sonar can be part of such an answer in the case of bats, in much the way saying that the vision of cats is sensitive to green and blue but not red can be part of an answer in the case of cats. It is true that when the question is *what it is like* to be a bat or a cat, the answer must try to characterize something on the lines of the creature's point of view. But the accounts that I envisage do that, to the fullest extent that makes sense, without warranting the thought that in the case of bats at least there are facts that elude our understanding. These accounts capture the character of the proto-subjectivity of the creatures in question, the distinctive ways in which they are alive to their environments.

We are familiar "from within" with what it is like to see colours. It is tempting to think that this equips us to comprehend a fully subjective fact about what the colour vision of cats is like, which we report when we say they can see green and blue but not red. There must then be parallel fully subjective facts about bat echo-location, but they defeat our understanding. But this is just another form of the Myth of the Given. The idea is that mere animals already enjoy perceptual experience in which the world strikes them as being a certain way, and the only difference our understanding makes for us is that we can impose conceptual form on the already world-representing but less than conceptual content that, like them, we receive in experience. Then the problem about bats is that our imagination cannot extend to how the conversion into conceptual form would go, in the case of the content yielded by the echo-locating capacity. So the picture is that mere animals only receive the Given, whereas we not only receive it but are also able to put it into conceptual shape. To think like that is to set one's foot on a familiar philosophical treadmill.[11]

7. How has it come about that there are animals that possess the spontaneity of understanding? That is a perfectly good question. There was a time when there were no rational animals. Suppose we had a credible account of how forces that are intelligibly operative in nature might have led to the evolution of animals with conceptual powers. That would definitively avert a form of rampant platonism: the idea that our species acquired what makes it special, the capacity to resonate to meaning, in a gift from outside nature. If we took that seriously, we would have to suppose that when succeeding generations are initiated into responsiveness to meaning, what happens is that upbringing actualizes a potential for the development of an extra-natural ingredient, a potential implanted in the species in the supposed extra-natural evolutionary event.

But this request for an evolutionary story need not look very pressing. Evolutionary speculation is not a context in which rampant platonism is somehow particularly tempting. Reflection about the *Bildung* of individual human beings should be enough to distinguish the naturalized platonism I have recommended from rampant platonism. And in this reflection we can regard the culture a human being is initiated into as a going concern; there is no particular reason why we should need to uncover or speculate about its history, let alone the origins of culture as such. Human infants are mere animals, distinctive only in their potential, and nothing occult happens to a human being in ordinary upbringing. If we locate a variety of platonism in the context of an account of *Bildung* that insists on those facts, we thereby ensure that it is not a rampant platonism. Mere ignorance about how

11. Nagel could have made many of the points he wanted without leaving the domain of subjectivity properly so called (by my lights). Perhaps Martians have an echo-locating capacity, which figures in the rational basis of their world-view in the way our senses do in the basis of ours. I have no need to deny that there might be concepts anchored in sensory capacities so alien to ours that the concepts would be unintelligible to us. What I am objecting to is only the way this point gets focused, in the case of bats, on a supposed non-conceptual content that we cannot convert into conceptual shape.

human culture might have come on the scene in the first place is hardly a plausible starting point for an argument that initiation into it must actualize an extra-natural potential in human beings.[12]

And in any case, if we do speculate about how animals might have evolved into a way of living that includes initiating their young into a culture, we must be clear that that is what we are doing. It would be one thing to give an evolutionary account of the fact that normal human maturation includes the acquisition of a second nature, which involves responsiveness to meaning; it would be quite another thing to give a constitutive account of what responsiveness to meaning is. I have been granting that it is reasonable to look for an evolutionary story. This is not a concession to the sort of constructive philosophical account of meaning that I discussed in my last lecture (§3): something whose point would be to make the relevant sort of intelligibility safe for a naturalism without second nature. That is a misbegotten idea, and there is no comfort for it here.

8. Michael Dummett has claimed that the fundamental tenet of analytic philosophy is that philosophical questions about thought are to be approached through language.[13] In these lectures, I have concerned myself with thought; I have tried to describe a way of conceiving how thought bears on the world that would be immune to some familiar philosophical anxieties. And so far I have scarcely mentioned language. So it might seem that I have enrolled myself as an opponent of analytic philosophy in Dummett's sense.

But any such impression would be quite superficial.

I have followed Kant in taking thought to be an exercise of the understanding: "the mind's power of producing representations from itself, the *spontaneity* of knowledge".[14] The power of spontaneity comprises a network of conceptual capacities linked by putatively rational connections, with the connections essentially subject to critical reflec-

12. It is true, however, that the good questions we can raise in the evolutionary context come as close as good questions can to the philosophical questions I want to exorcize.

13. See "Can Analytical Philosophy be Systematic, and Ought It to Be?", in his *Truth and Other Enigmas* (Duckworth, London, 1978), pp. 437–58. At p. 442 Dummett writes: "For Frege, as for all subsequent analytical philosophers, the philosophy of language is the foundation of all other philosophy because it is only by the analysis of language that we can analyse thought."

14. *Critique of Pure Reason*, A51/B75.

tion. I have claimed that experience must stand in rational relations to judgement if we are to be able to understand the very possibility of empirical content; and I have claimed that we can make sense of rational relations between experience and judgement only in the context of an equation between the space of concepts and the space of reasons. Thought can bear on empirical reality only because to be a thinker at all is to be at home in the space of reasons. And being at home in the space of reasons involves not just a collection of propensities to shift one's psychological stance in response to this or that, but the standing potential for a reflective stance at which the question arises whether one ought to find this or that persuasive.

Now it is not even clearly intelligible to suppose a creature might be born at home in the space of reasons. Human beings are not: they are born mere animals, and they are transformed into thinkers and intentional agents in the course of coming to maturity. This transformation risks looking mysterious. But we can take it in our stride if, in our conception of the *Bildung* that is a central element in the normal maturation of human beings, we give pride of place to the learning of language. In being initiated into a language, a human being is introduced into something that already embodies putatively rational linkages between concepts, putatively constitutive of the layout of the space of reasons, before she comes on the scene. This is a picture of initiation into the space of reasons as an already going concern; there is no problem about how something describable in those terms could emancipate a human individual from a merely animal mode of living into being a full-fledged subject, open to the world. A mere animal, moved only by the sorts of things that move mere animals and exploiting only the sorts of contrivances that are open to mere animals, could not single-handedly emancipate itself into possession of understanding. Human beings mature into being at home in the space of reasons or, what comes to the same thing, living their lives in the world; we can make sense of that by noting that the language into which a human being is first initiated stands over against her as a prior embodiment of mindedness, of the possibility of an orientation to the world.

This way of accepting the basic tenet of analytic philosophy is some distance from any Dummett considers. Dummett focuses on two "principal functions" of language: as "instrument of communication" and as "vehicle of thought". His conclusion is that we should take neither of them to be primary.[15] But that is because he thinks those functions of language are both fundamental. In the picture I am suggesting, they are secondary. The feature of language that really matters is rather this: that a natural language, the sort of language into which human beings are first initiated, serves as a repository of tradition, a store of historically accumulated wisdom about what is a reason for what. The tradition is subject to reflective modification by each generation that inherits it. Indeed, a standing obligation to engage in critical reflection is itself part of the inheritance. (See Lecture I, §5; Lecture II, §7.) But if an individual human being is to realize her potential of taking her place in that succession, which is the same thing as acquiring a mind, the capacity to think and act intentionally, at all, the first thing that needs to happen is for her to be initiated into a tradition as it stands.[16]

15. See "Language and Communication", in Alexander George, ed., *Reflections on Chomsky* (Basil Blackwell, Oxford, 1989), pp. 192–212. When I delivered this lecture, I wrongly attributed to Dummett the view that language's function as instrument of communication is primary. My point was just to lead up to language's function as repository of tradition, and I have felt free to recast what I say so as to arrive there without falsifying Dummett's position. I am grateful to Christopher Peacocke for setting me straight.

16. The concept of tradition is central in Gadamer's thinking about understanding; see *Truth and Method*, passim.

AFTERWORD

PART I

Davidson in Context

1. In the lectures, I use Davidson's coherentism exclusively as a foil to the view of experience that I recommend. Here I want to place Davidson's thinking about the epistemology of empirical thought in a historical context, constituted by a strand in the recent development of the American pragmatist tradition. I hope this will bring out something the lectures obscure: the extent to which I can count Davidson as an ally rather than an opponent.

2. The two dogmas of empiricism that W. V. Quine attacked in his celebrated essay of that title were, first, that there is a "fundamental cleavage" (p. 20) between the analytic, in the sense of statements true by virtue of meaning alone, and the synthetic, in the sense of statements whose truth is dependent not only on meaning but also on the world; and, second, that "empirical significance" can be parcelled out statement by statement among the body of statements that express our view of the empirical world.

What we ought to say instead of the second dogma, according to Quine, is this: "The unit of empirical significance is the whole of science" (p. 42: this is the source for the way I have put the second dogma). An alternative formulation is this: "our statements about the external world face the tribunal of experience not individually but as a corporate body" (p. 41). If these are two formulations of the same thought, Quine is implicitly glossing empirical significance in terms of being subject to the tribunal of experience. That makes it look as if Quine's conception of "empirical significance" corresponds to the Kantian conception of empirical content, or bearing on the empirical

world, that I defend in the lectures. According to that conception, the
fact that something, say a belief, or—more congenially to Quine—a
whole world-view, bears on the world, in the sense of constituting a
stand taken as to how things are, depends on its being vulnerable to
the world for a verdict on its acceptability; and the verdict can be
delivered only through experience.

The rejected first dogma claims that the truth of a synthetic statement depends on two factors, meaning and the world; an analytic
statement is one for which the "world" factor is null. Now Quine's
positive picture retains this duality of factors on which truth depends.
He says (p. 36): "It is obvious that truth in general depends on both
language and extralinguistic fact." His claim is not that there are not
those two factors, but just that we cannot separate them out statement
by statement. In the context of an apparently uncontentious empiricism, the "world" factor is just the answerability to experience that is
summed up as "empirical significance". So Quine can reformulate the
"obvious" dependence of truth on both language and extralinguistic
fact, in an expression of the thesis that rejects the second dogma, by
saying (p. 41): "Taken collectively, science has its double dependence
upon language and experience; but this duality is not significantly
traceable into the statements of science taken one by one."

This validates an impression that is anyway given by the structure
of Quine's essay: that rejecting the second dogma is the fundamental
point. Quine's positive thinking in the essay is encapsulated in the thesis that the unit of empirical significance is the whole of science. With
the duality of factors retained, the first dogma figures as something
that can be correct only if the second dogma is, so that rejecting the
second can suffice to reject both. The first dogma is the thesis that
there are true statements that are analytic in the sense that for them
the "world" factor—the factor of dependence on experience, "empirical significance"—is null. If "empirical significance" cannot be
shared out among individual statements anyway, that undermines the
very idea of a statement with no "empirical significance". "No empirical significance of its own" could only be a special case of "some
empirical significance of its own". If it makes no sense to suppose a
particular statement has its own positive quantity of "empirical
significance", a determinate share of the "empirical significance" of
the total world-view in whose expression the statement figures, then it

equally makes no sense to suppose there might be statements for which the quantity is zero.[1]

3. As I said, Quine's positive picture, his "empiricism without the dogmas" (p. 42), retains a counterpart to the duality that figures in spelling out the idea of analyticity. Truth—which we must now think of as primarily possessed by a whole world-view—depends partly on "language" and partly on "experience". "Language" here labels an endogenous factor in the shaping of systems of empirical belief, distinguishable—though only for whole systems—from the exogenous factor indicated by "experience". When we acknowledge this exogenous factor, we register that belief is vulnerable, by way of "the tribunal of experience", to the world it aims to be true of. So "language" figures, in Quine's holistic context, as a counterpart to "meaning" as "meaning" figured in the now debunked contrast between "true by virtue of meaning alone" (true in a way that involves no vulnerability to the world) and "true by virtue of both meaning and the way the world is".

"Empirical significance" registers the exogenous factor in this contrast, the answerability to something outside the system. And the nearest thing in Quine's positive thinking to the old notion of meaning is "language", which stands on the other side of the retained duality, as the endogenous factor. "Empirical significance" is not meaning as it figured in the idea that there might be statements true by virtue of meaning alone; and it is not a functional descendant of meaning, so conceived, in the novel environment of Quine's holism, but a functional descendant of what stood precisely in contrast to meaning in the old version of the duality.

The fact that Quine's "empirical significance" is one side of a holistic counterpart to the old duality means that, in spite of the convergence between Quine's talk of facing the tribunal of experience and my talk of a rational vulnerability to intuitions, we cannot gloss Quine's "empirical significance" in terms of bearing on the empirical world in the sense in which I use that phrase: what stand one takes on how things are in the world when one adopts a belief or a world-view. For Quine, the two factors are distinguishable, even though

1. The structurally parallel idea, the idea of statements for which the "meaning" factor is null, is clearly self-defeating.

only for whole systems, and that means that the "empirical significance" of a world-view cannot amount to its empirical content in the sense of how, in adopting the world-view, one takes things to be in the empirical world. That requires the other factor, the endogenous one, also.

So far, this might be merely a terminological oddity about Quine's use of the phrase "empirical significance". It is Quine's own point that "empirical significance" does not amount to content, in the sense of what stand one takes on how things are in the empirical world. In the thesis that translation is indeterminate, which is meant to elaborate the moral of "Two Dogmas", his aim is to stress "the extent of man's conceptual sovereignty" in the formation of world-views:[2] that is—to put it in a way that brings Quine into explicit contact with Kant—the extent to which the content of world-views is a product of spontaneity operating freely, uncontrolled by the deliverances of receptivity. And from Quine's point of view, it is a merit of the notion of "empirical significance" that it stands on the wrong side of the descendant duality to be a descendant of the old notion of meaning. Quine is no friend to the old notion of meaning, and the descendant notion, the notion of "language" as the endogenous factor, bound up as it is with "man's conceptual sovereignty", retains in Quine's thinking some of the intellectual dubiousness of its ancestor. In contrast, "empirical significance" is an intellectually respectable notion, because it is explicable entirely in terms of the law-governed operations of receptivity, untainted by the freedom of spontaneity. To put it in a more Quinean way, "empirical significance" can be investigated scientifically. "The extent of man's conceptual sovereignty", the extent to which the content of a world-view goes beyond its "empirical significance", is just the extent to which such a notion of content lies outside the reach of science, and therefore outside the reach of first-rate intellectual endeavour.

It is not just a verbal point that "empirical significance" is on the wrong side of the duality to be a descendant of the notion of meaning. We have to discount the rhetoric that makes it look, at first sight, as if Quine's notion corresponds to the Kantian notion of empirical content. Quine speaks of facing the tribunal of experience, which seems

2. *Word and Object* (MIT Press, Cambridge, Mass., 1960), p. 5. For the indeterminacy thesis, see chap. 2 of that work.

to imply a vulnerability to rational criticism grounded in experience. But he conceives experience as "the stimulation of . . . sensory receptors".[3] And such a conception of experience makes no room for experience to stand in rational relations to beliefs or world-views. The cash value of the talk of facing the tribunal of experience can only be that different irritations of sensory nerve endings are disposed to have different impacts on the system of statements a subject accepts, not that different courses of experience have different rational implications about what system of statements a subject ought to accept. In spite of the juridical rhetoric, Quine conceives experience so that it could not figure in the order of justification, as opposed to the order of law-governed happenings. This is all of a piece with the idea that "empirical significance" is a topic for natural science.

At one point in "Two Dogmas" (p. 43), Quine writes: "Certain statements . . . seem peculiarly germane to sense experience—and in a selective way: some statements to some experiences, others to others. . . . But in this relation of 'germaneness' I envisage nothing more than a loose association reflecting the relative likelihood, in practice, of our choosing one statement rather than another for revision in the event of recalcitrant experience." The only connection he countenances between experience and the acceptance of statements is a brutely causal linkage that subjects are conditioned into when they learn a language. It is not that it is right to revise one's belief system thus and so in the light of such-and-such an experience, but just that that revision is what would probably happen if one's experience took that course.[4] Quine conceives experiences so that they can only be outside the space of reasons, the order of justification.

It may still seem that Quine is subject at most to criticism of his rhetoric. But his talk of facing the tribunal of experience is not just a slip, which we could easily excise; it has roots that go deep in Quine's

---

3. This is from p. 75 of "Epistemology Naturalized", in *Ontological Relativity and Other Essays* (Columbia University Press, New York, 1969).

4. This must go for the concept of recalcitrant experience, which is central to Quine's celebrated image of "a man-made fabric which impinges on experience only along the edges" (p. 42). It is tempting to spell out the idea like this: an experience is recalcitrant if one cannot rationally take it at face value while continuing to believe everything one believes; it is rationally incumbent on one either to recast one's world-view (and the Duhemian point from which Quine starts is that there will be more than one way to do this) or to discount the experience. But for Quine what it is for an experience to be recalcitrant can only be that a subject who has the experience will probably change her beliefs.

thinking. We cannot simply register that "empirical significance" is not genuinely a kind of significance if experience is not in the order of justification, and leave the substance of Quine's thinking intact.

If experience is not in the order of justification, it cannot be something that world-views transcend or go beyond. But Quine needs that for his talk of "the extent of man's conceptual sovereignty". What a world-view might transcend, so that adoption of it might be an exercise of spontaneity or "conceptual sovereignty", is evidence that tells less than conclusively in favour of it. But if experience plays only a causal role in the formation of a world-view, not a justificatory role, then it does not serve as evidence at all.

And if experience does not stand to world-views as evidence to theory, that puts in question the capacity of Quine's picture to accommodate world-views at all. It is true that Quine wants the idea of a world-view to stand exposed as intellectually second-rate. But he does not want to abandon it altogether. That would be to abandon the point he wants to make by talking of "the extent of man's conceptual sovereignty". There would be nothing for the thesis of the indeterminacy of translation to be about if instead of talking about arriving at world-views we had to talk exclusively about acquiring propensities to feel comfortable with certain vocalizations. Now the idea of an interaction between spontaneity—"conceptual sovereignty"—and receptivity, which is Kantian so far as it goes, can so much as seem to make room for the idea of adopting a world-view only if the deliverances of receptivity are understood to belong with the adopted world-view in the order of justification. If we try to suppose that exercises of "conceptual sovereignty" are only causally affected by the course of experience, and not rationally answerable to it, there is nothing left of the idea that what "conceptual sovereignty" produces is something that is *about* the empirical world, a stance correctly or incorrectly adopted according to how things are in the empirical world. And if we lose that, there is nothing left of the idea that what is operative is "conceptual sovereignty". The notion of a world-view, formed in an exercise of "conceptual sovereignty", is not just the notion of a perturbation produced jointly by impacts from the world and by some force operating from within the subject, in a way that is partly (but only partly) determined by those impacts.[5]

5. Understandably, Quine's language often tries to have it both ways. A characteristic formulation is this (from p. 75 of "Epistemology Naturalized"): "The stimulation of his

If we clean up Quine's formulations by eliminating the juridical rhetoric, we deprive him of the very idea of "conceptual sovereignty", and the effect is to threaten the idea that we are in touch with the empirical world at all. It is not that this reading makes Quine suggest we may be wildly wrong about the world, like an old-fashioned philosophical sceptic. But without the "tribunal" rhetoric and its companion idea of "conceptual sovereignty", which have emerged as strictly illicit by Quine's own lights, he puts in question the very idea that we have the world in view at all, that anything that we do constitutes taking a stand, right or wrong, even wildly wrong, on how things are in it.[6]

4. The awkward position of experience in Quine's thinking has implications for an otherwise attractive reading of what he is doing when he rejects the first of the two dogmas. In the lectures, I derive from Sellars, and trace to Kant, a rejection of the idea that something is Given in experience, from outside the activity of shaping worldviews. The attractive reading has Quine making a counterpart point, rejecting the idea that something is Given from within the very structure of the understanding.[7]

Sellars says: "empirical knowledge, like its sophisticated extension, science, is rational, not because it has a *foundation* but because it is a self-correcting enterprise which can put *any* claim in jeopardy, though not *all* at once."[8] We must think of empirical rationality in a dynamic way, in terms of a continuing adjustment to the impact of experience.

To reject the idea of an exogenous Given is to follow this prescription in part. It is to refuse to conceive experience's demands on a sys-

---

sensory receptors is all the evidence anybody has had to go on, ultimately, in arriving at his picture of the world." This sentence begins with a formulation that would fit only something outside the order of justification, but continues ("has had to go on . . . in arriving at his picture of the world") in a way that would make sense only of something within the order of justification. What one goes on in arriving at one's picture of the world is not the stimulation of one's sensory receptors, experience as Quine officially conceives it, but how things appear to one, which belongs in a quite different conception of experience.

6. For a much fuller discussion of Quine's thinking on these lines, see chap. 6 of Barry Stroud, *The Significance of Philosophical Scepticism* (Clarendon Press, Oxford, 1984), to which I am much indebted.

7. This is how Rorty reads Quine; see chap. 4 of *Philosophy and the Mirror of Nature*. (I capitalize "Given", as throughout, to contrast the problematic conception with one that is innocuous; see Lecture I, §4.)

8. "Empiricism and the Philosophy of Mind", p. 300.

tem of beliefs as imposed from outside the activity of adjusting the system, by something constituted independently of the current state of the evolving system, or a state into which the system might evolve. The required adjustments to the system depend on what we take experience to reveal to us, and we can capture that only in terms of the concepts and conceptions that figure in the evolving system. What we take experience to tell us is already part of the system, not an external constraint on it.

That is to say that nothing is Given from outside the evolving system of belief. The counterpart claim—the claim that nothing is Given from inside the understanding, the intellectual capacity that is operative in the continuing activity of shaping the system—is in Sellars too; it is implicit in the remark about the rationality of science that I have just quoted. It is true that when Sellars debunks the Myth of the Given in detail, he focuses on the supposed external constraint, but he begins "Empiricism and the Philosophy of Mind" by saying (pp. 253–4) that the idea of something Given in experience is a specific application of a conception that is much more general. It can easily seem that rejecting an endogenous Given requires us to say what Sellars says in the remark I have quoted: that any of our beliefs, including beliefs about structures that must be instantiated in intellectually respectable belief systems—the beliefs that implicitly or explicitly govern adjustments in belief systems in response to experience—are open to revision. And this has a distinctly Quinean ring.

But there is one thing wrong with reading Quine like this, as claiming that nothing is Given from inside the evolving system either, and that is the word "either". We cannot without qualification take it that Quine fills out the attack on the Given with a counterpart to Sellars's focus on the idea of something Given from outside. The trouble for this reading comes from the uneasy status of Quine's juridical rhetoric. From one perspective Quine leaves the external Given in place: on his official conception, experience would have to lack the putative rational bearing on belief that is distinctive of the Myth of the Given, but the "tribunal" rhetoric, which is not mere decoration, implies a rational link between experience and belief. So Quine's thinking looks like an awkward combination: he tries to reject an endogenous Given without definitively rejecting an exogenous Given. In Quine's picture, "man's conceptual sovereignty" has no internally generated limits to its freedom of play, but it operates within limits set from outside its domain.

5. Davidson's recommendation of coherentism, which I have used as a target of criticism in these lectures, is a response to a genuine and important insight, which we can identify with the point I have made about Quine: Quine's play with (in effect) spontaneity and receptivity impossibly tries to have it both ways—to exploit the idea of experience as a tribunal that stands in judgement over beliefs, while conceiving experience so that it has to stand outside the order of justification. Davidson is also, admirably by my lights, hostile to any philosophy that generates problems about how we can be in touch with the empirical world at all, as I have claimed Quine's does.

Davidson argues that the duality of endogenous and exogenous factors, as it persists into Quine's "empiricism without the dogmas", is "itself a dogma of empiricism, the third dogma".[9] He attacks this persisting dualism, "the dualism of conceptual scheme [Quine's "language"] and empirical content [Quine's "empirical significance"]",[10] from both sides.

In "On the Very Idea of a Conceptual Scheme", the attack is from the side of the endogenous factor. A vivid expression of Quine's idea of "conceptual sovereignty", a freedom only partly constrained by the exogenous factor, is the thesis that there might be world-views that are mutually unintelligible—that different exercises of "conceptual sovereignty" might diverge that far. But Davidson argues that the idea of mutually unintelligible world-views does not make sense.

In "A Coherence Theory of Truth and Knowledge", the attack is from the other side. There Davidson argues that experience cannot constitute "a basis for knowledge outside the scope of our beliefs" (p. 310). The argument is reminiscent of Sellars. In the terms I have used, Davidson's point is that experience cannot be both inside the space of reasons, as it would need to be if it were to constitute "a basis for knowledge", and outside it, as Davidson claims it would need to be if it were to be "outside the scope of our beliefs".

9. "On the Very Idea of a Conceptual Scheme", p. 189. Davidson continues: "The third, and perhaps the last, for if we give it up it is not clear that there is anything distinctive left to call empiricism."
10. "On the Very Idea of a Conceptual Scheme", p. 189.

Now Davidson's aim in these thematically connected writings is to exorcize a style of thinking whose effect—even when this is not the intention—is to make a mystery out of thought's bearing on the empirical world. He ends "On the Very Idea of a Conceptual Scheme" like this (p. 198): "In giving up the dualism of scheme and world [that is: world conceived as the source of demands imposed on our thinking in experience, from outside thought], we do not give up the world, but re-establish unmediated touch with the familiar objects whose antics make our sentences and opinions true or false." Focusing on this remark, we can see that the image I recommend in the lectures, in which thought is unbounded, should be fully congenial to Davidson. The rejected image, with a boundary that encloses thought and sets it off from the world, would give pictorial expression to the idea that there are philosophical problems about the relation between thought as such and its objects. Rejecting the image is refusing to let our "unmediated touch" with the familiar world be threatened by a set of philosophical assumptions that give only the illusory appearance of being compulsory. Viewed in this light, Davidson's response to Quine's continuing dualism of scheme and world looks like something that ought to be a model for me.[11]

And indeed it is, up to a point. I gladly acknowledge that Davidson has the essential point, that philosophy must not be allowed to make a mystery out of thought's bearing on its objects. And he is right that Quine cannot have it both ways: experience as Quine conceives it cannot be a tribunal. But the aspiration of eliminating mystery is one thing; realizing it is another. In my view Davidson resolves the tension he finds in Quine in the wrong direction, and the result is precisely to leave us with the philosophical problems he wants to eliminate.

Davidson sees that Quine has no coherent way to make something out of, in effect, the idea that systems of empirical belief result from the co-operation of spontaneity and receptivity. He goes wrong by my lights in concluding that there is nothing to be made of the idea: that it can only reflect an unworkable dualism. As I said (§3 above), the idea of an interaction between spontaneity and receptivity can so much as seem to make it intelligible that what results is a belief, or a

---

11. Christopher Hookway and, in a different way, Aryeh Frankfurter urged this on me.

system of beliefs, about the empirical world—something correctly or incorrectly adopted according to how things are in the empirical world—only if spontaneity's constructions are rationally vulnerable to the deliverances of receptivity. Quine's official view of experience disrupts Quine's attempt at a version of that picture. And Davidson shares that view of experience: for Davidson, receptivity can impinge on the space of reasons only from outside, which is to say that nothing can be rationally vulnerable to its deliverances.[12] Davidson differs from Quine only in that he is explicit about this, and clear-sightedly draws the consequence: we cannot make sense of thought's bearing on the world in terms of an interaction between spontaneity and receptivity. If we go on using the Kantian terms, we have to say that the operations of spontaneity are rationally unconstrained from outside themselves. That is indeed a way of formulating Davidson's coherentism.

Of course Davidson's thinking does not obliterate all forms of the idea that empirical thinking is rationally vulnerable to the course of experience. "The course of experience" might be interpreted to mean the succession of circumstances that consist in its appearing to one that things are thus and so, and appearings do impinge rationally on the activity of shaping one's world-view. That is something we can say without confusion, by Davidson's lights, because its appearing to one that things are thus and so is, as such, already within the space of concepts, and hence qualified to stand in rational relations to other inhabitants of that space. But what we cannot say without confusion, according to Davidson, is that sensory impressions, impacts of the world on our senses, impose rational demands on our empirical thinking. Or if we can say that, it is only by dint of packing some complexity into "impose". Perhaps a sensory impression causes it to appear to a subject that things are thus and so, and the appearing has implications for what the subject ought to think. But sensory impressions

---

12. The point does not turn on the detail of Quine's conception of experience, as stimulation of sensory surfaces. There can be less resolutely anti-mentalistic conceptions of experience that nevertheless match Quine's conception at a more abstract level, in that they take experiences to be deliverances of receptivity. Davidson's general thought is that if experience is understood as what receptivity provides us with, then, whatever the details of the conception, experience is *eo ipso* understood in a way that removes it from the space of reasons.

themselves, as Davidson conceives them, cannot stand in rational relations to what a subject is to think.[13]

I have not put this thought in Davidson's own terms. Davidson
does not talk about appearings, and he writes as if only beliefs can fill
the role that I have suggested appearings can fill, for instance when he
expresses his coherentism by the remark I quote in the lectures: "nothing can count as a reason for holding a belief except another belief"
(p. 310).[14] If Davidson wants to acknowledge a grounding role for
appearings, this focus on beliefs seems unhappy, at least as a matter of
terminology. Its appearing to me that things are thus and so is not
obviously to be equated with my believing something. Certainly not
with my believing that things are thus and so. No doubt when it appears to me that things are thus and so, I usually (at least) believe that
it appears to me that things are thus and so, but it is not obvious that
the appearing *is* the belief; and whether it is or not, we can innocu-
ously credit the appearing itself with rational implications for what I
ought to think. But for my immediate purposes, there is no substantial
issue here. Davidson's terminology fits what looks like an overly simple formulation that he chooses for his coherentist position. He could
have made the same substantial point if he had said: nothing can
count as a reason for holding a belief except something else that is also
in the space of concepts—for instance, a circumstance consisting in its
appearing to a subject that things are thus and so. (There is a more
substantial problem with Davidson's formulation, which I shall come
to in due course.)

The echo of Sellars that I mentioned earlier sounds here.[15] Sellars
devotes part of "Empiricism and the Philosophy of Mind" to defending a notion of sensory impressions.[16] The point of the defence is to

13. At least in "A Coherence Theory of Truth and Knowledge", Davidson seems to
reserve the word "experience" for sensory impressions as distinct from appearings. See, for
instance, p. 313, where he formulates a view he opposes like this: "whatever there is to
meaning must be traced back somehow to experience, the given, or patterns of sensory
stimulation, something intermediate between belief and the usual objects our beliefs are
about." ("Belief" here serves as a code for "things in the space of concepts"; see the next
paragraph in my text.) But how we should use the word "experience" is not the point here.

14. See "A Coherence Theory of Truth and Knowledge", p. 311: "The trouble we have
been running into is that the justification seems to depend on the awareness, which is just
another belief."

15. In fact I have formulated what is innocuous by Davidson's lights in terms that are
more Sellarsian than Davidsonian.

16. The defence occupies most of the concluding part of the essay, from §45.

distinguish impressions from bits of the Given, and Sellars effects this by carefully refusing to attribute any direct epistemological significance to impressions. They have an indirect epistemological significance, in that without them there could not be such directly significant circumstances as seeing that things are thus and so, or having it look to one as if things are thus and so. But it is only in that indirect way that impressions enter into the rational responsiveness of empirical thinking to the course of experience. We can have an innocent interpretation of the idea that empirical thinking is rationally responsive to the course of experience, but only by understanding "the course of experience" to mean the succession of appearings, not the succession of impressions.

Impressions are, by definition we might say, receptivity in operation. So the picture that is common to Sellars and Davidson is this. Receptivity figures in the explanatory background of circumstances that belong together with evolving world-views in the order of justification. But receptivity itself cannot rationally interact with spontaneity, in the way that Quine's rhetoric implies, though his official conception of receptivity precludes such interaction.

Against this, I claim that although Quine's half-hearted attempt to picture world-views as products of a rational interaction between spontaneity and receptivity is unacceptable, as Davidson sees, that is no reason to discard the very idea of such an interaction. The trouble lies not in the idea itself, but in the half-heartedness—in the fact that while the rhetoric depicts the interaction as rational, Quine conceives receptivity in such a way that it cannot impinge rationally on anything. We can have a whole-hearted version of the idea if we can see our way to saying that the impressions of the world on our senses, the deliverances of our receptivity, are—as such—the appearings (or at least some of them) that, as Davidson and Sellars agree, can innocently be taken to belong together with our world-views in the space of reasons, since they are already in the space of concepts. That way, we can hold on to the attractive thought that Quine only half-heartedly embraces. There really is a prospect of finding empirical content, as possessed by exercises of spontaneity, unmysterious if we can think of it on the lines that Davidson and Sellars disallow, and that Quine is officially committed to disallowing. We ought to have no problem about how an exercise of "conceptual sovereignty" can bear on the empirical world—can constitute taking a stand on how things are, a posture correctly or incorrectly adopted according to the way the world is arranged—if "conceptual sovereignty" is rationally answerable to how the world impresses itself on the subject in experience.

It is not enough to say, with permission from Sellars and Davidson, that the exercise of "conceptual sovereignty" in shaping world-views is rationally responsible to the succession of appearings to the subject. Not that that is wrong. But if we follow Sellars and Davidson in distancing the appearings from the impressions, saying what they will let us say does not entitle us to find no philosophical mystery in thought's bearing on the world.[17]

According to Davidson and Sellars, we can place appearings within the space of concepts, so that they can coherently be taken to stand in rational relations to beliefs, only by distinguishing them from the world's impacts on our senses. Appearings are just more of the same kind of things beliefs are: possessors of empirical content, bearing on the empirical world. And now we cannot make the question "How can beliefs (say) have empirical content?" look any less pressing by talking about a rational interplay between appearings and beliefs. The question is really "How can anything have empirical content?", and it is no good just helping ourselves to the fact that appearings do.

Contrast how things look if we manage to conceive the rational answerability of beliefs to appearings as a rational answerability to receptivity itself. Now we cannot be accused of merely shifting the mystery of empirical content from beliefs to appearings. Now there is no mystery. If the rational answerability is to receptivity itself, not just to something linked with receptivity only in that receptivity figures in its explanatory background, then in being subject to the tribunal of experience, exercises of "conceptual sovereignty" are rationally answerable to the world itself. (Recall the image of experience as openness to the world.) There cannot be a problem about the idea of a stand as to how things are, correctly or incorrectly adopted according

17. "Entitle" matters here. Rorty (whom I shall come to shortly) is very good at debunking the moves that are available if we suppose there are such problems for philosophy. Perhaps the uselessness of the moves indicates, as it were from the outside, that this conception of philosophy's task must be mistaken. But this external approach can easily leave the philosophical questions still looking as if they *ought* to be good ones, and then the result is continuing philosophical discomfort, not an exorcism of philosophy. Exorcism requires a different kind of move, which Rorty is much less good at.

to the layout of the world, if shaping a world-view is rationally answerable, by way of experiential openness, to the world itself.

This conception of experience contrasts with one that pictures experiences as emissaries from the world. Davidson remarks ("A Coherence Theory", p. 312) that if we picture experiences as emissaries, putatively informing us about the world, we have the problem that they "may be lying . . . we can't swear intermediaries to truthfulness". But the real trouble with conceiving experiences as intermediaries is that we cannot make sense of experiences, so conceived, as purporting to tell us anything, whether truthfully or not. When we take receptivity itself to impinge rationally on belief, we equip ourselves to understand experience as openness to the world. And now the problem of making it intelligible that experience is endowed with content lapses, and the question of truthfulness takes on a different look. We achieve an intellectual right to shrug our shoulders at sceptical questions, if they are asked with the usual philosophical animus, namely, to point up a supposed problem about whether our thought is in touch with its purported topics. Of course we are fallible in experience, and when experience misleads us there is a sense in which it intervenes between us and the world; but it is a crucial mistake to let that seem to deprive us of the very idea of openness—fallible openness—to the world, as if we had to replace that idea with the idea of emissaries that either tell the truth or lie. It is only because we can understand the notion of appearings constituted by the world's making itself manifest to us that we can make sense of the empirical content, the bearing on the world, embodied in the idea of a misleading appearance. When we are not misled by experience, we are directly confronted by a worldly state of affairs itself, not waited on by an intermediary that happens to tell the truth.[18]

From this angle we can see that there is more than an excess of simplicity in Davidson's formulation "nothing can count as a reason for holding a belief except another belief". I suggested this emendation: nothing can count as a reason for holding a belief except something else that is also in the space of concepts. In fact the emended wording is fine by my lights. It need not give expression to what, in the lectures, I call "unconstrained coherentism", the thesis that there are no external rational constraints on exercises of spontaneity. The emended wording allows that exercises of spontaneity can be ration-

18. See Lecture VI, §3.

ally constrained by facts, when the facts make themselves manifest in experience; that is a constraint from outside exercises of spontaneity—from outside the activity of thinking, as I put it in the lectures, though not from outside what is thinkable, so not from outside the space of concepts (Lecture II, §3). But this idea of external constraint is genuinely available only if we can contrive to accept a rational engagement with spontaneity on the part of receptivity itself, and Davidson thinks that is impossible. So when Davidson says that only beliefs can stand in rational relations to beliefs, that is not just the terminological awkwardness that I discounted earlier—the easily discarded implication that an appearing is a belief. Davidson's formulation reflects something deeper: he cannot countenance external rational requirements on exercises of spontaneity, so his coherentism is genuinely unconstrained. Even if we do not take the word "belief" very seriously, the restriction to beliefs conveys something on these lines: only subjective things belong together with evolving world-views in the space of reasons. My claim is that this is disastrous: it ensures that we cannot refuse to find a mystery in the bearing of belief, or anything else, for instance appearing, on the empirical world.

The conception of impressions that is common to Sellars and Davidson does not completely remove impressions from the domain of epistemology, even apart from their indirect relation to what one should believe. The way impressions causally mediate between the world and beliefs is itself a potential topic for beliefs, and these beliefs can stand in grounding relations to other beliefs. Consider a belief that credits an observable property to an object. In the context of a rationally held theory about how impressions figure in causal interactions between subjects and the world, such a belief might be rationally grounded in a belief about an impression. One might be justified in believing that the object has the property by the fact that one has an impression of a type that is, according to one's well-grounded theory, caused in suitable circumstances (for instance the prevailing illumination) by an object's possessing that property.[19]

19. Compare Sellars's discussion of the authority of observation, "Empiricism and the Philosophy of Mind" pp. 296–8. This passage comes before Sellars has undertaken to rehabilitate the notion of impressions; it makes the authority of an observational judgement that something is green turn on the subject's knowledge that her own report "This is green" is reliably correlated, in the right conditions, with something's being green. But once the impression of green is in view, it can figure in a parallel grounding, in a position corresponding to that of the report in the kind of grounding Sellars envisages.

But that is quite distinct from saying, as my picture allows and the picture common to Sellars and Davidson does not, that the belief that an object has an observable property can be grounded in an impression itself: the fact's impressing itself on the subject. In my picture impressions are, so to speak, transparent. In the picture common to Sellars and Davidson they are opaque: if one knows enough about one's causal connections with the world, one can argue from them to conclusions about the world, but they do not themselves disclose the world to one. They have an epistemological significance like that of bodily feelings in diagnosing organic ailments. And my claim is that that undermines Davidson's aim of eliminating mystery. If we cannot conceive impressions as transparent, we distance the world too far from our perceptual lives to be able to keep mystery out of the idea that our conceptual lives, including appearings, involve empirical content.

In the style of thinking I have been attacking, impressions need not be separated from appearings as causes and effects. Another version of the picture might allow one form of the claim that appearings (at least some of them) *are* impressions. What would make this still a version of the picture that I am attacking would be an insistence that something's being an appearing must be at a conceptual remove from something's (perhaps, in this version of the picture, the same thing's) being an impression. The identification of one and the same thing as both an impression and an appearing would straddle the boundary between two radically different modes of conceptualization; we would have to insist that it is not by virtue of being the impression it is that an item is the appearing it is. This version of the picture might be more congenial to Davidson than the version I have been working with, according to which impressions belong in the explanatory background of appearings; that seems to be Sellars's line.

As my counting it a version of the same picture implies, I do not believe identifying appearings with impressions in this way makes any difference to the main point. It will still be true, in the context of the identification understood like this, that impressions as such are opaque. If an item that is an impression is credited with empirical content, because it is said to be also an appearing, it is not supposed to be by virtue of being the impression it is that it possesses that content. This is just another way of refusing to countenance a rational engagement between spontaneity and receptivity as such, and I think it still leaves us short of an entitlement to find empirical content unmysterious.[20] What that requires is that we see our way to accepting that an impression as such can be an appearing, a circumstance constituted by the world's making an appearance to the subject.

In the picture I recommend, although the world is not external to the space of concepts, it is external to exercises of spontaneity. Although we are to erase the boundary that symbolized a gulf between thought and the world, the picture still has an in-out dimension. Linkages between what is further in and what is further out stand for the availability of rational groundings, and the world—which is as far out as possible—is ultimate in the order of justification. What I have been urging, against Davidson and Sellars, is that we must find a place for impressions, the deliverances of receptivity, along this in-out dimension. They must figure in the order of justification. Of course there are other dimensions along which we can trace connections between mental items and the world, and we can interpret phrases such as "the impact of the world on the senses" so as to apply to items that stand between minds and the world only along one of these other dimensions. But we must not suppose, with Sellars and Davidson, that that is the only sort of sense we can give to the idea of deliverances of receptivity.

6.   A clearer target for my criticism than Davidson himself would be Rorty's reading of Davidson, in "Pragmatism, Davidson, and Truth". There Rorty singles out for commendation precisely the aspects of Davidson's thinking that I have objected to. Playing them up yields a reading that makes no room for other aspects of Davidson's thinking. And the effect is to provide an object lesson in how not to rid ourselves of the illusory intellectual obligations of traditional philosophy.

In presupposing that this is the aim, I assume Rorty is right to discount "the fact that Davidson . . . does not present himself as repudiating the skeptic's question, but as answering it" (p. 342).[21] I also assume that philosophical concerns about the possibility of knowledge express at root the same anxiety as philosophical concerns about how

---

20. The point here is of a piece with something I suggest in Lecture IV, §4.

21. In "Afterthoughts, 1987" (in Alan Malachowski, ed., *Reading Rorty* [Blackwell, Oxford, 1990]), Davidson attributes to Rorty the claim that "I should not pretend that I am answering the skeptic when I am really telling him to get lost", and says "I pretty much concur with him".

content is possible, an anxiety about a felt distance between mind and world. Davidson and Rorty usually focus on concerns of the former sort, whereas I focus on concerns of the latter sort; I take it that the underlying thought is the same, that we ought to exorcize the feeling of distance rather than trying to bridge the felt gap.

Rorty is very strong in his conviction that the supposed obligations of traditional philosophy are illusory, and I have every sympathy with that. My objection to Davidson is not that he does not answer the question how anything can have empirical content, but rather that he does not ensure, as he wants to, that the question lacks urgency. But Rorty gives expression to the conviction in a way that spoils the point. What he praises Davidson for recommending is a way of thinking within which, on inspection, it turns out to be unintelligible how empirical content can be anything but a mystery. It is true that Rorty resists the blandishments of traditional philosophy, but the effect of the framework he assumes is that he can do that only by plugging his ears, like Odysseus sailing past the Sirens.

Rorty puts the point of Davidson's coherentism, which he endorses, like this: we must hold apart the view of beliefs "seen from the outside as the field linguist sees them (as causal interactions with the environment)" and the view of beliefs seen "from the inside as the pre-epistemological native sees them (as rules for action)" (p. 345). We must "abjure the possibility of a third way of seeing them—one which somehow combines the outside view and the inside view, the descriptive and the normative attitudes" (p. 345).[22] The outside view, the field linguist's view, is descriptive; it links beliefs with objects and circumstances in the believer's environment, in a structure whose constitutive relations are causal. (In the outside view, beliefs are "seen . . . as causal interactions with the environment".) The inside view is normative: it is "the . . . point of view of the earnest seeker after truth" (p. 347), a point of view in which beliefs are linked with what is taken to give them their rational credentials, that is, located in the space of reasons.

Rorty thinks different uses of the notion of truth can be shared out between these points of view. He commends Davidson for a "contri-

22. The abjured third view is what Rorty earlier describes as "a confused attempt to be inside and outside the language-game at the same time" (p. 342). Compare also the criticism of Hilary Putnam for wanting "a synoptic vision which . . . will somehow bring the outside and the inside points of view together" (p. 347).

bution to pragmatism" that "consists in pointing out that ["true"] has a disquotational use in addition to the normative uses seized on by James" (p. 342). The contrast with "normative", which, as we have seen, Rorty associates with the inside point of view, licenses us to read this as assigning the disquotational use of "true" to the descriptive view, the outside view.

That anyway fits the fact that Rorty identifies the outside view with the field linguist's view. Davidson's field linguist aims to construct theories of truth for this or that language in the style of Tarski, and such theories use "true" disquotationally, in an extended sense. We have disquotation strictly so called in the theorems of a Tarskian theory of truth formulated in a minimal extension of the language for which it is a theory: what Davidson calls "neutral snow-bound trivialities",[23] in a reminder of the notorious example "'Snow is white' is true (in English) if and only if snow is white". Here disquoting is what one needs to do in order to get from the left-hand side of a theorem to what should figure on the right-hand side. But that idea easily generalizes to the idea of cancelling semantic ascent; that need not be effected by a move in the language from which the ascent was made, as with disquotation strictly so called.[24] Davidson's field linguist aims at theories of truth whose theorems are disquotational in the generalized sense: they are inter-language counterparts to what figure, in the intra-language case, as the "neutral snow-bound trivialities". And Rorty's idea is that such theories are constructed and understood from the outside point of view, the point of view whose concern is descriptive as opposed to the normative concern of the "earnest seeker after truth".

Now this holding apart of the two points of view is quite unsatisfying, both in itself and as a reading of Davidson.

We can appreciate how unsatisfying it is in itself by considering a move Rorty makes against Hilary Putnam. Objecting to a position like the one Rorty finds and applauds in Davidson, Putnam once wrote:

> If the cause-effect-description [of our linguistic behavior qua production of noises] is complete from a philosophical as well as from a behavioral-

23. From p. 51 of "True to the Facts", in *Inquiries into Truth and Interpretation*, pp. 37–54; quoted by Rorty at p. 343.

24. For the generalization, see pp. 10–13 of Quine's *Philosophy of Logic* (Prentice-Hall, Englewood Cliffs, N.J., 1970).

scientific point of view; if all there is to say about language is that it consists in the production of noises (and subvocalizations) according to a certain causal pattern; *if the causal story is not to be and need not be supplemented by a normative story* . . . then there is no way in which the noises we utter . . . are more than mere "expressions of our subjectivity".[25]

Rorty responds as follows, in a passage I have already quoted from:

The line I have italicized suggests that disquotationalist theorists of truth think that there is only one story to be told about people: a behavioristic one. But why on earth should such theorists not allow for, and indeed insist upon, supplementing such stories with "a normative story"? Why should we take the existence of the outside point of view of the field linguist as a recommendation never to assume the inside point of view of the earnest seeker after truth? Putnam, I think, still takes a "philosophical account of X" to be a synoptic vision which will somehow synthesize every other possible view, will somehow bring the outside and the inside points of view together.

Until the last sentence, this strikes me as refusing to listen to Putnam's concern. Admittedly the concern is not well expressed in the passage Rorty exploits. But it takes only minimal charity to see what Putnam is driving at. Putnam does not suppose that wanting to tell a story about causal relations between human vocalizations and the environment is, in itself, enough to debar someone from so much as having a story to tell that represents the vocalizers as expressing thoughts and making assertions, trying to get things right.[26] What he objects to, as the last sentence I have quoted from Rorty in effect acknowledges, is precisely the thesis Rorty finds and applauds in Davidson, that the two stories must be held apart. But the acknowledgement comes too late. By saddling Putnam with a different target for his complaint, Rorty contrives to make it look legitimate for him to cap a series of supposedly well-placed rebukes to Putnam, to the effect that the one story does not exclude the other, a point that is in fact irrelevant, with an unargued reaffirmation of the thesis Putnam really means to question, that the two stories have to be kept separate.

Putnam's worry cannot be squelched by merely insisting that both

25. "On Truth", in Leigh S. Cauman et al., eds. *How Many Questions?* (Hackett, Indianapolis, 1983), p. 44; quoted by Rorty at p. 347. (The interpolation and emphasis are Rorty's.)

26. See the passage Rorty quotes from Putnam's *Realism and Reason,* at pp. 345–6.

stories are there to be told; the worry is precisely about the thesis that they cannot be told together. That implies that if we occupy a standpoint from which our beliefs are in view along with their objects and our causal engagements with the objects, then we cannot, from that standpoint, bring the beliefs under the norms of inquiry. And Putnam's worry about this is well placed: the result is to make it a mystery how what we are talking about can be beliefs, stances with respect to how things are in the world, at all. It does not help to insist, as Rorty does, that there is another standpoint from which beliefs are seen as subject to the norms of inquiry. If the view from this second standpoint is not allowed to embrace the causal interactions between believers and the objects of their beliefs—since those interactions are the preserve of the outside view, which has to be held separate—then it simply becomes mysterious how we can be entitled to conceive what organizes the subject matter of the second standpoint as the norms of inquiry.

The point comes out vividly in the way Rorty deals with disquotation. There is an obvious connection between disquotation, whether in the strict or in the extended sense, and a straightforward notion of getting things right. It is because "La neige est blanche" is true in French if and only if snow is white that, since snow is indeed white, I shall be getting things right if I express a belief in French by saying "La neige est blanche". Rorty's remarks about disquotation give the field linguist, the occupant of the outside point of view, responsibility for the question whether beliefs achieve truth in the sense of disquotability. The question whether a belief achieves disquotability is supposed to be descriptive as opposed to normative, and Rorty's picture keeps it apart from any question we address in our capacity as "earnest seekers after truth"—in our efforts to be responsive to what we should like to think of as the norms of inquiry. But this severs what we want to think of as responsiveness to the norms of inquiry from any connection with that unproblematic notion of getting things right. And the effect is to make it unintelligible how it can be norms of inquiry that are in question. Norms of inquiry are normative for the process of inquiry precisely because disquotability is the norm for its results.

Amazingly enough, Rorty seems to think it is merely routine to separate what we want to think of as norms of inquiry from the straightforward notion of getting things right that is connected with the notion of disquotability. At p. 336, he says, without ceremony, that it "seems paradoxical" to suggest that "There are rocks" is implied by "At the ideal end of inquiry, we shall be justified in asserting that there are rocks", because "there seems no obvious reason why the progress of the language-game we are playing should have anything in particular to do with the way the rest of the world is". But that is an extraordinary thing to say. It is the whole point of the idea of norms of inquiry that following them ought to improve our chances of being right about "the way the rest of the world is". If following what pass for norms of inquiry turns out not to improve our chances of being right about the world, that just shows we need to modify our conception of the norms of inquiry. Rorty implies that to say that sort of thing is to succumb to the attractions of traditional philosophy. But the world as I invoke it here, in this expression of the thought that Rorty's separation of viewpoints is intolerable, is not the world that is well lost, as Rorty sees, when we follow Davidson in rejecting "the dualism of scheme and world".[27] It is the perfectly ordinary world in which there are rocks, snow is white, and so forth: the world that is populated by "the familiar objects whose antics make our sentences and opinions true or false", as Davidson puts it. It is that ordinary world on which our thinking bears in a way that Rorty's separation of viewpoints leaves looking mysterious, precisely because it separates relatedness to the world from the normative surroundings that are needed to make sense of the idea of bearing—rational bearing—on anything. It is loss of that ordinary world that Rorty threatens us with, when he insulates norms of inquiry from disquotability.

Once one has adopted a style of thinking that has that effect, it is too late to refuse to listen to expressions of philosophical discomfort. We should indeed want philosophical problems about how thought can be in touch with the world to stand revealed as illusory, but Rorty deprives himself of the right to take that attitude. His own thinking makes those problems urgent, so that his refusal to address them can only be an act of will, a deliberate plugging of the ears. In one sense the refusal is well justified, since Rorty has such an excellent appreciation of how hopeless our predicament is if we try to address the ques-

27. I echo the engaging title of Rorty's "The World Well Lost", in his *Consequences of Pragmatism* (University of Minnesota Press, Minneapolis, 1982), pp. 3–18. That paper stands to Davidson's "On the Very Idea of a Conceptual Scheme" much as "Pragmatism, Davidson, and Truth" stands to "A Coherence Theory of Truth and Knowledge".

tions. But in another sense the refusal is arbitrary, since Rorty's own thinking, so far from being shaped so that the questions cannot arise, positively exacerbates their apparent pressingness.

Rorty's assignment of truth as disquotability to the outside point of view is also quite unsatisfying as a reading of Davidson.

It is true that the data available to a Davidsonian field linguist, when she begins on radical interpretation of a language, are restricted to vocal or otherwise putatively linguistic behaviour, with its causal connections to the environment. As long as the language, if that is what it is, has not been interpreted, the linguist has no handle on what, if anything, its speakers count as a reason for what, though she can observe which environmental circumstances are likely to prompt them to which vocalizations or other putatively linguistic actions. While the interpreter is in this position, it cannot yet stand quite firm for her that what is in question is linguistic behaviour at all; that depends on the behaviour's turning out to be interpretable—that is, capable of being intelligibly placed in the space of reasons.

But that is how it is only at the outset of radical interpretation. The field linguist's aim is not merely to codify those causally connected data, or to construct a theory that postulates further connections of the same kind, so as to make the data intelligible in the way a theory in the natural sciences makes intelligible the data it is based on. Exactly not: Davidson's field linguist aims to work into an appreciation, as from within, of the norms that constitute the language she investigates: the specific sense of when it is right to say what according to which that language-game is played. That is what she aims to capture in a theory for the language that is disquotational in the extended sense. She begins as an occupant of the outside standpoint, but if she succeeds in her aim, she ends up equipped to give expression in her own terms to part of how things look from the inside standpoint her subjects occupied all along. When Rorty suggests that the results of the field linguist's endeavours employ a notion of truth unconnected with norms, and hence separated—by the supposed gulf between the two standpoints—from, for instance, a conception in which the truth is seen as what ought to be believed ("the normative uses seized upon by James"), he obliterates the significance of the transition from starting predicament to achieved interpretation.

The outside standpoint as Rorty conceives it is a standpoint from sideways on. (For that image, see Lecture II, §4.) Davidson's radical interpreter starts with a sideways-on view of the relation between her subjects and the world. But she finishes with a theory whose point is exactly that it is not from sideways on: a theory that enables her to capture some of her subjects' relations to the world from their own point of view, though in her terms rather than theirs. It is just the beauty of the notion of disquotation in the extended sense that it is available for this capturing of the inside viewpoint. When Rorty separates disquotation from the standpoint of the speakers of the language, as "earnest seekers after truth", he precisely misses what makes a disquotational notion of truth suitable for summarizing the results of interpretation.[28]

7. When Rorty insists that the two points of view must be kept separate, that is an expression of a dualism of nature and reason. In this version of the dualism, nature figures as the subject matter of the outside view, and the space of reasons figures as the normative organization that things have when they are seen from the inside view; what is dualistic is insisting that the two modes of organization cannot be combined.

In the lectures, I point to the dualism of nature and reason as the source of the merely apparent difficulties confronted by traditional philosophy. I find the dualism operative in Davidson's thinking: it accounts for his attitude to the idea that spontaneity interacts rationally with receptivity. So I am not in a position to dissent outright from Rorty's reading of Davidson. But in my reading, Davidson's vulnerability to the dualism is a defect; it is out of line with his better thinking on interpretation, and it ensures failure in the aim of exorcizing traditional philosophical anxieties. In contrast, Rorty centres his reading of

---

28. Rorty is not alone in supposing that the sideways-on character of the radical interpreter's starting orientation—what makes the interpretation radical—persists into the results of radical interpretation. See Charles Taylor, "Theories of Meaning", in his *Human Agency and Language: Philosophical Papers, 1* (Cambridge University Press, Cambridge, 1985), pp. 248–92, especially pp. 273–82. Taylor takes it that Davidson's thinking excludes Gadamer's idea of a fusion of horizons. (See Lecture II, §4.) Like Rorty, Taylor thinks Davidson's approach to interpretation is inextricably committed to an outside point of view. And Cora Diamond seems to suggest something similar, at pp. 112–3 of "What Nonsense Might Be", in her *The Realistic Spirit: Wittgenstein, Philosophy, and the Mind* (MIT Press, Cambridge, Mass., 1991), pp. 95–114. I think such readings miss the distance between Davidson and Quine. (Davidson may be partly to blame for this, because of the way he systematically understates that distance. I say something about this at p. 73 of my "In Defence of Modesty", in Barry Taylor, ed., *Michael Dummett: Contributions to Philosophy* [Martinus Nijhoff, Dordrecht, 1987], pp. 59–80.)

Davidson on the dualism, and he applauds it as what it exactly is not, a way to escape from the obsessions of traditional philosophy.[29]

It is ironic that I can put things like this. Rorty begins "Pragmatism, Davidson, and Truth" with an admiring description of pragmatism, into which he wants to enrol Davidson, as "a movement which has specialized in debunking dualisms and in dissolving traditional problems created by those dualisms" (p. 333). But Rorty's own thinking is organized around the dualism of reason and nature, and that means he can be at best partly successful in being a pragmatist in his own sense. No wonder his attempt to dissolve traditional problems has the aspect of refusing to listen to questions that still stubbornly look as if they ought to be good ones, rather than supplying a way of thinking within which the questions genuinely do not arise.

Of course Rorty does not cast his view about nature and reason as a dualism. He speaks, for instance, of "patiently explaining that norms are one thing and descriptions another" (p. 347). That sounds like calmly drawing a distinction; it is not the obsessive mode of utterance characteristic of a philosopher insisting on a dualism. But I have been urging that if we try to think as Rorty says we must, we are stuck with the philosophical anxieties that he wants to avoid. Cultivating a non-obsessive tone of voice is not enough to ensure that philosophical obsessions are out of place.

I cited Rorty's suggestion that Putnam wants "a synoptic vision which will somehow synthesize every other possible view, will somehow bring the outside and the inside points of view together". Rorty means to accuse Putnam of the grandiose aspirations of traditional philosophy, which he thinks we should discard: thought is to be brought into alignment with its objects, minds with reality. My suggestion has been that bringing the outside and the inside points of view together (not "somehow", which suggests a mystery) is exactly the sort of dualism-debunking and problem-dissolving move for which Rorty himself admires pragmatism. So what I recommend in

---

29. I do not mean to suggest that we can easily isolate the dualism's role in motivating Davidson's coherentism. It is also at work elsewhere in his thinking: notably in the thesis that causal relations can hold between occupants of the space of reasons only because they can be identified with elements in the realm of law. (Compare Rorty's analogue to this thesis: it is only in the inside view that items are placed in the space of reasons, and causal relations are not present in that view at all.) This Davidsonian thesis is at issue in Lecture IV, §4.

the lectures could be represented as a pragmatism in Rorty's sense, even though, in trying to give expression to it, I borrow from thinkers such as Kant, whom Rorty finds utterly suspect.[30] And I am claiming that Rorty's own pragmatism is half-baked, according to standards set by his own account of what pragmatism is.

8.   Davidson's objection to the third dogma of empiricism is this: even as it tries to make out that sensory impressions are our avenue of access to the empirical world, empiricism conceives impressions in such a way that they could only close us off from the world, disrupting our "unmediated touch" with ordinary objects. Now Rorty generalizes that thought into rejecting a whole array of candidate intermediaries between us and the world, on the ground that to accept them is just to saddle ourselves with pointless anxieties about our hold on the world. He speaks of "such *tertia* as, in Davidson's words, 'a conceptual scheme, a way of viewing things, a perspective' (or a transcendental constitution of consciousness, or a language, or a cultural tradition)" (p. 344).

In the lectures, I explain how the notion of impressions can be innocuous. We can take it that spontaneity is rationally vulnerable to receptivity without the unwelcome effect that receptivity seems to get in the way between us and the world, if we reject the framework that is the real source of the problems of traditional empiricism, namely, the dualism of reason and nature. In the context of a full-blown pragmatism, impressions can come into their own as precisely a mode of openness to the world. And something similar goes for at least some of Rorty's other *"tertia"*. Conceptual schemes or perspectives need not be one side of the exploded dualism of scheme and world. Thus innocently conceived, schemes or perspectives can be seen as embodied in languages or cultural traditions. So languages and traditions can figure not as *"tertia"* that would threaten to make our grip on the world philosophically problematic, but as constitutive of our unproblematic openness to the world.[31] (This Gadamerian conception of

---

30. This might give one pause about Rorty's attitude to such thinkers. Moves in the language of traditional philosophy can be aimed at having the right not to worry about its problems, rather than at solving those problems. I think Rorty is insufficiently alive to this possibility.

31. The idea of a transcendental constitution of consciousness sounds harder to rehabilitate, but perhaps even that would not be impossible; see the previous footnote.

tradition figures at the end of Lecture VI.) Rorty suggests (p. 344) that "intentionalistic notions" just as such breed unhealthy philosophical worries ("inserting imaginary barriers between you and the world"); in the context of a pragmatism less half-baked than Rorty achieves, that suggestion can stand exposed as absurd.[32]

9.   I think if we follow Davidson in rejecting the third dogma of empiricism, that has a devastating effect on the familiar cornerstones of Quine's philosophy. Here I evidently diverge from Davidson himself: with respect to the distinction between the analytic and the synthetic, and to the indeterminacy of meaning, he declares himself "Quine's faithful student" ("A Coherence Theory of Truth and Knowledge", pp. 312–3).

Quine's thesis that translation is indeterminate gives vivid expression to his notion of "conceptual sovereignty". The indeterminacy is supposed to mark how far the products of "conceptual sovereignty" fall short of being determined by the scientifically treatable facts about "empirical significance". Now the point Quine is aiming to make here is inextricably bound up with the persisting dualism of the endogenous and exogenous factors ("conceptual sovereignty" and "empirical significance"), the very thing Davidson rejects as the third dogma. Quine's point is precisely to insist on how far the exogenous factor falls short of determining meaning in the intuitive sense, bearing on the world. When we discard the third dogma, we discard the very framework within which this point seems to make the sort of sense Quine wants. Now it should stand revealed as unsurprising that meaning is undetermined by "empirical significance"—so called. That just reflects the fact that "empirical significance" cannot really be a kind of significance at all, since, conceived as dualistically set over against "conceptual sovereignty", it is excluded from having anything to do with the order of justification.

That meaning is indeterminate with respect to "empirical significance" has no tendency to show, what would indeed be interesting, that meaning is indeterminate, period. That would require that we have an ineliminable freedom of play when we look for a kind of

---

32. No doubt Rorty is encouraged here by the example of Quine. But to the extent that Quinean suspicion of the intentional is more than mere scientism, its basis is thoroughly undercut by the debunking of the third dogma. See §9 below.

understanding that takes us outside the ambit of "empirical significance": a kind of understanding that involves seeing how the phenomena of our subjects' lives can be organized in the order of justification, the space of reasons. If meaning is indeterminate in this interesting sense, that is not something one could learn at Quine's feet.[33]

As for the distinction between the analytic and the synthetic, here Quine is on the track of a real insight. But once the insight is properly formulated, it undercuts that way of trying to give it expression. The insight is the one that comes to explicitness only in Davidson's correction to Quine: it is the rejection of the third dogma, "the dualism of scheme and world". The suspect notion of the analytic is the notion of truths that are such by virtue of being constitutive of conceptual schemes in the suspect sense, the sense in which schemes are conceived as dualistically set over against the world. The world plays no role in accounting for the truth of these statements, though it is supposed to help account for the truth of others. But once we have discarded the dualism of endogenous and exogenous factors, that can no longer seem a good interpretation for the idea of statements that are true by virtue of their meaning. Meaning is not to be identified with the endogenous factor. If we embrace the picture I recommend in the lectures, in which the conceptual realm is unbounded on the outside, we make it unintelligible that meaning's impact on determining what we are to believe is endogenous as opposed to exogenous. (Not that it is exogenous instead, or even jointly endogenous and exogenous; the need to make this kind of determination simply lapses.) That is to say: when we reject the dualism of scheme and world, we cannot take meaning to constitute the stuff of schemes, on the dualistic conception of schemes. But that does not deprive us of the very idea of meaning. So if I am right that Quine's insight is really a glimpse of the unacceptability of the dualism, perhaps we can rehabilitate the idea of statements that are true by virtue of their meaning, without flouting the real insight.

If, as I suggested (§8), the notion of a conceptual scheme need not belong to the dualism, meaning can constitute the stuff of schemes in

---

33. I say more about this at pp. 245–6 of "Anti-Realism and the Epistemology of Understanding", in Herman Parret and Jacques Bouveresse, eds., *Meaning and Understanding* (De Gruyter, Berlin, 1981), pp. 225–48.

an innocent sense. We can reject the two factors without threatening the idea that there are limits to what makes sense: that our minded-ness, as Jonathan Lear puts it,[34] has a necessary structure. The idea of a structure that must be found in any intelligible conceptual scheme need not involve picturing the scheme as one side of a scheme-world dualism. And analytic truths (in an interesting sense, not just definitionally guaranteed truisms such as "A vixen is a female fox") might be just those that delineate such a necessary structure.[35]

This need not involve backtracking from what is right about the Sellarsian thought that I considered in §4 above. Sellars claims that nothing is Given, and argues in detail against the idea of an exogenous Given. My topic there was a reading of Quine's attack on analyticity, according to which the claim is that nothing is endogenously Given either. The point was that there is a problem with "either": it suggests, falsely, that Quine is with Sellars in firmly rejecting the exogenous Given.

The Sellarsian thought in full is that nothing is either exogenously or endogenously Given. This need not tell against rehabilitating an idea of analyticity in the way that I have suggested. It would be wrong to conceive what is necessary in any intelligible conceptual scheme as fixed because it is Given, either exogenously or endogenously. That very distinction has lapsed. Sellars claims, in a Hegelian spirit, that all forms of Givenness are to be overcome; Davidson rejects the dualism of the endogenous and exogenous factors. Perhaps these are just two different expressions for the same insight. In that case Sellars's thought, general though it is ("all forms of Givenness"), did not re-quire him to claim that absolutely everything we think is up for revi-sion. Immunity to revision, come what may, is a mark of Givenness only if it is understood in terms of the two factors, and it need not be.

The idea that any intelligible conceptual scheme has a necessary structure needs care. If we find ourselves inclined to take the thought that the structure is necessary as a reassurance that our thinking must be on the right track, I think we have gone astray, in the direction of supplying a solution, rather than a dissolution, of traditional philo-sophical problems. As far as I can see, such reassurance is the point of

---

34. See "Leaving the World Alone", *Journal of Philosophy* 79 (1982), 382–403.

35. Perhaps this is the category in which we should place at least some of the "hinge propositions" to which Wittgenstein attributes a special significance in *On Certainty* (Basil Blackwell, Oxford, 1969).

the vestigial transcendental idealism that Lear finds in the later Wittgenstein.[36] A full-blown transcendental idealism reassures by affirming, to put it crudely, that we cannot be fundamentally wrong about the world we think about, since it is constituted by us. Lear's vestigial transcendental idealism affords a version of the same reassurance by affirming that the "we" who figure in the idea of "our conceptual scheme" "disappear"; the effect is that there cannot be a general worry about how we suppose things to be, a worry that this is just our line (as if there might be another). I think there is something right about the idea of the disappearing "we", but (though this is admittedly a fine distinction) the disappearance of the "we" should not take on the aspect of a reassurance, but should rather figure as part of the reason why a reassurance should never have seemed to be needed.

One way to discover the limits of what makes sense is by an activity characteristic of the later Wittgenstein: working out towards them in thought-experiments, and noting the extent to which one finds oneself losing one's grip. I borrow that image from Bernard Williams, in a paper called "Wittgenstein and Idealism".[37] Lear is following Williams when he takes it that the role of "how we go on" in Wittgenstein reveals his view as a form of transcendental idealism. But it is difficult to make this fit. "How we go on" summarily introduces what Lear describes as our mindedness, and we might begin by trying to find in Wittgenstein a thought on these lines: world and mind, or mindedness, are transcendentally made for each other. What makes it appropriate to call the Kantian version of such a thought "idealism" is, to put it crudely again, that the constituting of this harmony between world and mind is supposed to be a transcendental operation of mind: not, of course, the empirical mind, which is in constituted harmony with the world, but an off-stage transcendental mind. But nothing matches that in Wittgenstein. "How we go on" is just our mindedness, which is *ex hypothesi* in constituted harmony with our world; it is not something that constitutes the harmony, as it were from outside. And now we should be struck by the thought that there is nothing in Wittgenstein's picture to do the constituting of the harmony. The appearance of a piece of vestigially transcendental philosophy is hard to sustain.

36. See "Leaving the World Alone" and Lear's contribution to the symposium "The Disappearing 'We'", *Proceedings of the Aristotelian Society,* supp. vol. 58 (1984), 219–42.
37. In his *Moral Luck* (Cambridge University Press, Cambridge, 1982), pp. 144–63.

In §2, I cast Quine's rejection of analyticity as a corollary of his claim that "empirical significance" cannot be apportioned between statements: if there is no such thing as the "empirical significance" of an individual statement, it does not make sense to suppose that some statements may have null "empirical significance". Now once we appreciate the peculiarity of Quine's notion of "empirical significance", we can see a gap between the premise that "empirical significance" cannot be apportioned among individual statements and the conclusion that we cannot make sense of analyticity. An analytic statement should be a statement with no vulnerability to experience, and it is true that we cannot make sense of that if we cannot make sense of the idea that an individual statement might have its own vulnerability to experience. But here we must gloss "vulnerability to experience" in terms of rational answerability. When Quine speaks of facing the tribunal of experience, that sounds as if it expresses the idea of rational answerability, but the rhetoric is hollow; that is the point Davidson fastens on. So if "empirical significance" in Quine's sense cannot be apportioned between statements, that does nothing to show that rational answerability to experience cannot be apportioned between statements.

And in fact, once we understand experience so that it really can be a tribunal, we commit ourselves to conceiving it in such a way that rational answerability to it *can* be apportioned between statements. Consider an experience with a content partly capturable by "Here's a black swan". Such an experience poses a rational problem for the statement, or belief, that there are no black swans; there is a germaneness relation between them that is not restricted, as in Quine's picture, to the likelihood that the belief will be abandoned.

Quine's argument for the indeterminacy of translation exploits a familiar Duhemian point, which we can put like this: vulnerability to experience cannot be shared out among the statements of a theory. If the invocation of vulnerability is not just empty rhetoric, but alludes to a rational relation, this claim can indeed figure in an argument for an indeterminacy of meaning. The argument can work only if the language in which we capture experience can be held separate from the language of the theory, so that the relevant experience does not, as it were, already speak the language of the theory. In that case we can put the Duhemian point by saying that individual statements of the theory are indeterminate in meaning with respect to the observational statements on which the theory is grounded. Now it may be that in some of the contexts in which we think of theory as based on experience, the language of theory can indeed be held separate from the language of observation; so we can argue on those lines that the observational significance of individual theoretical statements is indeterminate. But we cannot extract a general indeterminacy of meaning from these considerations. We might hope to do so, but only by falling into the confusion of the third dogma of empiricism. That way we embrace, at the general level, a limiting case of the separation of languages. We push all meaning into theory, and we leave experience not speaking any language at all, not even metaphorically. But this defeats the hope, because it eliminates the rational relation that figures in the cogent Duhemian argument for indeterminacy. The cogent argument can at best be local. So if we see our way through the third dogma, we cut the Duhemian point down to size.

PART II

Postscript to Lecture III

1. In the lectures, I claim that we can coherently credit experiences with rational relations to judgement and belief, but only if we take it that spontaneity is already implicated in receptivity; that is, only if we take it that experiences have conceptual content. Evans's thinking stands as an obstacle to this: he undertakes to conceive experiences as a rational basis for judgements, even while he excludes experiences from the conceptual sphere. In Lecture III (§4), I argue that Evans's position is unacceptable, because it is a version of the Myth of the Given.

This can seem difficult to sustain. The very idea of representational content brings with it a notion of correctness and incorrectness: something with a certain content is correct, in the relevant sense, just in case things are as it represents them to be. I can see no good reason not to call this correctness "truth". But even if, for some reason, we reserve that title for correctness in this sense when it is possessed by things with conceptual content, it seems a routine thought that there can be rational connections between the world's being as a possessor of one bit of content represents it and the world's being as a possessor of another bit of content represents it, independently of what kind of content is in question.

Christopher Peacocke aims to exploit this routine thought in *A Study of Concepts,* when he argues for a position like Evans's in that it takes certain judgements and beliefs to be rationally grounded in non-conceptual content possessed by experiences. At p. 80 he defends the claim that the non-conceptual content he attributes to experiences can afford "not merely reasons but good reasons" for judgements and beliefs. The defence, for one representative case, involving an experiential basis for judging that something is square, goes like this: "If the thinker's perceptual systems are functioning properly, so that the non-conceptual representational content of his experience is correct, then when such experiences occur, the object thought about will really be square." Peacocke comments: "In this description of why the linkages are rational linkages, I make essential use of the fact that the non-conceptual content employed in the possession condition [the condition for a subject to possess the concept *square*] has a correctness condition that concerns the world. The account of the rationality of this particular linkage turns on the point that when the correctness condition of the relevant nonconceptual contents is fulfilled, the object will really be square."

But this falls short of establishing what Peacocke needs: namely, that non-conceptual content attributable to experiences can intelligibly constitute *a subject's reasons for* believing something.

There is a familiar style of explanation for circumstances that involve a subject (such as the circumstance of someone's believing something): an explanation of the sort I mean shows how it is that the explanandum is as it should be from the standpoint of rationality (for instance true, if the explanandum is a belief). Now this is not *eo ipso* to give the subject's reasons for whatever the explanation explains. The subject may not even have reasons. Consider, for instance, the bodily adjustments that a skilled cyclist makes in rounding curves. A satisfying explanation might show how it is that the movements are as they should be from the standpoint of rationality: suited to the end of staying balanced while making progress on the desired trajectory. But this is not to give the cyclist's reasons for making those movements. The connection between a movement and the goal is the sort of thing that *could* be a reason for making the movement, but a skilled cyclist makes such movements without needing reasons for doing so. Why would it not be similar with experience and judgement, if experiences had the non-conceptual content that Peacocke says they have?

The routine thought shows that the linkages between experience, conceived as Peacocke conceives it, and belief are rational linkages, but only in the sense in which the linkages between considerations about what is required to keep one's balance and the cyclist's adjustments are rational linkages. This does not establish that something with non-conceptual content can intelligibly figure on the in-out dimension I mentioned earlier in this Afterword (Part I, §5). That is: the routine thought does not entitle Evans to his talk of judgement and belief as "based upon" experience, or Peacocke to his counterpart talk of beliefs being formed for reasons constituted by experience's being as it is.[1]

How could we ensure that a story like Peacocke's displayed experience not just as part of the reason why, but as yielding reasons for which a subject forms her beliefs?

One way would be to have it that the subject accepts the story, and uses it in deciding what to believe, or at least would be disposed to cite it if challenged. Suppose we are told that someone argues to the conclusion that an object she can see is square, from the premise that in seeing it she enjoys an experience with a certain non-conceptual content. Its having that content involves a correctness condition rationally linked to believing that the object is square in the way that figures in Peacocke's exploitation of the routine point. The correctness condition is that the object is indeed square. In this version, the story clearly depicts someone who forms the belief, with its conceptual content, for a reason supplied by an experience, with its non-conceptual content. But this is not what Peacocke needs. This subject would have to be in command of Peacocke's more or less abstruse conceptual apparatus for talking about non-conceptual content: the concepts of scenario content, protopropositional content, and so forth. But Peacocke wants the supposed rational grounding in experience to figure in an account of conceptual capacities exploited in the observational judgements of quite ordinary subjects, not just those who are philosophically speaking in the know.[2]

---

1. See, for instance, p. 7: "The thinker must . . . be disposed to form the belief for the reason that the object is so presented." Here it is not something with non-conceptual content that is said to lie further out than a belief on my in-out dimension. But when, in a context in which non-conceptual content is in play, Peacocke writes of "perceptual experiences that give good reasons for judging . . . [certain conceptual] contents" (p. 66), he must mean that the judging is done *for* those reasons, as in the formulation on p. 7.

2. Similarly with "for the reason that" at p. 7, where it is not non-conceptual content that is supposed to figure further out than belief on my in-out dimension. A parallel defence of "for the reason that" here would require the subject to have the concept of sensational properties of regions of the visual field. Peacocke is sketching a candidate account of what it is to possess the concept *red,* and he would not dream of suggesting that anyone who possesses that concept must have the concept of sensational properties of regions of the visual field.

And it seems right not to require possession of the theory, even independently of the fact that the rational connection with experience is supposed to figure in accounts of what it is for *anyone* to possess this or that observational concept. If theory were needed to mediate the rational connection of experience to judgement and belief, that would undercut the very point of placing experience between belief and the world on the in-out dimension. If we restrict the role of experience in empirical thought to its being something from which we can argue to a conclusion about the world, given that we know the relevant theory, then we cannot conceive experience as itself constituting access to the world. Something whose role is to yield premises for arguments about the world could only be opaque, as I put it in a parallel context when I was discussing the conception of impressions that is common to Sellars and Davidson (in this Afterword, Part I, §5).

Once we are clear how far the routine point is from what Peacocke needs, it becomes possible to see how unattractive Peacocke's position really is. In the reflective tradition we belong to, there is a time-honoured connection between reason and discourse. We can trace it back at least as far as Plato: if we try to translate "reason" and "discourse" into Plato's Greek, we can find only one word, *logos*, for both. Now Peacocke cannot respect this connection. He has to sever the tie between reasons for which a subject thinks as she does and reasons she can give for thinking that way. Reasons that the subject can give, in so far as they are articulable, must be within the space of concepts.

I do not mean to suggest any special degree of articulateness; that would be just as unsatisfactory as requiring command of Peacocke's theory. But suppose one asks an ordinary subject why she holds some observational belief, say that an object within her field of view is square. An unsurprising reply might be "Because it looks that way". That is easily recognized as giving a reason for holding the belief. Just because she gives expression to it in discourse, there is no problem about the reason's being a reason for which . . ., and not just part of the reason why. . . .

In that simplest kind of case, what the subject says counts as giving a reason for her belief because the way the object looks is the way she believes it to be. In other cases the connection between reason and belief is less simple. A minimally articulate reply to the request for a reason might have to be less specific, perhaps "Because of the way it looks". But this makes no difference to the essential point. Here, too, the reason is articulable (even if only in the form "It looks like *that*"), so it must be no less conceptual than what it is a reason for.

The routine point is really no more than that there can be rational relations between its being the case that P and its being the case that Q (in a limiting case what replaces "Q" can simply be what replaces "P"). It does not follow that something whose content is given by the fact that it has the correctness condition that P can *eo ipso* be someone's reason for, say, judging that Q, independently of whether the content is conceptual or not. We can bring into view the rational relations between the contents—its being the case that P and its being the case that Q—only by comprehending the putatively grounding content in conceptual terms, even if our theory is that the item that has that content does not do its representing in a conceptual way. A theory like Peacocke's does not credit ordinary subjects with this comprehensive view of the two contents, and I think that leaves it unintelligible how an item with the non-conceptual content that P can be someone's reason for judging that Q.[3]

2. Why is Peacocke convinced that the rational grounding of belief and judgement in experience has to set up links between the conceptual realm and something outside it?

The conviction is largely sustained by a requirement of non-circularity that he imposes on accounts of what it is to possess this or that concept. Avoiding circularity, in the relevant sense, does not require that the concept in question not be used within the account at all, but just that it not be used in a specification of the content of a conceptual state. An account that violates this requirement "will not have elucidated what it sets out to elucidate" (p. 9).

Now if we set out to give an account of what it is to possess an observational concept, we shall have to exploit the way judgements

3. Evans appropriates "seem" as "our most general term for the deliverances of the informational system", that is, items with non-conceptual content (*The Varieties of Reference*, p. 154; see also p. 180). It is certainly an easy thought that seemings can be our reasons for judgements and beliefs. But I think that is only because we understand the content of seemings as conceptual; Evans's appropriation just undermines the intelligibility of "seem". For the content of seemings (specifically lookings) as conceptual, see Sellars, "Empiricism and the Philosophy of Mind", pp. 267–77.

and beliefs that employ it can be rationally grounded in experience.[4] So if we hold that the content of the relevant experiential appearings already involves the concept in question, we cannot satisfy Peacocke's requirement of non-circularity. When we set out to give an account of what it is to possess, for instance, the concept *red*, we shall find ourselves saying things like this: to possess the concept *red* one must be disposed—if one takes it that the lighting conditions and so forth are of the right sort—to make judgements in whose content that concept is applied predicatively to an object presented to one in visual experience, *when the object looks red to one*, and for that reason.[5] But this use of "looks red" presupposes, on the part of an audience to whom the account might be addressed, not just the concept *red*, which would be innocent, but the concept of possession of the concept *red*, which is implicit in the idea of being able to have things look red to one. And that is just what the account was supposed to be an account of. It is obvious how this motivates the thought that the grounding experience must be characterizable otherwise than in terms of conceptual content.

But this just shifts the question. Why should we suppose that it is always possible to give accounts of what it is to possess concepts, in conformity with Peacocke's non-circularity requirement? Notice that what is in question is accounts of *what it is* to possess concepts. Perhaps we could give a condition satisfied by all and only those who possess a certain concept, without presupposing the concept of possession of that concept. For all I know, for instance, there may be a neurophysiologically specifiable condition that distinguishes those who possess the concept *red* from those who do not. But that speculation does not promise an account of *what it is* to possess the concept. The neurophysiological condition would not bear on the question

4. Of course the applicability of an observational concept is not restricted to cases in which one has the grounding type of experience. (A subject must understand that something can be red without looking red to her.) This point is implicitly covered by the wording in the text. Suppose someone took a predication of "red" to be warranted only when she had an experience like those we describe in terms of something's looking red to us. Such a person would not qualify as possessing the concept *red*; that is not how judgements and beliefs exploiting that concept are rationally grounded in experience. (Things could not even look red to such a person; that is why I needed the circumlocution "an experience like those. . .".)

5. Compare the first clause of Peacocke's sketch at pp. 7–8.

what someone thinks when she thinks that something is red. And Peacocke wants his accounts to bear on such questions. That is why an account of an observational concept must place employments of the concept in the space of reasons, even though the non-circularity requirement compels Peacocke to hold that the experiences that constitute the rational basis of employments of such concepts are outside the space of concepts.

What is at issue here is whether it is in general possible to give sideways-on accounts of concepts, in the sense that figures in Lecture II, §4, and in my discussion of Rorty earlier in this Afterword (Part I, §6). The non-circularity requirement is in effect an insistence on sideways-on accounts. In Lecture II, I deny, in effect, that sideways-on accounts of concepts are in general possible. I cannot see that Peacocke gives any reason to suppose that is wrong. In fact this seems to work the wrong way round for him. In §1 above, I urged that it is difficult to see how experiences, conceived as Peacocke conceives them, could constitute a believer's reasons for believing something. This suggests I was right to deny that sideways-on accounts are possible; the problem for the motivated thought tends to undermine the motivating thought.

Peacocke's proposed accounts are indeed offered as accounts of what it is to possess this or that concept, and they talk of beliefs or judgements, which figure in the accounts as having contents that employ the concepts in question. But that does not mean that the accounts are not from sideways on in my sense. What is true is that the accounts explicitly represent themselves as being about thinkers, users of the concepts in question. But they do not say—indeed they carefully refrain from saying—*what* the thinkers think when they use the concepts in question. Avoidance of circularity requires the accounts to come at what the thinkers think only from the outside, identifying it as something that one thinks when . . ., where what follows "when" is a condition external to possession of the concept. The accounts embody the claim that there is an inside view, but they are not given from it. Peacocke is responsive to the suspicion that this externality threatens the project of capturing content. He thinks he can meet the threat by linking the external condition to the thinking not just with "when" but also with "for the reason that". However, I have urged, in §1 above, that the required externality undermines the very intelligibility, here, of "for the reason that". So I see no reason to give up, or qualify, the claim I made in Lecture II. I see no reason to suppose, and plenty of reason not to suppose, that it is always possible to give accounts of concepts in conformity with the non-circularity requirement.[6]

Non-circular accounts might be available, so far as these considerations go, in cases where what follows "when and for the reason that . . ." can be a mention of conceptual states whose content involves concepts other than the one of which an account is being given; that is, cases in which a concept can be captured in terms of how employments of it are rationally grounded in employments of other concepts. But that is of course exactly not how it is with observational concepts. These non-circular accounts would be given not from a sideways-on orientation to the whole conceptual realm, but only from outside the conceptual capacities of which they are accounts; whereas Peacocke's proposed accounts of observational concepts would be given from outside the conceptual realm altogether.

Is my scepticism about accounts that do everything Peacocke wants some kind of obscurantism? Peacocke makes a suggestion to that effect at pp. 35–6:

> Theories are developing in the literature of what it is to possess certain specific concepts: the first person, logical notions, and many others. While there is much that is still not understood and not all of what has been said is right, it is hard to accept that the goal of this work is completely misconceived. On the contrary, there are often phenomena specific to the concept treated that are explained by these accounts. McDowell would not let us say that these accounts are theories of what it is to possess these concepts. But I cannot see what else they can be, and we can hardly just dismiss them.

A lot depends here on what "the goal of this work" really is. We are not restricted to just two options: either accepting that the presuppositions of this undismissable work are made explicit in Peacocke's desiderata for a theory of concepts, avoidance of circularity and all; or

---

6. What I was driving at in "In Defence of Modesty" was this denial that the sideways-on perspective can capture concepts. I cannot recognize my side of the debate in Peacocke's representation, at pp. 33–6. As Peacocke puts what he takes to be my point, it ought to be satisfiable by a sideways-on story, so long as the story announces itself as being about thoughts. My point was that one cannot fix *what is thought* from the outside, identifying it only as something that one thinks when . . .; and I do not believe it helps to add "for the reason that. . . ". (Dummett makes much of the claim that the connections are rational in his response to me: see pp. 260–2 of "Reply to McDowell", in Taylor, ed., *Michael Dummett: Contributions to Philosophy*, pp. 253–68.)

refusing to acknowledge that there might be anything to be said about, for instance, the specific rational connections between first-person thinking and experience.

That case is worth considering in a little more detail. As Peacocke remarks (p. 72), it does not individuate the concept of the first person to say that it "is that concept *m* such that judgements about whether *Fm* display a certain sensitivity to experiences that represent *Fm* as the case". But we do not have *that* problem if we identify the relevant judgements, for a given subject, as judgements that display a certain sensitivity to experiences that represent *F(herself)* as the case. Of course this violates the non-circularity requirement. But we can leave the violation standing and still have plenty of room for substantive inquiry into the character of the "certain sensitivity". No doubt the amended formulation is much too simple. But the possibility of locating its substantive promise in the "certain sensitivity", leaving the circularity undisturbed, is suggestive. Peacocke is here aiming to co-opt Evans's discussion of the first person as an example of work directed towards an account of the sort Peacocke envisages. But I think Evans is much better read as primarily concerned with the "certain sensitivity", and not particularly interested in avoiding circularity.

3.   Evans claims that we do not have enough concepts of, say, colours for it to be possible that the content of our visual experience is conceptual. In Lecture III, §5, I urge, against that, that we can express all the concepts we need, in order to capture the finest detail of our colour experience, by utterances of "that shade". We do not have all these concepts in advance, but we do have whichever we need, exactly when we need them.

An utterance of "that shade" depends for its meaning on the identity of a sample shade. We might lay down the rule that something counts as having *that* shade just in case it is indiscriminable in colour from the indicated sample. (Of course we can actually say something in these terms only in the presence of a sample.)

Now there is a familiar pitfall here. It may be tempting to lay down a second rule as well: that something counts as having a shade if it is indiscriminable in colour from something else that counts as having that shade. But if we say that, we run afoul of a sorites paradox: we undermine the idea that utterances of "that shade" can express a determinate meaning at all, because indiscriminability in colour is not transitive. With an artfully arranged series of samples, we could work out from the original sample to one that would have to count as having the shade in question, by repeated applications of the second rule, even though it is discriminable in colour from the original sample, contrary to the first rule. The two rules do not cohere.

So we should restrict ourselves to the first rule, and resist the temptation to endorse the second. Something that counts as having a shade does not thereby count as a *sample* of the shade, bringing into the shade's extension anything indiscriminable from it; that is what leads to the familiar collapse. The status of a sample, a determinant of the extension of the concept expressed by "that shade" in the relevant use, must be reserved for the original sample, or at least for things whose promotion to that status would not contribute to slippage in the concept's extension.[7]

In the lecture I allow that a shade concept can be given overt expression later in the duration of the recognitional capacity that constitutes possessing it, if experience happens to provide something to anchor the reference of a later utterance of the demonstrative "that shade". In view of the point I have just made, we need to treat that thought with some care. If there are things that would be indiscriminable in colour from the new anchor but would have been discriminable in colour from the original sample, then even if one is not wrong in recognizing the new anchor as an exemplifier of the shade in question (since it would be indiscriminable from the original sample), one would be wrong if one supposed it would do as a *sample* of the original shade. And it is hard to suppose that when it anchors the reference of an utterance of "that shade", it can be serving as anything but a sample of whatever shade is in question. This case brings out the possibility that a putatively recognition-based conceptual capacity can lapse. One can suppose one is employing a recognitional capacity, but wrongly because one's propensities to arrive at what one takes to be recognitions have been skewed; and one way that can happen is that one has promoted an unsuitable example to the status of a secondary sample. In this kind of case, the subsequent utterance of "that shade" does not express the original shade concept. The subject has lost the original shade concept without realizing it.

7. I see no need for the apparatus Peacocke introduces in response to the sorites threat, pp. 83–4.

4. What makes it recognizably a concept that is made available by the presence to experience of the original sample is a capacity of memory; so I claim in the lectures. A person can retain a capacity to recognize things as having that shade, and while this recognitional capacity persists, possibly for quite a short period, the subject can embrace just that shade in thought. (It is redundant, in my usage, to say "conceptual thought".) The most direct manifestation of the conceptual capacity after its onset is a judgement in which the recognitional capacity that constitutes it is directly employed: something seen later is judged to have the shade in question. But this kind of memory-based capacity to embrace a precise shade in thought can also be exercised in thinking that is not geared to present experience. Consider, for instance, someone who remembers the colour of a rose that she no longer has in view, and thinks "I should like the walls of my room to be painted that shade".

The kind of thought I mean here needs to be distinguished from one that might be expressed by something like "I should like the walls of my room to be painted the shade of the rose that I saw on such-and-such an occasion". One can have a thought of this second kind without remembering the shade itself, as we can naturally put it. Perhaps one remembers that it was a shade of pale apricot, and that it struck one as ideal for the walls of one's room. In the case I mean, one has the shade itself in mind, as we can naturally put it: it does not figure in one's thinking only as what fits some specification. One way of capturing this is to say that one sees the shade in one's mind's eye.

In the presence of the original sample, a subject who has the concept of a shade is enabled to classify items as possessing the relevant shade or not, by direct inspection for colour match. We can retain, for a while at least, a capacity to classify items as possessing the relevant shade or not, in a way that corresponds with the verdicts we would have given on the strength of direct inspection for colour match, even after the original sample is no longer in view. (In fact this capacity of memory is drawn on even while the original sample is still in view, if a candidate for being credited with the shade cannot be juxtaposed with the sample in a single overview.) We can be confident, and with good grounds, that the verdicts, or potential verdicts, of the memory-involving capacity correspond with the verdicts direct comparison would have yielded, and that fact is at least part of what underlies how natural it is to say things like "I see it in my mind's eye". It is as if a sample is still available for comparison with any candidates for being credited with the shade.

The idiom is a fine way to make the distinction between having the shade itself in mind and bringing one's thinking to bear on it by way of a specification. But it can elicit a familiar and dubious philosophical thought, according to which the idiom's obvious rightness points to a mechanism by which the retained classificatory capacity operates. The idea is that the subject attributes the shade by comparing things she sees with a retained inner sample of the shade; it is like checking things for match in colour with, say, a paint manufacturer's sample, except that here the sample is before an inner eye. Wittgenstein warns against ideas like this (see, for instance, *Philosophical Investigations,* §604). "I see it in my mind's eye" is a natural way to affirm one's capacity to embrace the shade itself in one's thinking, a capacity that would be overtly displayed, given a suitable opportunity, in verdicts as to whether things exemplify the shade. The idiom does not allude to psychological machinery that would be operative in one's production of those verdicts.[8]

5.   What brings into being the recognitional capacities that constitute abilities to embrace determinate shades in one's thinking? In the lectures I consider only confrontations with exemplifiers of the shades in question. But recall Hume's question whether a subject could form, in pure thought, the idea of a shade that has been missing from her colour experience.[9] That introduces what may be a different possibility. I am already committed to claiming that we have all concepts of the relevant kind potentially, just by virtue of having the concept of a shade. But Hume's question is about possession of such a concept in actuality: the suggestion is that a subject might equip herself to see the missing shade in her mind's eye, by an exercise of imagination alone.

---

8. "I see it in my mind's eye" embodies a picture. The proper attitude to it is like the one Wittgenstein expresses, in *Philosophical Investigations,* §427, to the picture embodied in saying things like "While I was speaking to him I did not know what was going on in his head." Wittgenstein says: "The picture should be taken seriously. We should really like to see into his head. And yet we only mean what elsewhere we should mean by saying: we should like to know what he is thinking." Taking *this* picture literally, and even supposing it is somehow intellectually obligatory to do so, is depressingly common in contemporary philosophy of mind.

9. *A Treatise of Human Nature,* ed. L. A. Selby-Bigge and P. H. Nidditch (Clarendon Press, Oxford, 1978), 1.1.1.

Perhaps this is indeed possible; I have no thesis that the possibility would threaten, in the way it seems to threaten Hume's empiricism about concepts. The main thing to insist on is that if it is possible, this is just another possibility for the genesis of the sort of recognitional capacity we can claim by saying "I see the shade in my mind's eye". There is no extra support here for the idea that exercises of the associated recognitional capacity are based on comparison with an inner sample.[10]

10. If there is a possibility here, the point is that imagination can fill gaps in a repertoire of concepts of shades. But the repertoire must be mainly initiated by experience, in the way I discuss in the lecture. Shade concepts in general must still be constitutively dependent on intuitions, in the way that, according to my speculation in the lecture, underlies the fact that Evans does not even consider them as a possible range of concepts.

Postscript to Lecture V

1. According to Crispin Wright, Wittgenstein commits himself to elaborating a certain conception of meaning, though his "quietism" prevents him from discharging the commitment. In Lecture V, §3, I suggest that the consequences Wright himself attributes to that conception of meaning are intolerable. I leave the suggestion undefended, and turn instead to urging that we must miss Wittgenstein's point if we read him in a way that makes his "quietism" an awkward fact about a set of texts that actually set substantive tasks for philosophy, and even give hints as to how to execute them.

This does not strike me as a real gap. If we form a proper understanding of Wittgenstein's "quietism", the doctrines Wright finds him committed to can collapse of their own weight. It is only under pressure from philosophy that anyone could dream of thinking there is any problem about the idea of how things are anyway, independently of communal ratification.

Wright thinks Wittgenstein reveals just such a philosophical compulsion. According to Wright, Wittgenstein poses a genuinely urgent question about how meaning is possible: a question of a sort philosophy characteristically addresses, in a kind of activity whose very point is bound up with our not being able to rule out in advance the possibility of affront to what passes for common sense. And Wright thinks a conception of meaning can be legitimized, in the face of the problem Wittgenstein supposedly elaborates, only if we are willing to rethink what passes for common sense about the idea of how things are anyway. So Wittgenstein's "quietism" looks like an embarrassing failure to acknowledge the character of his own philosophical achievement.

But it is a mistake to think Wittgenstein points up a good question about how meaning is possible.

The "quietism", the avoidance of any substantive philosophy, is really the point. Questions such as "How is meaning possible?" express a sense of spookiness, and Wittgenstein's point is that we should not indulge the sense of spookiness, but rather exorcize it. The question looks like an urgent one from the standpoint of a world-view that is inhospitable to meaning: a standpoint from which it looks like a task for philosophy to shoehorn into the world something as close as we can get to our previous conception of meaning. But philosophy's task is rather to dislodge the assumptions that make it look difficult to find a place for meaning in the world. Then we can take in our stride meaning's role in shaping our lives. We do not need a constructive legitimizing of its place in our conception of ourselves.

Wittgenstein aims to cast suspicion on an aura of mystery that certain thoughts about meaning acquire in an uncongenial environment. The thoughts are thoughts like this: the meaning of, say, an instruction that specifies an arithmetical series, for instance the instruction "Add 2", "determines the steps in advance" (compare *Philosophical Investigations*, §190), in such a way that—to bring the thought into direct connection with Wright's concerns—the fact that such-and-such a move is the correct one at a certain point in the expansion of the series does not depend on ratification by the relevant community, those who count as understanding the instruction. Such a thought can seem uncanny, as if it credited meaning with magical powers. Wright's mistake is to take it that Wittgenstein means to cast suspicion on such thoughts themselves. But Wittgenstein's target is the atmosphere of uncanniness. The thought itself is all right.[1]

The contrast between rampant and naturalized platonism helps to bring out this possibility. The relevant thoughts are platonistic, and if we can envisage only a rampant platonism the aura of uncanniness is inescapable; our only recourse is a philosophical construction in which we pull in our horns, about objectivity or whatever. But the

---

1. Compare *Philosophical Investigations*, §195. An interlocutor voice says: "But I don't mean that what I do now (in grasping a sense) determines the future use *causally* and as a matter of experience, but that in a *queer* way, the use itself is in some sense present." The responding voice says: "But of course it is, 'in *some* sense'! Really the only thing wrong with what you say is the expression 'in a queer way'. The rest is all right."

problem is not with the platonistic thoughts themselves. Within a naturalized platonism they do not have the aura of uncanniness. So another way of putting Wright's mistake is to say that he is blind to the possibility of a naturalized platonism.[2]

2. In the lecture I credit Wittgenstein with the aspiration of seeing through the apparent need for ordinary philosophy. This needs to be taken with care. I do not mean to suggest that Wittgenstein seriously contemplates a state of affairs in which ordinary philosophy no longer takes place. The intellectual roots of the anxieties that ordinary philosophy addresses are too deep for that. This point comes out dramatically in the multiplicity of voices in Wittgenstein's later writing, its dialogical character. The voices that need to be calmed down, recalled to sobriety, are not alien voices; they give expression to impulses he finds, or at least can imagine finding, in himself. When he writes, "The real discovery is the one that makes me capable of stopping doing philosophy when I want to" (*Philosophical Investigations*, §133), we should not take him to be envisaging a post-philosophical culture (an idea that is central to Rorty's thinking). He is not even envisaging a future for himself in which he is definitively cured of the philosophical impulse. The impulse finds peace only occasionally and temporarily.[3]

But I do not think it follows that there can be no role, in a style of thinking that is genuinely Wittgensteinian in spirit, for the sort of diagnostic move I propose in the lectures. What I suggest is that our philosophical anxieties are due to the intelligible grip on our thinking of a modern naturalism, and we can work at loosening that grip. It is a way of making this suggestion vivid to picture a frame of mind in which we have definitively shrugged off the influences on our thinking that lead to philosophical anxieties, even if we do not suppose we

2. I elaborate a reading on these lines, with more detailed reference to Wittgenstein than seemed appropriate in these lectures, in "Meaning and Intentionality in Wittgenstein's Later Philosophy", in Peter A. French, Theodore E. Uehling, Jr., and Howard K. Wettstein, eds., *Midwest Studies in Philosophy*, vol. 17: *The Wittgenstein Legacy* (University of Notre Dame Press, Notre Dame, 1992), pp. 42–52. For kindred thoughts, see Cora Diamond, *The Realistic Spirit*. At p. 6, she describes one of her targets like this: "Wittgenstein's criticism of . . . mythology or fantasy—in particular, his criticism of the mythology attached to logical necessity—is read as if it were rejection of the mythology as a *false* notion of how things are."

3. I have been persuaded here by James Conant and Lisa Van Alstyne.

could ever have such a frame of mind as a permanent and stable possession. Even so, this identification of a source for our apparent difficulties can be one of our resources for overcoming recurrences of the philosophical impulse: recurrences that we know there will be.

3.   When I describe the relaxed platonism made possible by a naturalism of second nature, I say things like this: the structure of the space of reasons is not constituted in splendid isolation from anything merely human. Wittgenstein's "quietism", properly understood, is a good context in which to stress that remarks like that should not invite the question "So what does constitute the structure of the space of reasons?" If we take ourselves to be addressing that question, my invocation of second nature, sketchy and unsystematic as it is, will seem at best a promissory note towards a proper response. But that would miss my point. I think the response we should aim at being entitled to, if someone raises a question like "What constitutes the structure of the space of reasons?", is something like a shrug of the shoulders. It is a thought well expressed by Rorty that questions like that should not be taken to be in order without further ado, just because it is standard for them to be asked in philosophy as we have been educated into it. Their sheer traditional status cannot by itself oblige us to take such questions seriously. Rather, there is an assumed background that is supposed to make them urgent. When I invoke second nature, that is meant to dislodge the background that makes such questions look pressing, the dualism of reason and nature. It is not meant to be a move—which could be at best a first move—in constructing a response to that question.

4.   In Lecture V, §5, I discuss Kant's suggestion that the continuity of self-consciousness embodies only a formal conception of persistence. It is worth comparing the suggestion Wittgenstein makes in a well-known passage (pp. 66–7 of *The Blue Book*): that "the use [of "I"] as subject" does not refer. We can formulate what Wittgenstein suggests there, in a way that brings out the resemblance to the Kantian thought, like this: the reference-plus-predication structure in, say, "I have a toothache" is merely formal. The considerations that induce Wittgenstein to make this suggestion seem closely similar to those that are operative in the Paralogisms. And our verdict should be the same. The motivation for the suggestion—to undermine the basis for

a Cartesian conception of the ego—is admirable, but once we understand the wider context in which the use of "I" as subject functions, the suggestion can be detached from its motivation. There is no obstacle to supposing that my use of "I" as subject refers to the human being I am.[4]

5. It may be helpful to juxtapose my remarks on reference to particulars, in Lecture V, §6, with what I say in Lecture II, especially §3.

In Lecture II, I exploit Wittgenstein's "truism" to discourage the idea of a gap between thought as such and the world. An objector might say something like this: "You can make it look as if your drift is not idealistic, so long as you consider the world only as something whose elements are *things that are the case.* In that context, you can exploit the claim that it is no more than a truism that when one's thought is true, what one thinks *is* what is the case. But as soon as we try to accommodate the sense in which the world is populated by *things,* by objects (and there had better be such a sense), it will emerge that your image of erasing an outer boundary around the realm of thought must be idealistic in tenor, perhaps in an extended sense. Even if the image allows for a kind of direct contact between minds and facts, it obliterates a certain possibility that we should not be willing to renounce, a possibility of direct contact between minds and *objects,* which must surely be external to the realm of thought. This possibility is what has been brought to our attention in the recoil from the generalized Theory of Descriptions."

Given the identity between what one thinks (when one's thought is true) and what is the case, to conceive the world as everything that is the case (as in *Tractatus Logico-Philosophicus,* §1) is to incorporate the world into what figures in Frege as the realm of sense. The realm of sense *(Sinn)* contains thoughts in the sense of what can be thought (thinkables) as opposed to acts or episodes of thinking. The identity displays facts, things that are the case, as thoughts in that sense—the thinkables that are the case. But objects belong in the realm of reference *(Bedeutung),* not the realm of sense. The objection is that Wittgenstein's "truism" yields an alignment of minds with the realm of sense, not with the realm of reference.

---

4. See Evans's discussion of the Wittgenstein passage in *The Varieties of Reference,* pp. 217–20.

I can indeed formulate a main point of my lectures in terms of the Fregean notion of sense, like this: it is in the context of that notion that we should reflect about the relation of thought to reality, in order to immunize ourselves against the familiar philosophical anxieties. This is just another way to put the thought I express in the lectures in terms of Sellars's image of the logical space of reasons. Frege's notion of sense operates in the space of reasons: the whole point of the notion of sense is captured by the principle that thoughts, potential senses of whole utterances, differ if a single subject can simultaneously take rationally conflicting stances towards them (say, any two of acceptance, rejection, and neutrality) without thereby standing convicted of irrationality. If failing to distinguish senses would leave us liable to have to attribute to a rational and unconfused subject, at the same time, rationally opposed stances with the same content, then we must distinguish senses, so as to make possible a description of the subject's total position that has different contents for the stances, and so does not raise a question about the position's rationality.[5]

The objector I have imagined thinks that if we take this Fregean view, that thought and reality meet in the realm of sense, then we can purport to accommodate thought's bearing on *objects*—a relation between minds and inhabitants of the realm of reference—only by embracing some version of the generalized Theory of Descriptions. We lose the insights of those who have insisted on a more direct relation than that allows between minds and objects.

Now what I say at the end of Lecture V can be seen as pre-empting any such objection. On a proper understanding of the Fregean apparatus, my exploitation of Wittgenstein's "truism" in Lecture II, which can indeed be reformulated by saying thought and reality meet in the realm of sense, already allows for what is right in the recoil from the generalized Theory of Descriptions. If the relevant senses are rightly understood, the role of sense, in a picture that leaves the relation of thought to the world of facts unproblematic, already ensures that there is no mystery about how it can be that the relevant thoughts bear on the relevant particulars, inhabitants of the realm of reference, in the non-specificatory ways that proponents of the recoil rightly insist on.

5. See Evans, *The Varieties of Reference*, pp. 18–19.

Postscript to Lecture VI

1. My talk of Aristotelian innocence may raise some suspicions. It may seem to fly in the face of an obvious fact: Aristotle explicitly discusses positions that are, in some respects, strikingly like modern naturalism.

It is true that the ancient atomists (to single out perhaps the best case for the objection) already have a somewhat modern-seeming conception of nature, in the sense of what is comprehended by the most fundamental understanding of things. They take nature, in that sense, to be empty of meaning and value. And it is true that Aristotle sticks to his different conception of nature in self-conscious opposition to conceptions like that. But in such ancient anticipations of the disenchanted conception of nature, the thesis that nature is empty of meaning and value lacks a certain status it has in modern thinking. It does not figure as another way to formulate a rightly entrenched view of the kind of understanding aimed at by properly scientific investigation: a view that is not open to dispute, but part of what one must take for granted if one is to count as an educated person.

As I insist in the text, we must recognize that when the realm of properly scientific understanding came to be generally seen as disenchanted, that marked an intellectual advance. That is why it is so difficult for us to get out from under the philosophical anxieties I have been concerned with. It can easily go unnoticed that what it is right for us to conceive as disenchanted need not be identified with nature. Aristotle's innocence consists in his not being subject to that intellectual pressure. Certainly he is aware that it is possible to see nature, identified as the topic of the most fundamental understanding, in a way that disenchants it. But for him that reflects a merely optional—and, from his intellectual standpoint, not very well supported—view of the most fundamental understanding. He does not have to resist a temptation to let the label "nature" affix itself to something that he is anyway intellectually committed to countenancing as what is comprehended by scientific understanding. Aristotle has no inkling of a perfectly correct thought that we can formulate like this: *if* we identify nature as the topic of scientific understanding, we must see it as disenchanted.[1]

2. In Lecture VI, §4, I refuse to credit non-human animals with orientations towards the world. Understandably, that raises some hackles.

It may help to stress that what I am committed to denying in the case of mere animals is precisely, and only, something correlative with possession of spontaneity. In the text of the lecture, I try to minimize any appearance that I am debunking animal mentality, by disowning a reductive conception of biological imperatives, which are what shape the lives of mere animals. And perhaps this talk of biological imperatives already suggests a harder line than I need, even without the reductive conception I disown. The point is just that dumb animals do not have Kantian freedom. That is perfectly compatible with acknowledging that they can be, in their ways, clever, resourceful, inquisitive, friendly, and so forth. I do not suggest that they are somehow "out of it". Indeed my whole point, in appropriating Gadamer's notion of an environment, is to provide language for saying quite the reverse, even while I deny that, lacking spontaneity as they do, dumb animals can possess the world. And it is important that the freedom I claim they lack is precisely Kantian spontaneity, the freedom that consists in potentially reflective responsiveness to putative norms of reason. No one without a philosophical axe to grind can watch, say, a dog or a cat at play and seriously consider bringing its activities under the head of something like automatism. But we can deny Kantian spontaneity while leaving plenty of room for the self-movingness that is plain to the unprejudiced eye in such a scene.

The risks of falling into philosophical anxiety that I am concerned with in the lectures arise in relation to a conception of orientation

1. This section responds to a question raised by M. F. Burnyeat.

towards the world that is correlated with spontaneity in the Kantian sense. They arise precisely because of what is peculiar about spontaneity in the Kantian sense, when it is viewed from the standpoint of the familiar modern conception of nature as the disenchanted realm of law.

If someone wants to work out a conception of orientation towards the world that is detached from spontaneity in the Kantian sense, with a view to making the language of world-directedness available for talking about the mentality of brutes, that is, so far, perfectly all right by my lights. I have no wish, apart from this context, to say anything at all about mere animals, and certainly no wish to play down the respects in which their lives are like ours. It is part of what I want to insist on that we are animals too, not beings with a foothold outside the animal kingdom. And in some respects, the lives of mature human beings simply match the lives of mere animals; it would be absurd to suppose that *Bildung* effects a transfiguration, so to speak, of everything that happens in a human life.[2]

What I do want to resist is the suggestion that such a neutral conception of orientation towards the world will do for all purposes. That would amount to rejecting all talk of a spontaneity that is peculiar in the Kantian way. This may be motivated by the conviction that if we let an acknowledged peculiarity of that kind lead to an outbreak of philosophy, our intellectual position is hopeless, and I have made it clear that I sympathize with this motivation. But in the lectures I aim to show how we can acknowledge that we have a spontaneity that is peculiar in the Kantian way, and that that fact is crucial to a special way in which we are in touch with the world, without thereby landing ourselves in that philosophical predicament. We do not need to stop this kind of philosophy before it begins, by refusing to allow that there is any basis for the fuss it makes about spontaneity (to echo something I say in Lecture IV, §4). When we acknowledge the peculiarity of spontaneity, we should be aware of how we thereby risk falling into unprofitable philosophical anxiety. But the risk need not be realized. We can understand and exorcize the philosophical impulse, not just repress it.

We can understand how it can seem that philosophical problems

2. Even those aspects of mature human life that are shaped by *Bildung* show unassimilated residues from their evolution out of mere nature (first nature). That is a way of putting a central thought of Freud.

are posed by a notion of orientation towards the world that is correlated with the Kantian peculiarity of spontaneity. It seems so because
of the pressure to suppose that spontaneity would have to be non-natural. But I have tried to show how this appearance of a philosophical
task can be revealed as illusory. There is no call for elaborate and,
outside the study, incredible philosophical apparatus to respond to
the question how it is possible for empirical thinking, understood as
an exercise of "conceptual sovereignty", to bear on the world, let
alone to yield knowledge of the world. This is a recipe for a potentially
satisfying exorcism of philosophical anxiety, because it fully acknowledges the thought that generates the anxiety. And we can go this far
with the philosophical impulse only if we draw a line between possessors and non-possessors of spontaneity, in the way I do throughout
the lectures.

3.   When I invoke tradition at the end of Lecture VI, I mean to do no
more than open the door to the topic, about which, no doubt, much
more needs to be said. I am not going to attempt a proper discussion
here. But it may help to clarify the note I mean to sound if I make
some remarks about the way my stance sets me in opposition not only
to Dummett, as I register in the lecture, but also to Davidson.

The Gadamerian note that the lectures end on is that understanding
is placing what is understood within a horizon constituted by tradition, and I suggest that the first thing to say about language is that it
serves as a repository of tradition. Initiation into a language is initiation into a going conception of the layout of the space of reasons.
That promises to make it intelligible how, beginning as mere animals,
human beings mature into being at home in the space of reasons. On
this view, a shared language is the primary medium of understanding.
It stands over against all parties to communication in it, with a kind
of independence of each of them that belongs with its meriting a kind
of respect.[3] We can understand communication across boundaries between traditions by moving out from this basic case, where the horizon is pretty much given (not Given!) by the tradition embodied in the

---

3. Not just the respect due to an effective instrument, which is enough to account for
recoiling when people misuse words like "disinterested" or "careen". The respect I mean is
the respect that is due to something to which we owe our being what we are. (Of course
what we do with our language can change it; for instance, what was misuse can cease to be
misuse. But that does not undermine the sense in which the language is independent of us.)

language, to the sort of case where horizons need to be fused, which may take hard work.

Davidson does not concede this kind of importance to the idea of a shared language. On the contrary, for Davidson communicative interaction stands in no need of anything to play the role of a medium in the sense I have gestured at. (Of course in a different sense there has to be a medium: speech, smoke signals, or whatever.) In Davidson's conception, the parties to communication are self-standing individuals. They do not need a language—a specific repository of tradition as to the shape of the space of reasons—to constitute them as potential parties to communication, or indeed participants in any other activity that requires conceptual capacities. In Davidson's view, the idea of a language shared between parties to communication is at best shorthand for an explicable degree of correspondence in idiolects. Such correspondence can make hypotheses for interpretation easier to come by between some pairs of people, but mutual understanding between people whom we think of as sharing a language is in principle no different from the most radical interpretation. The "shared language" is no more than an aid in a cognitive performance that could be undertaken without it; the capacity for mutual understanding needs no philosophically interesting background.[4]

I cannot properly argue against this vision here, but I shall allow myself a suggestion. Davidson conceives the kind of understanding of persons that is in question here in just the way that I do in the lectures: that is, in terms of placing what they think and do (including what they say) in the space of reasons. It was as much from Davidson as from Sellars that I learned to think that way. Where I use the Sellarsian image of the space of reasons, Davidson talks of "the constitutive ideal of rationality"; but the idea is clearly the same. (I exploit this correspondence in Lecture IV, §4.) So Davidson's mutual interpreters must come to their cognitive task already equipped with a sense of the layout of the space of reasons, a substantive conception of what "the constitutive ideal of rationality" requires. Now I think we should be suspicious of the thought that we can simply credit human individuals

---

4. See "A Nice Derangement of Epitaphs", in LePore, ed., *Truth and Interpretation: Perspectives on the Philosophy of Donald Davidson*, pp. 433–46. The germ of the thought is already present in Davidson's claim that "all understanding of the speech of another involves radical interpretation": p. 125 of "Radical Interpretation", in *Inquiries into Truth and Interpretation*, pp. 125–39.

with this equipment, without benefit of anything like my appeal to initiation into a shared language and thereby into a tradition. I think the idea that this cognitive equipment needs no such background is just another outcropping of Givenness. If we want to attack the Myth of the endogenous Given, in a counterpart to Sellars's Kant-inspired attack on the Myth of the exogenous Given, this would be a much better target than the idea of analyticity, or unrevisability come what may (see Part I of this Afterword, §§4, 9). To put it in Hegelian terms, Givenness is not unrevisability as such, but a supposed unrevisability that reflects absence of mediation from our picture; and Davidson renounces the only available mediation for the capacity of human beings to understand one another.

In recent work, Davidson has undertaken to build the concept of objectivity out of a "triangulation" between these self-standing subjects, pairwise engaged in mutual interpretation.[5] This comes into conflict with the Kantian thesis of interdependence that I consider in Lecture V, §5, and reconsider in Lecture VI, §4. By my lights, if subjects are already in place, it is too late to set about catering for the constitution of the concept of objectivity. We must take subjectivity and the concept of objectivity to emerge together, out of initiation into the space of reasons.

4. I shall end by saying something to avert a perhaps unreal risk: that by invoking tradition, I may seem to commit myself to a hidebound conservatism about the possibilities for intelligibility. At the close of the lectures, I repeat something I stress at various earlier points: that being at home in the space of reasons includes a standing obligation to be ready to rethink the credentials of the putatively rational linkages that constitute the space of reasons as one conceives it at any time. That leaves exactly as much room for innovation as there is. If a bit of, say, vocal behaviour is to constitute making a novel remark, as opposed to mere babble, it must be capable of being understood by people who would not have thought of saying that themselves. One kind of originality calls on those who understand it to alter their prior

---

5. See "Meaning, Truth, and Evidence", in Robert B. Barrett and Roger F. Gibson, eds., *Perspectives on Quine* (Basil Blackwell, Oxford, 1990), pp. 68–79. Davidson had sketched this exploitation of "triangulation" at the end of "Rational Animals", in Ernest LePore and Brian McLaughlin, eds., *Actions and Events: Perspectives on the Philosophy of Donald Davidson* (Basil Blackwell, Oxford, 1985), pp. 473–80.

conception of the very topography of intelligibility. A remark with this kind of originality is not just a move hitherto unimagined but still within the possibilities as they were already comprehended, at least in general terms. (That is how it is with even the most radical innovation in chess.) Rather, the remark changes a hearer's conception of the structure that determines the possibilities for making sense. But even in this kind of case, it can only be a matter of warping a prior conception of the topography of intelligibility. An utterance could not make a place for itself in a comprehending mind from scratch, reshaping wholesale its audience's conception of the possibilities. Even a thought that transforms a tradition must be rooted in the tradition that it transforms. The speech that expresses it must be able to be intelligibly addressed to people squarely placed within the tradition as it stands.

Index